A History of Theology

A History of Theology

Yves M.J. Congar, O.P.

Translated and edited by Hunter Guthrie, S.J.

Adelaide

2019

A History of Theology is based on the article "Théologie" by Fr. Congar which first appeared in Volume XV of *Dictionnaire de Théologie Catholique* published by Editions Letouzey & Ané, 87, Boulevard Raspail, Paris 6.

First published by Doubleday, New York 1968.

Front cover photo: Yves Congar OP, 1967. Photo from the Archives of the Province of France, with thanks to Fr Bruno Dominique La Fille OP

ISBN: 978-1-925612-76-9   soft
        978-1-925612-77-6   hard
        978-1-925612-78-3   epub
        978-1-925612-79-0   pdf

Published by:

An imprint of the ATF Press Publishing
Group owned by ATF (Australia) Ltd.
PO Box 504
Hindmarsh, SA 5007
ABN 90 116 359 963
www.atfpress.com
Making a lasting impact

Contents

Publishers Note

Hilary D Regan

The Congar section in the archives of the Dominican Province of France is in the basement at the Bibliothèque du Saulchoir (rue de la Glacière, Paris), next to the Couvent St Jacques. The section is on two sides of a very large series of compactors, and is full of boxes catalogued by year and often within that by subject. In addition, there is a handy reference folder detailing in summary the contents of each box. There are of course archives of material by many other members of the Province of France. Congar's is undoubtedly the largest of all the collections in the archives.

The Congar section in the archives takes up thirty metres in total with many, many boxes of files in folders with a simple classification system of numbers. Congar kept all his correspondence, envelopes included often, and it has been well indexed by one of the Provincial Archivists of the Province of France some years ago. Finding the right box with the correct documentation takes some time, but none-the-less it delivers results that are much needed in research and this is due to the work done by both Congar and the Archivists over time. Sifting through all the documents that he kept on a particular topic or book also takes time; he kept snippets from many sources, but also none-the-less it produces an incredibly rewarding result.

One finds carefully preserved original type-written letters of sixty or seventy plus years ago, complete with his hand-written notes on these letters, or notes he made for a response on matters for correction, addition or omission. Often these are very small pieces of paper. In looking at these documents, one gets a feel for Congar's mind, the developments in his thought on a project and his method of work, the respect (and the disputes) that others—publishers, theologians, other Dominicans—displayed towards him, as well as a deeper insight into his theology. In sum, these files are a necessary addition to our understanding of Congar.

Inside one of these boxes there is a set of documents, going back to the 1940's, regarding the original article and the then manuscript of what was to be entitled *A History of Theology*. The file includes at the top of the documents and correspondence a small piece of paper, almost a 'post-it' note where Congar noted the percentage of his original manuscript that had been omitted in the French Catholic Encyclopaedia article that was published some time before this new text. It amounted to about 1/3 of the original manuscript that was omitted. Congar used the original text he had written as the basis of an expanded manuscript of what was to be later translated; the re-write which he explains in the preliminary pages of this book.

As said, Congar was meticulous in keeping all correspondence, which have been assiduously archived, and these archives are and will always be an invaluable source for anyone researching Congar and his work and his many articles and books. It is in these same archives, for example, that one can find the original type written text, take from his notebooks, that became the book published of his journal of the Second Vatican Council. Both the original note books and the type written text are filed in a box in the archives, as is hand written text (on very fine paper), of his yet unpublished journal from the Second World War. His journal from the First World War, written as a child (and therefore before he was a Dominican) he did not put in the Provincial archives, which began to be gathered together before his death, but it was found in his room after he died.

The files, for what was to become *A History of Theology*, contain original correspondence, some in French and some in English, to and from Congar with the publisher and others (including hand written letters by **Étienne Gilson**, who played an instrumental role in encouraging Congar to re-write the text and publish the book), of how this work came to be published in English by Doubleday, with notes on the additions and corrections to be made by Congar and who was responsible for the translation and the final publication.

In the correspondence found in the Paris archives there is a letter of November 1959 from Anton Pegis, Editorial Director at Doubleday in New York, to Congar, while he was living in Strassbourg in 'exile', the first letter regarding the publication, which makes the connection with Gilson. 'Professor Gilson has forwarded to me your letter of October 16, 1959, in which you were kind enough to consider in a favourable way the publication of your article "Thélogie" in English.' The letter also deals with the issues around the fact the original publisher Letouzey 'suppressed about one third of your original text', and that 'it may be that the publisher has no rights in the circumstances' and adds 'however . . . it would be correct to inquire whether this is the case'. The letter leaves it to Conagr, as author, to make the inquiries, which he did, and he was allowed to rework the manuscript. (The correspondence between Congar and Letouzey is also in the archives.) The letter from Pegis finishes with a proposal that a Fr Eschmann of Toronto be the translator of the work once it was received. There is no note in the files from Congar about this proposal and presumably this is a Fr Ignatius Echmann OP (1898–1968), a German Dominican who was professor of philosophy at the Pontifical Institute of Mediaeval Studies in Torronto from 1942.

Some time elapsed before Congar completed the work, including (after his 'exile') the period of his involvement with the Second Vatican Council, and the final draft was sent to New York in 1966. By that time, for whatever reason, it was clear Fr Eschmann would not be the translator, possibly due to ill health or advancing age as he died in 1968 at the age of seventy.

In a letter, of May 1966, by JF Bernard (no mention of what his position is in the company) to Congar, and after Doubelday 'were delighted to receive the manuscript', he, Congar, is told who would now be the translator. 'You may be interested to know that the translator of the book will be Hunter Guthrie SJ, a former rector of Georgetown University and a most able and accomplished theologian and translator. Father Guthrie was, coincidentally, one of the censors of the Archdiocese of Paris who read (with highest approval) the original manuscript in 1939.' Guthrie makes no mention in the Doubleday book, published in 1968, of this earlier acquaintance with the Letouzey article.

Sadly, and somewhat oddly for Congar, the files in the Archives do not contain a copy of the original French manuscript from which the French translation into English was made. This publishing house has tried over a number of years with various sources to locate the original French manuscript so that a new French edition could be made, but this search has come up with nothing. Congar wrote it in a time before photocopiers, and it seems Congar did not keep a copy, not even a carbon copy, of what he sent to the American publishers to be translated. This does seem rather odd for Congar. Alas also it seems the translator, Guthrie (he died in November 1974), did not keep a copy or the copy in his personal files (held by his Jesuit Province in America), that is the original French document, and those responsible today for the Doubleday files do not have the files with the manuscript either.

Who has the original French text? Does it still exist somewhere? Was there only the one copy made by Congar and not kept by anyone? Was it not returned Congar by Doubleday? Was it returned to Congar by Doubleday, and later mislaid? However, if by chance the manuscript and the letter were there in the files, were they taken from the files at some stage and never returned, or kept in someone's personal files or, worse still, destroyed?

There are, thus, limitless possibilities as to what has happened to the text sent to New York in 1966

If the original still exists somewhere it is a mystery that has not been solved to date despite a number of years of research and contacting different groups and individuals including those who took over the Doubleday publication list.

But if it does exist somewhere, one day it may turn up in a cupboard or in a file that has long been forgotten. What a find it would be! Anyone who reads this who may know of its location, ATF Press would be very happy to hear from them!

The files in the archives of the Province of France do not refer to the possibility of a French edition. So, in a rather unusual situation for Congar this full text we have in English was never published in French and so is the only version of the full manuscript of this important text by him. However, we do have the English translation and with gratitude to all concerned, including Jean Michele Pontin OP, the current Provincial Archivist of the Province of France, we all owe a debt of gratitude, and now have this new edition including a preliminary piece by the American theologian Thomas O'Meara OP.

It is, then, a great pleasure and with much satisfaction after much work over a number of years, that ATF Press provides this new edition to the theological world.

Publisher
ATF Press
Adelaide, Australia
August 2019

Introduction

Thomas F O'Meara, OP

These pages offer a new edition of Yves Congar's *History of Theology*. This work began as a lengthy article appearing in the multi-volume *Dictionnaire de Théologie* in 1946 entitled '*Théologie*'.[1] Congar wrote that he, Fr M-D Chenu, and Fr Henri-Marie Féret in the 1930s planned to write a history of theology. Their work load, World War II, and Chenu's teaching in Canada interfered. He used some of his notes for that project for the article begun in 1938. The manuscript was completed by the Dominican priest as he was mobilized for service in the French army because World War II was just beginning.

After being captured by the Germans he attempted to escape; that was punished by internment in the stricter camps of Lübeck and Colditz. Those experiences of repression prepared him—he later observed—for the censorious measures to come in the 1950s from the Vatican because of his advocacy of ecumenism and historical approaches to ecclesiology. Later he did not hesitate to compare the Holy Office with the Gestapo.[2] Returning from the war, Congar looked at what had been published in the *Dictionnaire* and found that his text had been cut by about two-fifths. He edited and improved the original text, restoring many of

---

1. Congar, '*Théologie*', in *Dictionnaire de Théologie* 15: 1 (Paris: Letouzey et Ané, 1946), cols. 341–502.
2. Étienne Fouilloux, 'Un théologien dans l'Église du XXe siècle', in *Bulletin de literature ecclésiastique*, 106 (2005): 22. Fouilloux speaks of Congar's theology 'illuminating the path of the church traversing history' ('L'apport du Père Congar à la théologie du XXe siècle', in *Gregorianum*, 83 [2002]: 507).

the deletions; that work was not published in French but translated into English in 1968.

Yves Congar's family lived in Sedan in northeast France, although he was of a people whose native land was to the west, Celtic Brittany. Congar's mentor was the great medieval scholar of the structure and synthesis of Thomas Aquinas, M-D Chenu. He founded a school emphasising historical knowledge as well as contemporary ministry. In that French Dominican seminary of Le Saulchoir Congar studied and then taught. History was the way to bring past ages and thinkers to life and, equally important, let them contribute to contemporary renewal. Aquinas—not only in the thirteenth and sixteenth centuries but in the twentieth century—could be a force for leading the Roman Catholic Church in new directions. Congar spent his life studying the history of the structures and institutional theories of the *ecclesia.* He catalogued topics and ideas from publications in ecclesiology appearing in Europe and around the world. He was also a Roman Catholic pioneer of ecumenism with Protestant and Orthodox churches.

After World War II there was no lack of teachers and pastors, theologians and activists who said that the Roman Catholic Church needed to enter into a revitalisation to help present the Gospel in a positive and attractive way. That renewal energized a spectrum of ideas and church institutions. Not a few seminaries and schools north of the Alps broke out of the sterile intellectual framework imposed after 1850 by the Vatican, a monopoly of one philosophy and its related philosophical theology drawn from medieval scholasticism. The sole purpose of theology was to defend doctrinal definitions and ecclesiastical laws. Years passed, and that new version of 'school-thinking', a neo-medievalism, was dominant up to Vatican II. It was mainly philosophical, Aristotelian, a textbook collection of definitions and divisions. Some claimed it to be the thought of Aquinas, but the neo-Thomism from 1850 to 1950 was neither a medieval thought nor the prized theology of Aquinas. According to Otto Pesch, neo-scholasticism held the real theology of Aquinas 'under house arrest'.[3]

Franciscans and Benedictines, Dominicans and Jesuits, universities like Louvain and Munich—each developed after 1900 accurate, expansive, and Christian interpretations of medieval thinkers. That theological rebirth could serve the present and could be in dialogue with the approaches of modern philosophers. Christian ideas and church forms had the power to express in new ways the reality of the church, local and universal. 'Anyone who did not live during the years of French Catholicism after the war missed one of the finest moments in the life of the Church. Through a slow emergence from misery, one tried in the great freedom of a fidelity as profound as itself, to rejoin in a gospel way the world, a world of which the church could become an integral part for the first time in centuries.'[4] While Congar was composing the article, '*Théologie*', he was also organising a series of future books in ecumenism and ecclesiology, *Unam Sanctam*, and was writing the first volume for that collection, *Chrétiens désunis*, a pioneering study of Catholicism within the ecumenical movement.[5]

Congar's 'Preface' to the history published in 1968 discussed how theology since 1939 had unfolded as new approaches to theology began to replace neo-scholasticism. Patristic and biblical studies appeared in a considerable number. The related to a new secular appreciation of time and emphasised the historical structure of revelation. Theologies after 1950 faced new questions and areas

3. Pesch, *Thomas von Aquin, Grenze und Grösse einer mittelalterlichen Theologie* (Mainz: Matthias-Grunewald,1988), 197. Congar called Thomas Aquinas 'the master-teacher of realism', (Fouilloux, 'L'apport du Père Congar', 508).

4. Congar, *Dialogue between Christians. Catholic Contributions to Ecumenism* (London: G Chapman, 1966), 32.

5. Congar, *Chrétiens désunis* (Paris: Cerf, 1937). The series *Unam Sanctam* had over thirty-five volumes up to the time of Vatican II when it produced commentaries and studies on the Council. A new series began around 2014.

of discussion: some did this by employing the traditional, creedal arrangement of information (Michael Schmaus), while others fashioned a theology out of personal or social thought-forms and orientations drawn from contemporary philosophy (Karl Rahner). If Vatican II has opened the way further, 'it has given only a vague indication of the theological work of the future'.[6]

Congar's temporal overview of 1500 years of intellectual history, after a discussion of the history of the word, 'Theology', treats six periods, six cultural ages of Christian thinking. Here theology is a spectrum including, for instance, spirituality, moral theology, and ecclesiology along with the thought-forms behind all of them. Hervé Legrand sees Congar's overall method and approach as beginning with the history of doctrines but presenting and locating them in a wider realm of culture. He sees the unity of Christian teaching and of Catholicism to be a unity in diversity. The dialectic of revelation and culture, repressed in recent decades, is now being restored.[7] The New Testament follows this approach as do the first centuries of Christian teaching and thinking. While Congar's book has its limitations in terms of treating mainly the Western Church in Europe, the sections themselves are something vital and relatively new. They look at history as cultural periods, each with a beginning, a flourishing center, and a conclusion leading to the next epoch. Out of a moment of originality and newness a particular cluster of ideas has wide influence. In each age human activities from metaphysics to painting have an identity through a collection of particular forms. History is neither a rigid narration nor one age or philosophical expression. Faith and church are developmental, varied, vital, and organic.

---

6. Congar, *A History of Theology* (Garden City, NY: Doubleday, 1968), 18.
7. Hervé Legrand, 'Yves Congar (1904–1995): une passion pour l'unité', in *Nouvelle Revue Théologique*, 126 (2004): 549.

The six epochal chapters offer not only information but historical context and insight: they retain their value today. The Dominican historian treats somewhat the cultural context of these six periods of theology. For instance, patristic theology first existed in the world of pagan culture with its philosophies and religions. Christians were not arguing against some dubious teachings of religion, but they lived within a world of science and morality that was in various ways not Christian or Jewish. The second section, 'From the Sixth Century to the Twelfth Century', describes the little known age leading from the early theologians of the church (increasingly neglected) to the new kinds of European schools with some knowledge of Aristotle and literary figures like Alcuin. The twelfth century receives its own section, for that century sees the emergence of the school, the inquiring question, the open discussion, and the organic *summa*. The section of sixty pages on the thirteenth century (some of the final pages are dedicated to a decline in the fourteenth century) offers Congar in the realm he knows so well and has creatively formed, Thomas Aquinas and medieval theology in the universities. There follows a section on the Reformation. The pages on scholasticism in the sixteenth century and after Trent remain a valuable summary of that age with its theological method, organized textbooks, and theology as spirituality. The period from the seventeenth century is informative, and its understanding of thought forms like pyramid or descending Dionysian illumination are helpful for understanding the model of central church administration that has lasted up to the present time.

Neo-scholasticism yielded in the late sixteenth century to a 'Tridentinism'. That was not the Council of Trent (which has its place in tradition) but a system developed under the influence of popes after Trent. It sought to control and reduce to one ideology every aspect of Catholic life and faith, furthering Roman centralization and the repres-

sion of all that was new and extra-Roman.[8] There was a particular emptiness in the control exercised by Rome between
the end of the Baroque and Vatican II. Congar learned
from history to reject what he called the hyperinactivity of
the Vatican, the church as thoroughly defensive, and the
neglect of Christology and pneumatology.

The last section carries forward the movement of the
late Baroque and then looks at the nineteenth century, particularly at ecclesiology and theological method among
German theologians. It reaches the twentieth century by
surveying theologians and books that represent some dialogue between Catholicism and modern philosophy. This
concluding section ends with pages on 'Conditions of Theological Work and Progress'. They treat the relationships of
theology to the Christian spiritual life and to the universal
church. What are the contributions of theologians to the
church? Is not some freedom necessary for the theologian
to proceed? Congar, however, offers little here on theology
in the future, perhaps because that was considered in the
'Preface'.

History is omnipresent and liberating. 'Everything is
absolutely historical including the person of Jesus Christ.
The Gospel is historical; Thomas Aquinas is historical; Paul
VI is historical. Historical does not mean just that Jesus
came at a certain point in time but that one must draw today
the consequences of this fact, He is conditioned by the time

---

8. Bernard Lauret, editor, *Fifty Years of Catholic Theology.
Conversations with Yves Congar* (Philadelphia: Fortress, 1988), 3–5.
Congar rejected every reactionary fundamentalism in the church
fixated on this or that phrase or devotion. That *'intégrisme'* held a
false way of conceiving what was supernatural and rejected healthy
manifestations of human nature and subjectivity. 'A refusal of the
modern world, a taste for all that is determined by the mode of
authority comes basically from a contempt or a misunderstanding
in regard to that which is presented as view of humanity, a
development, and as emergence of new perspectives in history'
(Congar, 'Mentalité "de droite" et intégrisme', in *La Vie Intellectuelle,*
52 [1950]: 657).

in and through which he lives.'[9] At Vatican II among the theologian-experts, the '*periti*', Congar was remarkable for his influence, past and present. Illustrative is an entry in Congar's diary for the end of the Council on December 7, 1965. 'I left the Basilica slowly and with difficulty; a number of bishops congratulated me, saying that this was very much my work. Looking at things objectively, I did do a lot to prepare for the Council, to elaborate and diffuse the ideas the Council made its own. At the Council itself I worked a lot.' He lists sections of the documents on the church and on revelation that are from him as well as the introduction and the conclusion of the text on ecumenism and that on non-Christians. Parts of the documents on foreign missions, priests, and religious liberty hold his ideas. 'In short, this morning, that which was read came very extensively from me.'[10] Richard McBrien wrote: 'By any reasonable account, Yves Congar is the most distinguished ecclesiologist of this century and perhaps of the entire post-Tridentine era. No modern theologian's spirit was accorded fuller play in the documents of Vatican II than Congar's.'[11] Vatican II is a significant marker and goal in the history of Western Christian theology as presented in this book. The European ecclesiologist Hervé Legrand observes: 'It is very rare that the personal destiny of a theologian prefigures and influence the course of the life of the Church.'[12] In some ways the course of the recent history of theology in this volume is heading towards Vatican II.

Within this history of theology Congar's own theology is present: seminal, historical, global, and structural. The

---

9. Jean Puyo, *Jean Puyo interroge Yves Congar 'Une vie pour la verité'* (Paris: Le Centurion, 1975), 43.

10. Congar, *Mon Journal du Concile* II (Paris: Cerf, 2002), 510f. My translation.

11. McBrien, 'Church and Ministry. The Achievement of Yves Congar', *Theology Digest*. 32 (1985): 203.

12. Jossua, 'Yves Congar. La vie et l'oeuvre d'un théologien', in *Cristianesimo nella storia*, 17 (1996): 1.

Church was moving from a past, Latin set of precise doctrines and religious rituals back to the sources of the New
Testament and the early theologians. The institutions of
today are themselves products of the past. A biblical and
pneumatic reality may have grounded this or that papal
ritual. Sacramentality or ministry had a source and history
greater than Baroque episcopal vestments or Latin canons.
In the incarnational process of the Christian church under-
lying sources lead historical forms and ideas to becomes
concrete in new movements for social justice or in expanded
ecclesial ministries.[13] At the same time, an absence of philosophy as the inner dynamic (and not as another aspect of
a historical culture) is rather absent. The history of Christianity is very much a dynamic continuity of institutions
(including the papacy). An emphasis on important ideas
and perennial institutions is central, while schism and heresy and separation are to be avoided as abnormal. Thus
unity, church, tradition, and history emerge as aspects of
Congar's way of thinking and writing. They are, of course,
the titles of his important books.

For the Dominican, Vatican II was not a group of regulating documents but an event whose challenging time and
broadly influential creativity was beginning. When he was
asked about deliberations in the United States on ecclesio-
logical issues like a national pastoral council or a role for
members of the church other than archbishops in the selection of bishops he observed: 'The upheavals in the post-
conciliar era have their roots not in Vatican II but in the
constrictive decades or centuries before it . . . It is astonishing how the post-conciliar period has so little to do with the
Council. The post-conciliar questions are new and radical.

---

13. A collection of essays and talks by Congar from the end of the
    Council into the postconciliar years is René Rémond, editor, *Le
    Concile de Vatican II* (Paris: Beauchesne, 1984). A large history of
    theology but one focused on the theologies of the church is *L'Église
    de saint Augustin* à *l'époque modern* (Paris: Cerf, 1970).

"Aggiornamento" [now] means changes and adaptations to a new situation.'[14]

The Ecumenical Council liberated Christian realities for the church. This will not just be for Europe. 'The requests from Africa or Asia for a true inculturation are authentic requests from the church as its moves in the journey of the human race.'[15] In the 1950s Congar had called a 'wide world' the church's 'parish'.[16] Now he observed a new 'Catholicity' in the Church. It has two sources: the fullness of the grace of Christ, and the virtual infinity of creation and the development of the human species.[17] The challenge posed by the modern person and contemporary society is twofold: the perspective and creativity of the subject and the unfolding of history. 'It is not *in spite* of time and its course but in them that the Church brings forth the gifts of God and realizes them.'[18] Christians cannot avoid time with its expansion and its delays, for into that dynamic stream God's gifts come. Yves Congar spent his life serving history, and it rewarded him with change and even progress.

---

14. Letter to Thomas O'Meara (1970); see William W Bassett, editor, *The Choosing of Bishops: Historical and Theological Studies* (Hartford, CT: Canon Law Society of America, 1971); *A National Pastoral Council: Pro and Con* (Washington, DC: USCC, 1971).

15. Congar, 'Situation au moment de "Ecclesiam Suam"', in *Le Concile de Vatican II*, 32.

16. Congar, *The Wide World My Parish; Salvation and Its Problems* (Baltimore: Helicon, 1961) 17; a new French edition appeared in 2000.

17. Congar, 'Les religions non bibliques sont-elles des médiations de salut?', inEcumenical Institute for Advanced Theological Studies, *Year-Book 1972–1973* (Jerusalem: Tantur, 1973), 82.

18. Congar, 'Pour un sens vrai de l'Église', in *Cette Église que j'aime* (Paris: Éditions du Cerf, 1968, 94). 'The vision of the Council—that of *Lumen Gentium*—has been resolutely that of the history of salvation given a destiny by eschatology. The Council has taken in the best of biblical, patristic and theological studies of the past thirty years preceding it, but also it has been a pastoral council; doctrinal certainly but in a pastoral vision and directed by pastors' ('Situation au moment de "Ecclesiam Suam"', in *Le Concile de Vatican II*, 27).My translation.

Foreword

Hunter Guthrie, S.J.

In an ecumenical age, this is an ecumenical work, both in content and composition.

In content it presents a theology which is at once historical and modern. In composition it is the original work of a Dominican, translated and amicably edited by a Jesuit—nothing could be more ecumenical.

The work is truly a masterpiece. In this day of cloudy thinking it comes to grips with reality at every point that is important for man's relationship to himself and to eternity.

It is a work of scholarship and still a text geared to the student's needs and his problems. It is a basic orientation course for the start of a college curriculum in theology. For it introduces the student to all of the great names in Catholic thought, together with their methods and conclusions.

In keeping with the ecumenical age, Martin Luther has his say and, indeed, a very good one.

From its pages those of all faiths, or none, can come to an adequate understanding of the march of Christian theological thought during the last two thousand years.

May 1968

Preface

Yves Congar, OP

This book substantially reproduces the article entitled "Théologie" which appeared in the *Dictionnaire de Théologie Catholique* published at Paris in 1938–39. My manuscript was sent to the editor, Msgr. Amann, on the second of September 1939, just as I was preparing to leave for the general mobilization prior to World War II. Returning from the war at the end of May 1945, I was surprised to see that the editor had discarded about two-fifths of my text. It was a question at times of useful simplifications replacing long heavy arguments, and in these cases I have let the changes stand. At other times, however, there were deletions that weakened the text and its documentation, and in such cases I have restored the deleted passages. This fact alone is evidence that the present text is more complete than that published in the *Dictionnaire*.

It has, moreover, another claim to relative perfection. I have tried to update the present work, particularly in its historical section. Since 1939 there have been many books devoted to the object and method of theology. On these topics it was certainly my duty to provide a well-documented summary for my readers. I acknowledge the fact that the result is somewhat short of what I envisaged. Several paragraphs should have been rewritten, but time and opportunity were simply not available. My excuse is that I bowed to the friendly pleadings of eminent historians and of my editor. I have, however, introduced rectifications and sufficient and necessary additions, so that this revised edition meets the exigencies of honesty and, hopefully, answers a real, current need.

What has been published during the past thirty years on the life of the world and of the Church deserves more than a simple up-to-date bibliography. The theological situation, in fact, even the idea of theological endeavor, has changed in a quarter of a century. Nevertheless, it is well to remember that the continuities are more profound than the differences.

What has been called the "new theology" (radical as it may seem) is, in fact, more traditional than similar advances in other intellectual disciplines. Many eminent contemporary theologians are finding that their research turns up traditional leads and data in the economy or history of salvation, in eschatology, anthropology, etc. If we simply trace the evolution of theological ideas since 1939 we will discover an inspired and profound renewal of traditional Christian thought. This is not to say that no serious problems have arisen from the pact that Catholic theology seemed to have had with medieval or post-tridentine Scholasticism.

Let us therefore have a look at what has taken place since 1939 and thus find out where we are today.

In France, 1944–46 were years of intense fermentation. Two new collections of theological works appeared in print. The first was *Sources chrétiennes* (1942) which translated several books of the Greek Fathers, in particular those of Origen. The second series was called *Théologie*, which began in 1944 with *Conversion et grâce chez S. Thomas d'Aquin* by Fr. H. Bouillard, and *Corpus mysticum*, and two years later published Fr. H. de Lubac's *Surnaturel*. It was thought that these publications were the beginnings and first expressions of a "new theology," whose manifesto seemed to have been an article published by Fr. Jean Daniélou, "Les orientations présentes de la pensée religieuse," in *Études*, avril-juin 1946. In addition, new thinking on the nature of theology itself was expressed by Fr. M. D. Chenu in an essay entitled "Une École de Théologie" and a book by Fr. L. Charlier, *Essai sur le Problème Théologique*, published in 1938. Both of these works were put on the Index on February 6, 1942.[1] Fr. Charlier had outlined a critique of the nature and validity of theological conclusions, which it must be admitted never gained much support. Fr. Chenu's work examined the role of spiritual experience in the orientation of theology and also the value which the life of the Church has as a *locus theologicus*. The problem arose when, in a very questionable manner, these ideas of a vitalist religious conception of theology were grouped together and published, each in its own perspective, by Fr. Th. Soiron, G. Koepgen, and Fr. Hans Urs von Balthasar.

The choice of certain treatises translated in *Sources chrétiennes* (for example, the "Introduction" to one of Origen's works) strongly suggested that the typological, spiritual, and even allegorical exegesis of the Fathers was favored to the detriment of the literal sense. A chapter in the *Corpus mysticum* entitled "Du symbole à la dialectique" tried to encourage a return to a rich but wider interpretation in preference to the conceptual analysis on which Scholasticism thrived. Finally a sentence from Fr. H. Bouillard was cited: "When the spirit evolves, a truth remains immutable thanks only to a simultaneous and correlative evolution of all its ideas and to the fact that these preserve the same relation to each other. A *theology which is no longer in tune with its time is a false theology*."[2] Now this could be interpreted as a profession of historic and philosphic relativism, for it would seem that the invariant dogma, which the faithful profess formally to respect, remained foreign to ideas, that is, foreign to the concepts in which theology had given them a workable expression at some given date. Hence, it was left open to question what was to become not only of St. Thomas' theology but of theological science as he defined it. What, in brief, was to be the value of dogmatic formulas? Some professional Thomists, and particularly the Dominican Father R. Gar-

---

1. *AAS*, t. XXXIV, 1942, p. 37.
2. *Conversion et grâce chez S. Thomas d'Aquin*. Paris, 1944, p. 219. From this passage the usual quotation is simply the sentence I have underlined.

rigou-Lagrange, soon gave expression to their disturbance and their questions. The authors, and even more forcefully the Jesuit collaborators of *Sources chrétiennes* and *Théologie*, defended their position and explained it. They maintained that even though their position was basically modernistic, it was not necessarily destructive. It centered on two key points: (1) a distinction which was really a disjunction between *faith* and *belief*, the latter being the ideological structure in which faith finds expression; (2) the conception of the relation between dogmatic pronouncements and religious realities as a relation of symbol to reality, not as an expression *proper* (however inadequate) to reality.

The writings of 1944–46, which dealt with certain points of doctrinal history, had encountered to a certain extent the same problem as the Modernists, viz., the variations in the representations and the intellectual construction of the affirmations of faith. But this, of course, is a problem encountered in the pursuit of any historical knowledge. These authors solved the problem by distinguishing between an invariant of affirmations, and the variable usage of technical notions to translate essential truth in historic contexts differing culturally and philosophically. For them, first of all, the *invariant* was a set of affirmations having a real content of truth. And secondly, in the differing notional translations which the theologians had given, there existed an analogy of relations or a functional equivalence between the notions used to express that truth. In this way they escaped the accusation of ruinous anti-intellectualism and dogmatic relativism justly brought against the Modernists. There remained grounds, however, for suspecting that a penetrating philosophical analysis had furnished no clarification to the concept, reasoning, and systematization of theology.[3] Indeed,

---

3. The discussion had not gone as far as a philosophical reinterrogation regarding the place of the concept in our perception of the truth, its nature and value. Some interesting reflections on this subject by Fr. Ed. Schillebeeckx in *Approches théologiques*. I. *Révélation et Théologie*. Bruxelles, 1965, pp. 223–84, 340–45.

the simplified teaching of the schools and manuals, and even the authority of St. Thomas himself, seemed to have been infringed. Certain positions and formulations generally considered settled—and almost canonized—had been brought into question. The anxiety aroused was for the most part artificial. At the time, however, a certain few fashioned the fantastic idea of a "new theology" which moreover they were incapable of defining—as this author has learned from personal experience a good hundred times between 1946 and 1950.

It is true that Pius XII had used the expression "new theology" in his discourse of September 1946 to the general Congregation of the Jesuits.[4] The tenor of this discourse had been repeated to the general chapter of the Dominican Fathers (without a repetition of the expression "new theology").[5] Shortly after these two discourses, the Encyclical *Humani Generis* specified the precise points about which the Holy Father foresaw the danger of certain "novelties."[6] The dangers denounced arose from excessive concessions made to modern philosophies, dialectic materialism, existentialism, historicism, or—as is very evident today—irenics. They fostered a distrust of the use of reason in apologetics and theology, a weakening of speculative theology and of the value of dogmatic formulas, a neglect of the ordinary *magisterium*, and a failure to return to scriptural and patristic sources.

Today the crisis has passed, if indeed there was ever really a crisis. As always the problems remain. They are grounded in a situation whose component parts it may be

---

4. AAS, t. XXXVIII, 1946, pp. 384–86.

5. *Ibid.*, pp. 386–88.

6. AAS, t. XLII, 1950, p. 561 *sq.*; *Denz.* 3875–99. Fr. G. Weigel's article, "The Historical Background of the Encyclical *Humani Generis*," (*Theological Studies*, t. XII, 1951, pp. 208–30) would draw from my pen certain reserves. But "Gleanings from the Commentaries on *Humani Generis*" (pp. 520–49), a sort of bulletin on the Encyclical's commentaries, is well documented and instructive.

useful to outline briefly. I distinguish three principal elements, to which must be added the influence of ecumenism; but this latter is difficult to evaluate particularly with regard to the notion of theology.

The first is a renewal of the sources which nourish theological thought, at least by giving it incentive and appeal. Pius XII himself in the document where he undertook the defense of reason and speculative theology of the classical type recognized that "the study of the sources has always been a principle of rejuvenation for the sacred sciences, whereas speculation which neglects to delve again and again into the deposit of faith proves sterile."[7] Now the means of biblical and patristic source-research are incomparably better and more abundant today than in the nineteenth century. The deepening of our knowledge of history and philology have resurrected interest in more than one question. Contact with the primary sources has raised other questions dealing with the very nature of theological work: Revelation takes place in the framework of history or of an "economy." But are a conceptual-deductive method and an ordered plan of study following merely the formal sequences, sufficient and apt to amass and correlate all the data of Revelation?[8] And isn't it true that many of the concepts borrowed by St. Thomas from Aristotle and used by Scholasticism do not really convey exactly the concepts found in Sacred Scripture? Where in the great Scholastic syntheses are the biblical notions of *alliance, agape, flesh, know, hesed, justice,* and indeed the common notions of *word, kingdom,* and *truth*? There is definitely a gap between what we find under these headings in a good treatise or a good lexicon of biblical theology, and what we find in the great Scholastics or in our classic manuals.

---

7. *Aumani Generis: AAS,* pp. 568–69; *Denz.* 3886.
8. See my study on "Le moment 'économique' et le moment 'ontologique' dans la Sacra Doctrina," in *Mélanges M.-D. Chenu.,* Paris, 1966.

Finally, the questions and the difficulties raised by the Modernists, and again in 1944–6 in entirely other circumstances, basically refer to the concept of Revelation itself. The gap between notions which we have just pointed out exists primarily in that area. A one-sided approach to Revelation has considered it to be a collection of statements of a philosophical type dealing with realities which almost entirely escape our experience—as though it were a collection of theorems whose demonstration the teacher simply would not give. But for the past sixty years there has been a better understanding on the one hand of the economic and historic structure of Revelation, and on the other of its essential aim of alliance, i.e., to establish an interpersonal relation between God and His people. The dogmatic Constitution *Dei Verbum* of Vatican II (18 November 1965) has finally appropriated these values without the prejudice to a definite intellectual content. This is very important for the future of Catholic theology, since it solves many problems or at least renders them less problematic.

A second source of renewal which seems to be very efficacious is the new awareness which the theologians have not only of the real state of the world from the standpoint of faith, but also of their role with regard to this situation. The theologians have always worked in the Church and *for* the Church. For a long time, however, the majority of them produced their theology exactly as though the world had not become foreign to the affirmation of the faith which they distinguished and subdistinguished and over which they poured ratiocination. This is still the situation in certain schools and concerning certain questions (for example, aspects of Mariology). But a number of theologians have taken a better view of the link which binds theological work as a reflection on faith to the Church's duty of proposing the faith successfully to the men of this day and age. This link imposes on the theologian duties which transcend the service he can render by scientifically interpreting and theologically clarifying the realities of missionary activity or the pastoral ministry. In the theology of the Incarnation of the Son, for example, he must find room for the sacraments and eschatology, and even in the mystery of the Three Divine Persons he must examine the questions about human beings and propose solutions. Such a program is well within the directive proposed by Vatican I on the profit which our intelligence draws from contemplating the relation between the great mysteries and our final goal.[9] But this is not merely a question of enriching a treatise by the addition of a new paragraph. It is, rather, a question of establishing a new dimension of reality—a fifth dimension probably—which, in keeping with the nature of Revelation, embraces God and man and treats at length of the religious link between them.

I cannot exaggerate the importance of the new consciousness which theologians have acquired of their responsibility to the Church and to the internal credibility of the faith which the Church must offer mankind. There is less question today of technical details derived from standard theological systems; interest in a school's position—so often linked with Religious Orders—continues only in those rare, isolated spots not yet shaken by the great question, "What is our purpose in the world?" The passion for a conclusion-centered theology is also well in abeyance.

Thirdly, it should be noted that the most active currents of thought are those allied to the phenomenological method and to the philosophy of existence. Consequently, they tend to center reflection on man. Three great features or three great themes demand attention as a result of this reflection on the existential experience of man. First, the specificity of the personhood and all that pertains to it. People cannot be considered merely as simple things or objects. Beginning in this way, not only the consideration of certain realities (for example, the body, sacraments, the realities of conjugal love, the eschatological realities) appears in a new light,

---

9. Sess. Ill, cap. 4: *Denz.* 1796 (3016).

but also a certain *thingness* or *physicalness* of the classical theology become evidently unsatisfactory. *Thingness* and *physicalness* historically have been the consequence of the Scholastic method of interrogation: "What is a sacrament (and the answer: an instrumental cause); what is the fire of purgatory . . . etc." The point is that not only would the different treatises or chapters of theology be affected by this new consideration,[10] but also the *abordage*, the way of approach, the method of "theologizing." This new outlook was rich with possibilities. It was also fraught with dangers. It permitted an "existential approach," that manner of reference to human life which in its own fashion had sought out "kerygmatic theology." It ran the risk of attaching meanings to things only under the heading of existence, forgetting the ontology which ultimately gives them foundation, and neglecting to establish the relations between the affirmations of salvific faith and rational thought—something the Catholic Church has never failed to do. Secondly, after that as a start, an ontology was drawn up which was called "intersubjective" or "interpersonal." It is clear that this will affect not only the treatise on grace and sin, but also Christology and the doctrine of the Trinity. Thirdly, the historicity of the human condition has finally been brought to light in a new fashion, under the aspect of the condition of a being of the world and of a being with the other characteristics of the human person.

It is clear that all this introduces values for theological reflection other than those used by the Schools since the Middle Ages. It follows, of course, that the monopoly *de facto* exercised by Scholasticism has been called into question or, at least, that type of theology which has been called *Konklusionstheologie*. Even when it does not refuse to treat the classic themes with a reflection on the mysteries—such a refusal would be an abdication, practically treason—the

---

10. Fr. Schillebeeckx has drawn up a list of these renovations: "De nieuwe wending in de huidige dogmatiek," in *Tijdschrift voor theologie*, t. I, 1961, pp. 17–46.

new theology seeks rather to develop along the lines of a reflection on faith from the standpoint of its message to men, and then a reflection on faith before undertaking a reply to that fundamental question: how is faith—not in general, but the Christian faith—possible in a secularized world where it is universally questioned and where the "death of God" is at least practically admitted as an obvious condition for man to affirm himself? Hence theology tends to become a reflection on the totality of Revelation, on its fact *and content* insofar as it concerns man. For, from this viewpoint, nothing would have been gained if, with the ancient apologetic, the fact of Revelation had been simply established with man's consequent duty to submit to this Revelation without considering its content and the basic relation to man.

Following the suggestion of Fr. K. Rahner[11] these considerations can evidently be developed into a formal theology, introductory to the special theology where we find again our classical treatises simply completed where they seem most desirable. This formal dogma would thus assume, in part at least, the task of fundamental theology. It would involve a large development of "transcendental anthropology," that is, a study of the *a priori* conditions in which Revelation and faith are possible. But all of theology and the mode of "theologizing" would necessarily be affected.

It should be clear, then, that a classical type of theology can *adapt* and absorb the new questions and develop the new aspects, which, we have seen, refer to man and his existential experience. For example, this is what M. Schmaus has already done in his *Domatik*. We have here a renovation of the classic *De Deo* treatise, beginning with a study of the divine Persons, an insertion of theology into economy, a

---

11. See in the second edition of *Lex. f. Theol. u. Kirche* the articles *Dogmatik* (t. Ill, col. 449–51), *Formale u. Fundamentale Theologie* (t. IV, col. 205); at the head of *Schriften zur Theologie* (t. I, Frieburg, 1954, pp. 9–47) the plan for Dogma; P.G., An *interview. Karl Rahner. Theologian at Work*, in *The Amer. Eccles. Rev.*, t. CLIII, 1965, p. 217–30.

complete renovation of ecclesiology and eschatology, etc. This same new approach has been attempted by a series of monographs entitled *Le Mystère chrétien.*[12] In this series we try to give to the datum (revelation) its primacy and a large development. But from this datum previously and carefully established, theology is constructed as a rational organization and as an elaboration of it with the help—among others—of the elements of traditional philosophy eventually, and subsidiarily, with the help of the elements of modern philosophy.

Another type of theology appears in the wake of K. Rahner and his disciples. He makes no obeisance to the normal succession of *intellectus fidei* to *auditus fidei.* He makes no extended search into the annals of tradition to sift out the elements of an answer to new problems. Rather his position is a philosophical reflection on the relation which the global affirmation of faith has with man. When the questions of special dogma are considered; it must be remembered that the effort is not to establish or criticize certain treatises with reference to a documentary datum, but rather to establish a critique of the concepts engaged in the question and of the meanings of the affirmed propositions. In this way it is easy to arrive at a renewal of the concepts with respect to which the question is posed, or at the relation between its concepts. Give thought to problems such as nature and grace, lay status and functions of the Church, belonging to the Church, etc. . . . To answer these questions calls for a real theology, for reflection applies to realities testified to by our faith, but for a theology more philosophical and critico-reflective in character than historical.

In short, today we find differing manners of theologizing. Scholasticism: conceptual, argumentative, or deductive, exhausts the datum of tradition, not only of an *intellectus fidei*, rationally established, but of an application to differ-

---

12. First volume: *La Foi et la Theologie.* Toumai-Paris, 1962.

ent times and cultures. The reflective manner, on the other hand, philosophizes on the whole of Christian reality, illuminated, if you will, by the existential experience of man.

Vatican II has given us only a vague indication of the theological work of the future. The Council itself has used a theology sprung from the common tradition of the Schools in the Latin Church, but somewhat modified by its pastoral intention. During the first period of the Council, especially during the discussion on "the sources of Revelation" two mentalities came to the forefront.[13] On the one hand there was the conceptualist mentality, whose ideal is to define exactly the outlines of a notion carefully isolated from others and considered on the supra-temporal level. In this manner clean fishbone formulas are achieved without a chance of revision by recourse to a more profound tradition or without even a small margin permitting some embellishment. It is possible by pure reasoning to extend the consequences of the notion thus defined to new conclusions. But the Council followed another plan. It sought out a more concrete attack on reality, an overture of questions with the other Churches and approaches; often in this way the facts have preceded and guided the ideas. The Council has not worked toward propositions under the form of canons, but toward broad doctrinal statements often nourished by biblical and traditional sap. John XXIII outlined the path to take when, in his discourse of October 11, 1962, he said: "The Christian, Catholic, and Apostolic spirit awaits throughout the world a swift movement forward to a doctrinal penetration and a formation of consciences which corresponds more perfectly and more faithfully to the authentic doctrine, which must nevertheless be studied and set forth in accord with the methods of inquiry and presentation used by modern thought. One thing is the substance of the ancient doctrine contained in the *deposit*

---

13. M. Novak, *The Open Church. Vatican II, Act. II*. New York, 1964; I, pp. 67-69; Y. M.-J. Congar, *The Theologising of Vatican II, in The American Eccles. Rev.*, 1966.

of faith; its formulation is another thing altogether. This in its forms and emphases must be regulated by the needs of a *magisterium* whose character is dominantly pastoral."[14] The entire work of the Council echoes these words implicitly, but certain passages of its documents are quite explicit: as, for example, that theology must seek a language adapted to our times[15] and to achieve that we must borrow from different cultures the resources they continue to create.[16] The faculties or schools of theology must be in contact with other centers of human learning.[17] The teaching of theology to future priests must be centered on the mystery of Christ and nourished by a knowledge of the biblical and traditional sources.[18] Even while naming St. Thomas as the best guide in speculative theology, the Council ordains that philosophy must keep abreast of the most recent researches and that a place must be found for the study of other Christian theologies and eventually of other religions.[19]

From the standpoint of topics treated, the Council moved away from introspection on the nature of the Church and examined instead how the Church can truly benefit mankind. In the beginning it spent much time on the Church's life of prayer and ended up by speaking of the problems of man's life in the world, of his relation to God and the relation between his earthly work and the Kingdom of Heaven. With reference to both, it spoke of the Church, of divine Revelation, etc. Theology must study the God of Revelation and man in his concrete relationship to God. But the Council was equally precise in setting down theology's sources and norms. These, of course, will always be Scripture and

---

14. AAS, t. LIV, 1962, p. 792.
15. Cf. Const. *Gaudium et spes*, n° 62, 2. Comp., from the standpoint of preaching, the decree *Presbyterorum ordinis*, n° 4, 1.
16. Cf. Const. *Gaudium et spes*, n° 44; 58, 2.
17. Const. *Gaudium et spes*, n° 62, 7; Declar. *Gravissimum Educationis Momentum*, n° 10.
18. Decret. *Optatam Totius*, n° 14 and 16.
19. *Ibid.* n° 15 and 16.

tradition. And so, at the very moment when the Council was admitting the insertion of "the religion of man" into "the religion of God" (to reproduce the Pope's expressions in his discourse of December 7, 1965) as a major theological preoccupation, it recalled that even for that the decisive light must be sought in positive Revelation.

Strasbourg

Editor's Note

The following are the bibliographical abbreviations most commonly used throughout this book:

AAS   *Acta Apostolicae Sedis*

Denz.   *Enchiridion Symbolorum, Definitionum et Declarationum*, ed. Denzmger-Schönmetzer

PG   *Patrologiae Cursus completus, Series Graeca*, ed. J.-P. Migne

PL   *Patrologiae Cursus completus, Series Latina*, ed. J.-P. Migne

A History of Theology

Prologue
The Meaning of "Theology"

The term "theology" means a reasoned account about God. The theology presented in this work is Christian and Catholic. For a provisional start it may be defined as a body of knowledge which rationally interprets, elaborates and ordains the truths of Revelation.

Like many words of ecclesiastical usage, the term "theology" has passed from Greek to Latin to most modern languages with no significant alphabetical change. However, before settling on its actual meaning, the Greek term for theology, θεολογία, as well as the allied terms θεολόγος and θεολογεῖν, passed through variant significations which cannot be briefly classified.

In the Pagan Era

In pagan antiquity the term θεολογία seldom had the meaning it has historically developed in the Christian era with regard to a doctrine on God. For the pagans "divinity" was rather a convenient manner of explaining the things of this world. It enveloped the nymphs and dryads and the ambrosially busy characters on Mount Olympus. For them the "theologians" were the poets of the past like Orpheus, Homer, and Hesiod, who had drawn up detailed theogonies; in fact, any prose writer who speculated on the origin of the world was a "theologian." To these "theologians," who attributed a mythological explanation to the world, Aristotle in his history of philosophy set up an opposite group of thinkers whom he called "philosophers." These were historical figures like Thales, the first of the Milesians, and his

successor, Anaximander. Aristotle next classified the "phys-
iologists." These, according to him, looked for the explanation of things in the things themselves and in their physical
elements.

Plato was the first to use the term θεολογία,[1] to point
out the profound educational value of mythology. For this
reason the Neoplatonists and some of the early Fathers of
the Church classified him as a *theologian*.

In the *Metaphysics*,[2] Aristotle gives us this famous distinction, "There must, then, be three theoretical philosophies:
mathematics, physics, and what may be called *theology*,
since it is obvious that if the divine is present anywhere,
it is present in things of this sort. And the highest science
must deal with the highest genus." We have here Aristotle's
evident identification of theology with "first philosophy,"
later known as metaphysics.[3] Eventually, however, Aristotle settles on unidentified *being* as the "highest genus" and
abandons the eternal but determined, non-sensible reality
of a divinity as the object of his highest speculative science.
Hence, in his other works Aristotle employs θεολογία and
allied terms to designate mythology and not metaphysics.

The use of the term "theology" to signify a reasoned
account of God would seem then to be exceptional before
the advent of the Stoics. Zeno (334–264 B.C.) divided philosophy into logic, ethics, and physics. Cleanthes (third
century B.C.), his successor, by subdividing each division
into two, distinguished the last into physics and theology.
Toward the end of the second century B.C., Panaetius of
Rhodes (180–11o? B.C.), who helped establish Stoicism in
Rome, distinguished three kinds of theology. At least he

---

1. *Republic*, 379a
2. 1026a19–22.
3. The classification is repeated in Bk. K, 1064^{b}1–5, and finally, in Bk.
   A 1069^{a}17–1076^{a}6, where Aristotle devotes the entire ten chapters
   to establishing the existence of an eternal unmoved mover or the
   universe.

seems to be the author of that distinction found in the writings of Varro (116–27 B.C.). Tertullian (165–220) alludes to the text, which St. Augustine (354–430) has preserved for us: Theology, or the systematic treatment of the divine, may be divided into three parts, of which the first is called mythical, the second physical, and the third political . .,"[4] Hence, the Stoics were familiar with a use of the word *theologia* which meant, according to the explanation St. Augustine gives us, the systematic treatment of the divine. This means the reasoned account one gives of the gods and, as Panaetius points out, it can be taken from three viewpoints: (a) The *poetic* viewpoint, which returns us to mythology, (b) The *physical* or *rational* viewpoint, which elaborates the philosophical theories, thereby attempting to give value and tight formulation to the woodbine mythology. Varro called this *natural theology*, since it tended to make the gods personifications of the forces of nature. Moreover, this viewpoint lays a rational foundation for what follows, (c) The *ritual* viewpoint, which develops a public cult for the great Greek and Roman cities.*

Whence we learn the characteristic of all pagan "theology," in which the divinity is always treated as a transposition or an explication of mundane things, but never considered in His own personal mystery or His own intimate nature. St. Augustine sums it all up perfectly: They give us a *physiology* and not a *theology*.[5]

4. *The City of God*, bk. VI, ch. 5.
5. *The City of God*, bk. VI, ch. 8.
* *Translator's Note*. The reader should be warned against accepting Panaetius' triple division of theology as a program to come rather than as an account of what history offered. The tendency to exaggerate the role of the Stoic in the history of thought to which the author and his sources Stiglmayr, Kattenbusch, etc., were subjected, has been corrected and readjusted by later discoveries. Quite distinct from its mythological element, the ritual and cult element antedate the Stoics by a *millennium* or more, being well established for a fact in the areas of Mycenae, Knossos, Ur, and Sumer. Moreover, much of the fuzziness attached to mythology as opposed to a rational account of the gods is patently due to the haphazards of communication in ancient times. An unchanneled radio or unfocused TV gives us the same silly message today. The author's conclusion, however, is most valid.

Finally with the widespread development of public cult under the Roman Empire the meanings of the three terms θεολόγος, θεολογία, θεολογεῖν, became more definite and even approached or—better—prepared for some Christian meanings. For example, as applied to the Imperial cult, the terms could mean: to attribute the quality of god (to Caesar), to recognize or acknowledge as god, to praise and honor as god.

In the Christian Era

On the mystery of God the Christians had received a revelation: He is Father, Son, and Holy Spirit. Normally they would have understood the term *theology* as factual speculation about God Himself, if for so long a time they had not been indoctrinated by the pagan usage of the word. This is definitively observable in the cases of Clement of Alexandria and of St. Augustine. Under both authors the term is about to receive its definitive ecclesiastical meaning, but it still preserves a trace of its ancient pagan varnish. It is noteworthy that the Greek Fathers more quickly disengaged their thinking from this stabilizing factor of the ancient meaning of terms than did the Latin Fathers.*

A. *The Greek Fathers*

Clement of Alexandria (c. 150–220) in his *Stromateis* speaks of the "old theologians," viz., Orpheus, Linus, Musaeus, Homer, Hesiod, and the "Wise Men." He further tells us that they got their wisdom from the Hebrew prophets, embellishing it with allegories and thus they learned τὴνθεολογίαν (theology). The term θεολογία is here taken in an absolute sense and means the knowledge of divine things. It was Clement's opinion that the philosophers wanted to formulate a science of god which would be

---

*   *Translator's Note.* The Greeks were still searching terms for their meanings. The Latins were still trying to understand the meanings of terms. It was an instance of the perennial disparity between the *thinking* giver and the *thought receiver.*

"the true theology." "Philosophy, whether barbaric or Hellenic, has made eternal truth, not an offshoot of Dionysiac mythology but the theology of the eternally abiding Word."[6] "Hence it is evident why from a pagan meaning of the term 'theology' Clement could abstract a meaning which would be applicable to the Christian knowledge of God. But the pagan meaning is still the only one known and for this reason Orpheus is the prime theologian."[7]

Origen (c. 185–251), next in order, cites favorably the "old theologians of the Greeks," as well as "the theology of the Persians." For him "theologians" are pagan authors who have dealt with religion and, hence, whose doctrine is called "theology." However, if he does not use the term θεολόγος in a Christian sense, he certainly begins to purify the meanings of the terms θεολογία and θεολογεῖν, and uses them in a Christian sense. He proposes *theology* as a *veritable doctrine* about God, but more significantly he states it is a doctrine about Christ, the Saviour, Whom it presents truly as God. The knowledge of God Who is Spirit is the paramount act of the Christian life. This is presented as developing along three levels: an ethic, a religion, a true discourse on God. As for the term θεολογεῖν, when speaking of God or of Christ, it is quite positively employed to mean: to recognize, proclaim and confess as God, somewhat in the sense in which the pagans spoke of the divinization of Caesar.

By the time of Eusebius of Caesarea (c. 264–349) the sublimation of the terms and their Christian acceptance are accomplished facts. He calls St. John "the theologian," because his gospel is eminently a doctrine about God. He is aware of the pagan use of the term *theology*, nevertheless he deliberately gives the word a properly Christian meaning. In fact he announces this in the prologue to his great *Church History* when he states that what he is now beginning to record transcends anything that is merely humanly

---

6. *Strom.* I, 13.
7. Batiffol, *Ephem. theol. lovan.* t. V. p. 213.

possible, for this is to be a record of the Christian economy and theology. This obviously equates Christ and God. "For Eusebius the term 'theology' so exclusively means the science of the true God and of Christ, that after his time it was no longer possible to apply the word to the pagan gods without qualifying the term as false theology. Eusebius' constant use of the terms θεολογία and θεολογεῖν as meaning the science of the true God and of Christ makes way for an innovation which Eusebius himself is going to introduce. For he entitles one of his last works περὶ τῆς ἐκκλησιαστικῆς θεολογίας ('On Ecclesiastical Theology') (337 or 338). It was in this way that Eusebius consecrated the term which Denis, the Pseudo-Areopagite (c. sixth century) in his turn will use as a title, περὶ μνστικῆς θεολογίας ('On Mystical Theology')."

As for Denis, while he may be said to be part of the line of Greek Fathers who used the terms θεολογία, θεολόγος, to refer to Sacred Scripture and the authors inspired by Revelation, he did create that celebrated expression of "mystical theology" and formulated the classical distinction between a theology which was "hidden, mystic, symbolic but which united the mystic to God, while the other type (of theology) was evident, wider known, philosophic and demonstrative in character."[8] Obviously there is no question here of different parts or divisions of theology. Denis is simply talking about two different approaches to fathoming the same mystery. It is well to recall that in theological methodology he is still famous for his original conception of "negative theology." However, this is not so much a question of method as a doctrinal position which is fundamental to the Areopagite's thinking.

Henceforth, "theology" for the Greek Fathers is a "veritable doctrine about the true God." Naturally we must expect numerous distinctions, as to authors, viz. Athanasius, Gregory Nazianzen; as to doctrine, v.g., the trinitarian problem. Athanasius uses the term θεολογία five times and each time he refers it to the *sacra doctrina de Trinitate*

---

8. *Epistola IX.*

("the holy doctrine of the Trinity"). Again, St. Basil uses the term to signify the divinity common to the three Persons. Gregory Nazianzen, outliving the great champions of trinitarian orthodoxy, names them without further distinction "theologians." It was these Fathers of the late fourth century who fashioned a distinction which has remained classic in Byzantine theology. The distinction is between "theology" or doctrine dealing with the divinity of the three Persons of the Trinity and "economy" or doctrine dealing with the Word in the mystery of his Incarnation.[9]

The word θεολογία takes on a special meaning with the monks and mystical writers. For them it means a knowledge of God which is either the highest form of the gnosis or of that illumination of the soul by the Holy Spirit which is more than an effect since it is the very substance of its divinization or godlike transformation. For Evagrius Pontikus, followed by Maximus Confessor (580–662) and others, θεολογία is the third and the most elevated of the degrees of life. In short, it is that perfect knowledge of God which is identified with the summit of prayer.

---

9. On this general subject the principal Latin and Greek texts are furnished by Petau, *Dogmata Theologica*, prol. C. I, n. 2; see specially Eusebius *H.E.*, I, 1, 7; St. Basil, *Epist.* VIII, 3, *P.G.*, XXXII, col. 252C. In reality this VIIIth Epistle is by Evagrios Pontikos, cf. R. Melcher, *Der 8. Brief des hl. Basilius, ein Werk des Evagrius Pontikus.* Münster, 1923. Gregory Nazianzen, *Oratio* XXXVIII, viii, *P.G.*, t. XXXVI, col. 320B; Sévérien de Gabala, *De Sigillis*, 5, 6 (P.G., LXIII, 509–41); Cyril of Alexandria, *Comm. in Joan.*, lib. I, P.G., LXXIII, col. 149C; Maximus Confessor, P.G., XC, col. 1083; Métrophane Critopoulos, *Confession*, ch. I, ed. Michalcescu, p. 187; Gass, *Das patristische Wort* οἰκονομία, in *Zeitsch. f. wissenschaftl. Theol.*, 1874, pp. 465–504; A. Palmieri, *Theol. dogmat. orthodoxa*, I, Florence, 1911, p. 135 sq.; Fr. Lakner, *Das Zentral objekt der Theologie*, in *Zeitsch. f. Kathol. Theol.* LXII, 1938, pp. 12–13 & 21. Hence Fr. Pl. de Meester has a point in dividing his *Études sur la théologie orthodoxe* between theology proper and economic theology. He explains that distinction in *Revue bénédictine*, 1906, pp. 232–33 and in Bessarione, 1921, p. 47, sq. J. Haussleiter, *Trinitarischer Glaube und Christusbekenutuis in der alten Kirche*, 1920, G. L. Prestige, *God in Patristic Thought*, London, 3rd ed. 1956.

For Diadokus of Photikus (c. 450) θεολογία implies, along with a superior knowledge of God, a definite impulsion bolstered by grace to praise the sweetness and the glory of God in the communion of contemplation.

B. *The Latin Fathers*

Among the Latin Fathers up to and including St. Augustine, the term *theologia* did not attain its own ecclesiastical meaning. Several Fathers apparently do not even know the term; v.g., Minucius Felix, St. Cyprian, St. Ambrose, Arnobius, Boethius, and St. Gregory. Of course the term is used when arguing with the pagans, but always in the sense the latter give to it. Augustine, however, borrowing the term from the pagans, examined its etymological sense and stressed the fact that a *true* theology would lead them to Christianity.[10] But this *true* theology for him is still only a philosophy which he considers worthy of the name and he offers the example of Platonism. Beyond the *fable theology* of the poets and even the *natural theology* of Varro and the Stoics, which is little more than an interpretation of the world or, as we would say today, a sort of physics, St. Augustine points to a theology more faithful to God, its object, and for him this is Plato's philosophy.[11]

Indeed it seems we must wait for Abélard before the term *theologia* receives the meaning it has for us.[12] There is

---

10. *City of God* VI, c. viii.
11. *City of God* VIII, c. i & v.
12. Cf. C. J. Webb, *Studies in Natural Theology*, Oxford, 1915, pp. 205–06; J. G. Sikes, *Peter Abailard*, Cambridge, 1932, p. 27, n. 1.; J. Rivière, "*Theologia*," in *Revue des Sciences rei.* XVI, 1936, pp. 47–57, this gives us a detailed critical study of the question. He sets aside the authors who might seem to have a prior claim to the term, as Raoul Ardent and Honorius d'Autun with his *Elucidarium sive dialogus*, *P.L.*, CLXXII, whose subtitle, *De summa totius Christianae Theologiae*, is of doubtful authenticity. He shows that the titles "*Introductio ad Theologian*" and *Epitome theologiae christianae*" are due not to the author but the editors, and this last work, named by Abélard

still a wait, however, before the word gets its epistemological meaning. The turning point may definitely be placed
in the thirteenth century. And still even then and later we
will encounter the tired old preliminary expressions, viz.,
doctrina Christiana (St. Augustine), *sacra scriptura, sacra
eruditio, sacra* or *divina pagina*, and lastly *sacra doctrina*,
which is the term used by St. Thomas in the first question
of his *Summa*.

Since then the various editors of the *Summa* have introduced the word *theologia* into the titles of several articles
of this question, but in the original text the term occurs
only three times. On the other hand, the expression *sacra
doctrina* or *haec doctrina* occurs about eighty times. Moreover, *theologia* as a term is not taken in the modern sense of
theology but in its etymological sense of a treatment of or
discourse on God. In other works of St. Thomas, we meet
the term *theologia*, either in the modern sense of a defined
discipline exposing a rational explanation of revelation,[13]
or in the concrete objective sense of a consideration made

---

as a *Theologiae Tractatus* is a monograph on the Trinity dogma
in which *theologia* would not have the only meaning admitted by
several Greek Fathers. For Abélard had conceived a summary of
Christian doctrine of which he could only write out the first parts.
The work itself he called *theologia* and he permitted others to refer
to it by the same term. But it must be noted that the word is still
used to designate the concrete contents of a work bearing on the
ensemble of Christian dogmas and not, abstractly, on a discipline
like geometry or philosophy. Another point; in Abélard's school
tradition will preserve the usage that *theologia* pertains only to the
invisible God, One and Triune; whatever concerns Christology
and the Sacraments will be covered by the term *beneficia*. Thus
it is in the *Sententiae* Florianenses, ed. Ostlender, Bonn, p. 12; in
the *Sententiae Parisienses*, ed. Sandgraf, in *Écrits théologiques de
l'école d'Abélard*, Louvain 1934, p. 29; in the *Sententiae Rolandi*, ed.
Gietl, pp. 154–55. Finally cf. Abelard himself, *Introd. in theol.*, P.L.,
CLXXVIII, col. 986D and *Epitome* col. 1697 and 1730. The *Epitome*,
however, according to Ostlender, is the work of Hermann, one of
Abélard's disciples.

13. V.g., In *Boet. de* Trin, q. II, a. 3, ad 7um; *Contra Gent.* 1. IV, C. XXV.

from God's standpoint or that of a first cause rather than or over against a viewpoint derived from the nature of created things taken in themselves.[14] It is interesting, first, to note that St. Thomas makes use of Varro's distinction of the three theologies. Secondly, he goes to great lengths to avoid using the terms *theologia* and *theologus*, where the opposition between natural knowledge and supernatural knowledge is not expressed by the opposition between *philosophia* and *theologia*, but by the opposition between the *doctrine of philosophy* and the *doctrine of faith*, on one hand, and by *philosopher* and *believer*, on the other. Obviously only an exhaustive research would permit us to draw definite conclusions. What has been pointed out here is sufficient to show that circumspection is needed in interpreting St. Thomas' use of the terms under discussion.

A careful study of these remarks I think will settle the quarrel which has traditionally set St. Thomas' two greatest commentators at swords' points. For Cardinal Cajetan, *sacra doctrina* means supernatural teaching—that is, whatever in our consciousness springs from the supernatural magisterium as opposed to any teaching derived from rational enterprise. For John of Saint-Thomas, on the other hand, *sacra doctrina* means, from the first question of the *Summa*, theology properly understood and distinguished from simple, unquestioning faith. Moreover, he maintains that under this expression St. Thomas grouped not merely theological *science*, but everything opinionable or probable. For the theologian, progress would mean passing from these approximations to grounded and precise certitudes in the interior of this *doctrina sacra*. This interpretation of John of Saint-Thomas has certainly three important points against it and an adequate response does not seem possible:

(1) *Doctrina* means, for St. Thomas and his epoch, "teaching," either in the active sense of actual teaching or in the objective sense of content of teaching. *Doctrina sacra*

14. Cf. S. *Theol.*, Ia-IIae, q. lxxi, a. 6, ad 5[um].

means supernatural teaching. That is all. John of Saint-Thomas wrongly identifies *doctrina* and *probativa cognitio*.

(2) The mystery of John's misunderstanding deepens when we consider that St. Thomas himself posed the question,[15] *Utrum sacra doctrina sit scientia*? This, incidentally, is the type of question he frequently asks. It is not a question purely and simply of identifying the notion of Christian teaching and that of science, but only of asking whether in its originality and eminent perfection Christian teaching verifies, from some side, in some one of its parts or functions, the quality of science. This is an entirely different perspective from John's and later on we will see its importance.

(3) A simple reading of St. Thomas' text shows that from one end to the other of his first question, *sacra doctrina* contains *Sacra Scriptura* and is identified with it, at least, as with its principal parts. From one side to the other of this question, *sacra doctrina* represents *doctrinara quamdam secundum divinara revelationem*; that is to say, a teaching which proceeds from divine revelation, comprising at the same time the Scriptures of the two Testaments, the writings of the Fathers, the tradition of the Church, the catechism and Christian preaching—in short, the science of theology and then its lower forms which are dominated by opinion and by the probable rather than by the certain.

Now that those necessary clarifications and distinctions have been made, We are ready to begin the history of theology in its proper sense. There is a strong temptation in so doing to start with the end of the patristic period—i.e., with St. John Damascene (735) for the East, and with the period stretching from the death of Isidore of Seville (636) to that of the Venerable Bede (735) for the West. Such was the procedure followed, for example, by Martin Grabmann in his *Geschichte der Katholischen Theologie*. That approach, however, seems to be founded on a rather inflexible con-

---

15. *Summa* Ia, q. I, a. 2.

cept of theology as a systematic synthesis of Christian doctrine, and, indeed, on that premise it is easy to conclude that the Fathers did not write "theology" because no one of them offers a systematic synthesis of the whole of dogma. Instead, they composed—in the wake of the classical authors of Greece and Rome—special treatises, some of which were intended for the edification of the faithful, while others sought to defend this or that dogma from the threat of error.

Our approach will offer—and, we hope, will justify—a more generous treatment of the Fathers and will begin the history of theology with the very origins of Christianity.

Chapter One
The Patristic Age and St. Augustine

Before St. Augustine

Christianity came into the course of history as a *fact*. Moreover, it claimed to be a *new* fact. It was and is the fact of a
new life given by God through Christ and in the name of
Christ. This Christ was everything and in all orders so that
in Him could be found the total spread of the beautiful,
the true, and the good. Hence the first Christian sentiment,
finding everything in Christ, was to search for nothing outside of Him, i.e., outside of Christ crucified. The men who
had received the formation of a solid pagan culture were the
ones who exclaimed with Tertullian: "What is there in common between Athens and Jerusalem, between the Academy
and the Church? Too bad for those who have embraced a
Stoic, a Platonic, or a dialectic Christianity. As for us, we
have no need for curiosity after Jesus Christ, or for research
after the Gospel."[1] We admit, of course, that some seeking
must still be done and some questions asked, but "let us
seek and question among ourselves, and from our people,
and about our own affairs."[2] Another man formed by the
disciplines of paganism was Cyprian. His biographer, the
Deacon Pontius, tells us apropos of Cyprian's career as a
rhetorician: "The acts of a man of God must not be counted
until the day when he is born in God. Whatever have been
his studies, whatever influence the liberal arts have had
upon him personally, I will omit all that, for it will serve no
purpose except that of the world."[3]

---

1. *Praescr.*, 7.
2. *Ibid.*, 12.
3. *Vita Cypriani*, 2.

This idea of the total sufficiency of Christ is immediately echoed in the total sufficiency of the Sacred Scriptures. This view was common to the Fathers and the Scholastics. In the last analysis it meant that the believer's will was fixed in such a manner that not only would he not say anything *different* from what was to be found in the Sacred Scriptures, but perhaps even more important, he would say nothing *more*. This concept held sway from the early beginnings down to the Middle Ages. It is found in the writings of the Augustinians of the thirteenth century as well as those of Roger Bacon, Richard Fishacre, and St. Bonaventure. It must be quickly added, however, that this manner of treating the Sacred Scriptures enjoyed a rather broad interpretation. This was especially true in the case of those Christians engaged in the human sciences. While they accepted the principle of the sufficiency of Sacred Scripture, their understanding of it was not as radical as it was stated to be in the beginning.

The greatest opposition to this exclusive position of sufficiency came from philosophy and the philosophers. The opposition of the Fathers to philosophy's position stemmed not so much from the occasional suggestion of corruption or incompetence, as from the basic, radical, devastating position that the things of salvation belonged to an order superior to that of pagan wisdom. In short, that salvation is a matter neither of pure speculation nor of intellectual curiosity. On the other hand, it is a matter of record that Christian apologetics (borrowing a lead from Jewish speculation) declared that certain lofty truths expressed by the Greek philosophers were supposed to be borrowed from the Sacred Scriptures. This interesting idea was received by the Middle Ages either directly from St. Augustine or through the mediation of Cassiodorus' Institutions. It is also found in St. Thomas.

It is clear that in primitive Christianity there was a definite current of thought prejudicial to all attempts at speculation in matters of faith and, therefore, to the construction of a "theology." Be it noted in passing that Judaism certainly had a knowledge of God and of His wonderful works which was expressed in doxology but not systematically in a speculative manner. Nevertheless it is a fact that, within the early folds of Christianity, a *science* did proceed from the *faith*, and so quite soon there was a systematic conception with regard to God and the world. Such scholars as Harnack and Kattenbusch maintain that this development was a necessity and that the source of this necessity was the fact of Christ and the obligation to believe in Him. Together, these two factors naturally produced a mode of understanding the fact and the eventual intellectual construction of the mystery of Jesus Christ and the affirmation of His divinity.

It is true there were several good reasons which necessitated the expression and elaboration of the mystery of Christ and Christianity in a scientific manner that was properly theological. We see these reasons in effective operation in Christian antiquity.

First of all, pagan philosophy was a fact. There was a pagan culture. Inevitably there had to be a showdown between paganism and Christianity. The view that this philosophy and its culture were offshoots of Sacred Scripture and hence a foreshadowing of Christianity meant that they could not be totally rejected, that some sort of amalgam had to be fashioned with them. As a matter of fact this theory of close relationship was maintained by the Apologetic Fathers. Hence the Christianity their writings present to us, while it is basically that of the Apostolic tradition and the vital reality of the infant Church, is nevertheless intellectually reconstructed into categories homogeneous to those of pagan culture. This is particularly evident in Justin's works (who when attempting to express the Trinitarian faith wrongly uses the Stoic term *logos*), but it will also be found in Tatian, Athenagoras, and Minucius Felix. So it is that the Apologists have given the Church its first theological construction of the Christian faith.

However, it should be carefully noted that this construction did not arise solely from the need of a defense against paganism and a desire to set up a bridge between it and the faith. At this early date a second motive was at work: the personal spontaneous need of the believer to think out his faith in terms of his individual knowledge and the level of his culture. And this all the more so since he with his fellow Christians learned from St. Paul an ideal of knowledge, the *gnosis*, which they made to mean the experience of truth. This rises from the basis of faith to great salutary acts, which the Scriptures witness in reference to Jesus Christ, thereby presenting a complete and joyous summary of the Christian mystery. The best example of what we mean is Clement and his Catechetical School of Alexandria. "In Clement's view religious philosophy did not serve merely for apologetic and polemic purposes, but rather *it opened the door for thinkers to the understanding of Christianity*. He was conscious that his task consisted in adapting the content of that ecclesiastical tradition by submitting it to the grind and toil of philosophical thought. Faith is a gift. It must be translated into terms of gnosis, in other words it must turn into a doctrine which can satisfy the exigencies of an ethic and a philosophical conception of the universe."[4]

Clement came forward with a positive relation between Christianity and the activity of reason. If he was not perfectly clear, at least he was resolutely positive. And he has left us a concise formula of his position, "Greek philosophy purifies the soul and prepares it to receive the faith on which truth constructs knowledge."[5] In his opinion philosophy and the social sciences were propaedeutic to that contemplation or gnosis, which was the most elevated state of faith in the Christian life. In this preliminary manner philosophy assisted in the apprehension of truth which is secured or attained on the basis of ordinary faith but also beyond it in that developed and perfect faith which was the gnosis.

---

4. Hamack, Adolf. *Précis de l'histoire des dogmes*. Trad. E. Choisy, 1893, p. 97.
5. *Stromateis*, vii, 20.

Clement defined the relations between faith and gnosis in a way which shows that his notion of gnosis and ours of theology are quite akin. "Faith is a kind of elementary and summarized knowledge (*gnosis*) of necessary things. The gnosis itself is a sound and solid demonstration of what has been received by faith. It is erected on faith by the teachings of our Lord and passes to a state of firm, intellectual apprehension."[6] We are far from the stiff, intransigent attitude of Tertullian.

This does not mean that for Clement Christianity was not self-sufficient. As for the others, so for him, Christianity was "the true philosophy"; moreover, for him also, Christ was our only teacher. "Since the Word Himself has come to us from heaven, we no longer need to seek out a human teacher or search the secrets of Athens or Greece or even Ionia . . . For now the true Master teaches and so thanks to the Word henceforth every place is Athens and Greece for us."[7] Nevertheless he maintains that the act of faith itself becomes a form of intellectual contemplation which superlatively develops its intelligibility and its virtualities. The portrait of the gnostic or perfect Christian is also that of a contemplator of the faith and could be quite acceptable as the ideal portrait of the theologian.

It must be noted, however, that if Clement outlined a theory of theological speculation, he never composed that synthetic and systematic exposé of Christian truth which his program seemed to promise. The *Stromateis*, as their name indicates, are simply "frameworks." However, they set afoot a movement neatly defined: the propaedeutic value of philosophy and the human sciences in relation to the contemplative activity of the believer. This theme is discussed over many years and in many places. Toward the end of the second century in the East there are *schools* of theology

---

6.　*Ibid.*, vii, 57; cf. also vii, 55.
7.　*Protreptikos*, 112.

in Cappadocia, Edessa, Jerusalem, Caesarea, Antioch, but especially at Alexandria, where the "didascalos of sacred science" can be traced back beyond Pantaenus. Rome under Justin, Tatian, and Rhodo had already started a sort of catechetical and apologetic school, but at this date in the East there are respectable schools of religious speculation each with its distinctive tradition and spirit.

Origen is the creator of the first grand synthesis of speculative theology.

In the history of theology, from the standpoint of methodology, he occupies a position quite as important as that of Irenaeus, and that for three reasons, (a) He founded the scientific exegesis of the Scriptures; (b) he formulated a theory of religious knowledge; (c) he is the author of the first work of theology which can be properly called systematic.

(a) Origen faithfully remained, even in his most hazardous speculations, a biblist. His systematic work, *Principles* (*περὶαρχῶν), is a commentary on the scriptural texts which presented the groundwork for theological speculation. Athanasius and the Cappadocians will develop them in a profoundly ecclesiastical sense.

(b) Origen proposed and put in practice a theory of religious knowledge which emphasized the distinction made by Clement between faith and gnosis. Much less a philosopher but much more a cleric or churchman than Clement, Origen separated still further the superior knowledge of the gnosis and the common faith and set these two types of knowledge in relation to the two senses of the Scriptures, the material sense and the allegorical or spiritual sense. For him, then, the gnosis represents at once a mode of knowledge and a motive of adherence different from the mode and motive of simple faith. As pure faith, however, it is obviously concerned with the mysteries but not on the level of historical facts or significant announcements. Rather it approaches them and is nourished by them on the high level of ideological speculation, where wisdom alone can survive.

(c) Origen composed the first great work of systematic theology, the *Principles*, in four volumes, in which he
discussed in order, God and Celestial Beings, the Material
World and Man, Free Will and Its Consequences, and, finally,
Sacred Scripture. In the prologue, he first of all distinguishes
between the objects which ecclesiastical preaching imposes
on our credence and the large domain of elaborations and
explanations left free to the initiative of the scholar. Origen
profits richly from the liberty of research which he has thus
outlined. However, be it carefully noted that Origen knew
how and when to correct himself, so that in his own person,
we may say, the believer and the churchman knew how on
several occasions to straighten out the philosopher and the
rash speculator. In his work he was most careful to assume
whatever it was reasonably possible to assume. A master
of exacting and exact thought, a man anxious to assimilate
synthetically into religious thought every element of truth
and to profit from everything in order to grow spiritually,
such is Origen as preserved for us by his disciple, Gregory
Thaumaturgus, Bishop of Neocaesarea, in his detailed and
faithful memoire.[8]

Despite their outstanding importance from a dogmatic
standpoint, we will have little to say about the Cappadocians, who, having devoted themselves in a notable manner to speculation, had little to say from the standpoint of
methodology. It must be noted, however, that Basil very

8. *Oratio panegyrica*, n. 8, 11, 13, 14, etc. but esp. P.G., X, col. 1077. (As
to Origen's position in theology cf. F. Prat, *Origène, le théologien,
l'éxegète*, Paris, 1907; L. Lebreton, *Le désaccord de la foi populaire et
de la théologie savante dans l'Église chrétienne du IIIe siècle*, in *Revue
d'hist. ecclé.* XIX 1923, pp. 481–506; XX, 1924, pp. 5–37; *Les degrés
de la connaissance religieuse d'après Origène*, in *Rech. de science relig.*
XII, 1922, pp. 265-96; J. Bonnefoy, *Origène, théoricien de la méthode
théologique*, in *Mélanges F. Cavallera*, Toulouse, 1948, pp. 87–145;
H. de Lubac, *Histoire et Esprit. L'intelligence de l'Ecriture d'après
Origène.* Paris, 1950; H. Crouzel, *Origène esti-il un systematique?* in
Butt. Litter, ecclés. 1959, pp. 81–116; F. H. Kettler, *Der ursprüngliche
Sinn der Dogmatik des Origenes.* Berlin, 1966.)

force-fully asserted the necessity of the *primacy of faith*.[9] If
the student studies this *Epistola XXXVIII*, just cited, he will
be impressed by the sureness and exactitude with which
Basil distinguishes the terms "essence" and "hypostasis."
It is obvious from this that Christian thought is equipped
to elaborate, construct, and systematize revelation on the
basis of faith. Like St. Athanasius he develops his thought
beginning with the Sacred Scripture and in constant reference to it. They both stress the prime necessity of belief;
intelligence follows faith. But due to their formation in the
schools and the necessity of combatting heresy, the Fathers
were disposed toward refined and subtle concepts. For
example, in *Epistola* XXXVIII of St. Basil, note the firm-
ness and subtlety with which he distinguishes the notions
of essence and hypostasis. Far beyond a mere repetition of
scriptural affirmations, far beyond, too, an apologetic concordat made with pagan philosophy, we find here, serviced
by a most precise perception and expression of the Christian
data, a use of reason and its resources which is an authentic
theology. Moreover, Gregory Nazianzen expressly says that
for the sake of clarity there should be no fear or hesitation
in formulating new terms or expressions.[10]

About St. Jerome we make no comment beyond the
mention of his famous letter[11] to Magnus who was called
the "Orator of the city of Rome." This letter, as a matter
of fact, in which Jerome justifies the use of pagan literature, became for the Western Church and in particular for
the Latin Middle Ages the *locus classicus* proclaiming and
rationalizing the use of humane sciences, pagan literature,
and, in general, rational elements in the sacred sciences.
For Gregory Nazianzen theology is a spiritual function
reserved to the priests and practically identical with the

---

9. *Hom. in psalmum CXV*, n. 1, P.G., XXX, col. 104 sq.; *Epistola*
   XXXVIII, n. 5, P.G., XXXII, col. 336.
10. *Oratio* XXXIX, n. 12.
11. P.L., t. XXII, col. 664–68.

theory. This, of course, is not a *pure* theory but it is sufficient to engage a total spiritual life and any spiritual experience. With regard to the previous text we need cite only two
typical references: Abélard, to justify the use of "*testimonia
philosophorum*,"[12] and St. Thomas in discussing theology
and secular knowledge.[13]

St. Augustine

St. Augustine conceived a theory of theological contemplation. His presentation of it was forceful because he had
applied it to himself and his personal problems. For this
reason his theory had an absolutely preponderant influence
on the development of theology in the Western Church.[14]

St. Augustine is a man who found the light, life, and
joy of his intelligence in faith. He himself painstakingly
underwent the experience that faith opens the interior eyes
of the soul. There is an approach to faith in which reason
and its reasons play a role and there is through and in faith
an advance, a broadening, a deepening of the spirit by an
effort of intelligence and contemplative activity, which latter constitute what is properly called theology. These two
approaches to a fulfillment of knowledge have been neatly
formulated in the well-known phrases: *intellige ut credos,*

---

12. *Introd. ad theol. P.L.*, CLVIII, col. 1035 sq.
13. *In Boet, de Trin.* q. II, a 3; *Sum. Theol.* 1a q. 1, a. 5, obj. 2; *Contra Impugn.* C. XII, etc.
14. The texts on this conception of theology are scarce, but there are several explicit and formal exposés which can be studied, for example, in *Sermo XLIII, P.L.*, XXXVIII, col. 254 sq. (Commentary on *Nisi credideritis, non intelligetis*); *Sermo CXVII*, c. 5 and 6, col. 665 sq. (On the use of similes); *Epist. cxx and consentium, P.L.*, XXXIII, col. 452 (462 on the relations between *reason* and *faith*); *Enarr, in Ps.* CXVIII, *Sermo XVIII*, specially n. 3, *P.L.*, XXXVII, col. 1552 (on the relations between *credere* and *intellectus*); *De Trinitate* (written between 398 and 416) specially book XV, *P.L.*, XLII, col. 1057–98; *De doctrina christiana, P.L.*, XXXIV, col. 35–66 (written in 397, revised in 427).

crede ut intelligas ("understand that you may believe";
"believe that you may understand").[15]*

We see no point in expanding St. Augustine's treatment of
the first activity of the spirit in its preliminary steps toward
an embracing of the faith. That those steps were taken in
nature is sufficient condemnation of any who thought that
Augustine belittled nature.

Faith having been received into the soul is not present
there without life or movement. On the contrary, faith is
a penetration into the realm of eternal life and its internal
movement there is one of assimilation, apprehension, and
finally intelligence of its object. Augustine calls *intellectus*
the fruit of faith.

Moreover, he makes careful note of the fact that this
intellectus is not the fruit of any sort of faith, neither a pure
knowledge, nor a pure flash of information. It is the fruit
of a "pious" faith, by which he means that God is not a
mere object of knowledge but is also an end to be loved and
toward which one's whole life should be dedicated. It is this
pia fides, which cloaks us with piety, which heals the soul
(probably from the stains of original sin) and finally leads it
to that vision or to that intelligence which is the beginning
of the celestial life.

---

15. *Serm. XLIII*, c. vii; *Serm. CXXVI*, n. 1.
*   Translator's Note. H. I. Marrou in his *Saint Augustin et la fin de la
     culture antique*, Paris, 1938, has satisfactorily established the point
     that when St. Augustine was converted in 386 he was in search of
     a wisdom exclusively concerned with the polarities of himself and
     God. The liberal arts and the sciences were less than secondary in
     his search for knowledge at the time. But then in 391, an ordained
     priest and a bishop, he realized that he should open himself to the
     reality of the otherness of action and of science in the temporal
     order. In his De doctrina Christiana and in the second part of
     the *De Trinitate* we find his first acknowledgment of scientia as a
     possible research aid in the development of *sapientia*. However, his
     notion of "wisdom" in its relation to the *intellectus fidei* remains so
     unchanged that we may still accept the De doctrina Christiana and
     the *De Trinitate* as the final development of his thought without
     pointing to a "scientific" change in 391.

Such is the Augustinian *intellectus*: it is the contemplation of a soul which believes, which loves and whose vital contemplative activity is purified and expanded in proportion to its faith and its love. Faith here plays its full role as the total form of human life. Man perfects himself, even in his human intelligence, by believing and paying obeisance to the movement of faith. This is a tenet specifically Augustinian and consists in a refusal to separate knowledge, whether it be "science" or "wisdom," from its use or application and from its moral value, but, above all, it is a refusal to sublimate knowledge into a pure epistemological reality, comprising in its very substance no particle of reference to the last end or to beatitude; in short, it is the denial of an autonomous or separated philosophy.

Nevertheless, to embrace the moral life in its total reality, the theological, Augustinian approach makes every effort to use all of man's resources both on the sensible and intellectual levels. On this point, Augustine worked out a dialectic of the ascension of man's mind toward God. The vision at Ostia is its immortal example and the *De Trinitate* contains its systematic presentation. To climb up to God in the Augustinian sense of wisdom employing research, the soul first uses its corporeal objects, then the treasures of its memory which are its intellectual acquisitions, finally it finds God in itself, viz., in the superior part of the memory.

What we find interesting here is the use, first, of sensible similitudes and, then, of all the resources of the sciences and arts and, this, mind you, by the soul in its search for an understanding of the mysteries. It is this aspect of theology which Augustine qualifies as scientific, because it is directly concerned with the use of created things as a help to a comprehension of the divine. Moreover, he claims that faith, that is, salvific faith which leads to beatitude, is engendered, nourished, defended, and reenforced by these lowly truths.

Still more interesting is the fact that St. Augustine has used this entire process of created things nourishing theological contemplation with reference to the mystery of the Trinity. In this context the plan of the *De Trinitate is* quite significant. The first seven books represent rather well the first step in the process which is *credere*. Here St. Augustine establishes the existence of the three Persons, studies Their attributes and answers objections made against the dogma. At the same time he presents the sources of his doctrine, which are first the Sacred Scriptures and then the Fathers.

Books eight to fifteen form a second part in which St. Augustine himself says that he will proceed *modo interiore*. This corresponds well enough to the operation of the *intellectus*, which in its attempts to understand the mystery presents for our analysis extremely complicated images and analogies. This *intellectus* of the faith, Augustine describes as the mind's translation of the faith's facte, bk. XV, c. xxvii, n. 49, col. 1096. It is presented in a series of analogies of increasing complexity, all chosen from images of man's natural activities, bk. IX–XI, with a passing reference to images chosen from the moral activity of a Christian, bk. XII–XIII, which increase in perfection until they attain the perfect image of wisdom, bk. XIV. Of course, these analogies are not proofs. They have values only for the intelligent ears of the believer. In fact they are heard only by the "ears of the Christian people" and the Bishop of Hippo presents them only to the *faithful*. Bk. XV, c. xxvii, n. 48, col. 1095–96. And it can never be underlined too often that his thinking and writing are always in the ambiance of the faith, hence the *intellectus* reposes essentially on the *credere*, of which it is the fruit, while, in its turn the *credere* is essentially regulated and defined by the Sacred Scriptures.

It is in this atmosphere and this perspective that St. Augustine very firmly proclaims the legitimacy and the practical utility of profane studies even for the development of Christian wisdom. Church bells can ring over this deci-

sion because this is the capital position—more or less—
which will determine the doctrinal attitude of the Middle
Ages and of the Occidental Church. I say "more or less"
because strangely enough an extreme anti-intellectualism
claimed this attitude for its parentage, while at the same
time it engendered the Christian humanism of St. Anselm
and the Victorines, Hugh and Richard, not to mention its
definitive confirmation in the doctrine of St. Thomas.

The important text is found in his *De Doctrina Christiana*, 1. II. Here St. Augustine wishes to name and elicit every
possible assistance for the plenary understanding of the
Scriptures. He lists these as knowledge of sacred languages,
knowledge of the nature of being, knowledge of dialectics,
which can discover and refute sophisms and which teaches
the art of definition and of the proper division of the matter
to be considered, without which, he explains, no presentation of truth is possible. To this list he adds the knowledge
of eloquence, the science of numbers, history, and law.

This is a staggering program which St. Augustine and
even the Middle Ages actuated only in part. The *theological*
Middle Ages for the most part participated in Augustine's
program only from the standpoint of grammar and dialectics. St. Augustine, then, without rejecting the principle
of the sufficiency of Christianity and the Scriptures, called
upon the wisdom of antiquity to assist both in the practical
application and study of this new Revelation. The program
and the encyclopedic spirit of the Middle Ages proceed
directly from this Clement-Augustinian position.

Chapter Two
From the Sixth Century to the Twelfth Century

The Heritage of the Sixth Century

It is in the sixth century that Latin Christianity receives its formal determination both as to the concept and the practice of theology. This formulation endured for some ten centuries and it had two main components. The first was the heritage of the Fathers, in which we must incontestably affirm the religious hegemony of St. Augustine. The second was the philosophical heritage received from antiquity and in particular from certain writings of Aristotle translated and passed on by Boethius (d. 525).

A. *The Patristic Heritage*

Before we begin the history of the notion of *theology* in the Pre-Scholastic and Scholastic Middle Ages, it would perhaps be useful to point out some of the intellectual characteristics of the epoch particularly in its regard to the theological *datum*. As we have said, these characteristics in great part were determined by the patristic tradition and here St. Augustine's influence was preponderant. Martin Grabmann in his *Geschichte der Scholastichen Methode* summarizes this influence in four salient points. (1) Dialectics has a propedeutic value; (2) the rational suitableness of an authority dealing with the relations of reason and faith and establishing a positive method of summarizing these relations; (3) the influential example of a strongly systematized synthesis formulated in certain works which could be used as models; (4) the elaboration of several broad questions, the creation of a procedure to be followed in any controversy, the invention of kinds of arguments, of a new theory of religious knowledge, and lastly a dogmatic language.

From the author's viewpoint the patristic heritage should be credited with the following points.

1. USE OF THE SCRIPTURES. Theological activity is simply an effort to penetrate the meaning and the contents of Scripture which is the work of God. The principle of the sufficiency of the Bible is the first legacy of the Fathers. This principle will be maintained and concretely observed by the Middle Ages without extenuation. For example, St. Anselm would not introduce speculation into his writings without first stating that speculation was allowed by Scripture, and Abélard presents his theological synthesis, replete with speculation, as an "Introduction to Sacred Scriptures":

> Please read the Sacred Scriptures frequently and relate your other reading to them.[1]

Up to the end of the twelfth century theology is essentially and, we may truthfully say, exclusively biblical. It is properly called *sacra pagina* or *sacra scriptura*.

The Middle Ages also inherits from the Fathers, and especially from St. Augustine and St. Gregory, the methods of approach to and the manner of treating the scriptural text. These were handed down in the original texts, in the anthologies, the great *Sententiae,* and even the glosses. This exegesis has the following characteristics:

(a) *Allegorical transpositions* which going well beyond the historical meaning of the text furnish us with a second way of reading and understanding it. For example: From the fact that the proportions assigned by *Genesis* to Noah's Ark are the same as those which tradition attributes to the human body, Augustine deduces that the Ark is the figure of man *par excellence,* Who is Christ Jesus, to Whom we owe salvation as did Noah to his wooden vessel.[2]

---

1. *P.L.*, t. CLXXVIII, col. 1760.
2. *De Civ. Dei*, 1. XV, c. XXVI, n. 1; *PJL.,* t. XLI, col. 472.

A treatment of the biblical text in which the resources of Latin grammar have a preponderance over the simple facts of history, over a knowledge of Hebrew and Greek, and the geographical, historical, and cultural milieu in which the biblical facts took place and the biblical accounts were recorded. This produces a labored, if subtle, sort of interpretation of a text which could be understood exactly and without mystery if the commentator knew the history involved. For example: St. Augustine's interpretation of the Hebraism: "What is man that Thou art mindful of him? or the son of man that Thou visitest him?"[3]

Nevertheless, the exegesis transmitted by the Fathers, being always a part of the Christian reality, even in the absence of adequate philological resources, developed a valuable science of Sacred Scripture; all is by no means allegory. Moreover, their exigencies which have become those of the modern exegetical method beginning with André de Saint-Victor (d. 1175), then Hugues de Saint-Cher (d. 1263), who drew up a Latin verbal concordance and schemed a revision of the text of the Vulgate. Then we have St. Thomas Aquinas, whose admirable commentaries on St. Paul and St. John search a literal understanding of the text by a happy understanding of parallel passages.

2. Use of the Liberal Arts. The Fathers and especially St. Augustine gave the Middle Ages the idea that the sciences or the profane arts and the liberal arts rightfully belonged to Christ and that they should be put to the service of their true Master by making them assist in a better— more profound, if you will—understanding of the Sacred Scriptures. In the beginning of this period there were occasional anathemas against human knowledge which did not become too general and fortunately did not last. For quite soon it became evident that the so-called pagan reason was needed to elaborate the self-sufficiency of Christianity as well as coordinate and classify the new and absolutely

---

3. *Ps.* 8, 5; *Enarratio in psalmum VIII*, n. 10, *P.L.*, t. XXXVI, col. 113.

original character of Christian facts. In this frame of reference the allegory of the Hebrews walking off with the gold and silver vessels of the Egyptians, *Ex.* xi, 2; iii, 22; xii, 35, was quickly exploited. Then again there was the allegory of David killing Goliath with his own sword, and, lastly, following Philo, there was the allegory of Sara and Agar. Agar, an Egyptian concubine, gave Abraham his first child. This represents human knowledge which Abraham had to have before he had a son from a free woman. These symbols illustrate the concept of the propaedeutic and auxiliary value of the profane sciences. This notion dominates the thought of the Middle Ages and we find it in full force in the thirteenth century.

Formulated by St. Augustine,[4] we find it repeated in the *Institutiones* of Cassiodorus, in St. Gregory's exposition of the first *Book of Kings,* and in St. Isidore's *Etymologies.* Alcuin elevated it to a principle of education in his writings and the schools he guided. More generally, the helpful, propedeutic value of profane knowledge was a structural concept of the culture of the Middle Ages, which was characterized by the subordination of all the elements of knowledge to the sacred science which latter was essentially conceived as the explanation, the penetration, and the illustration of one text, the Bible. This is characteristic of the Middle Ages and of its essentially theological civilization. However, this is not to deny that this civilization embraced many lay tendencies nor assert that the profane and scientific elements of culture were conceived or practiced only in a subordinate reference to theology. In general medieval culture can best be characterized by its total reference to Revelation and salvation. Moreover it is essentially a thing of the Church, a gift of Christianity, since the cultivated world is practically identified with that of the clerics and teaching is exclusively in the hands of the Church. The schools and universities obeyed more or less the law of

---

4. *De Ordine* 1. II, c. XVI, PJL., t. XXXII, col. 1015.

theological culture and rendered obeisance to the theological queen, who was served and chaperoned by the arts and sciences, her servants. Again we find in that pure Augustinian line of the thirteenth century, the letter of Gregory IX to the University of Paris and the brochure of St. Bonaventure, with its astonishingly suggestive title—even if the title is not from Bonaventure himself, *Reductio artium ad theologiam* ("The Reduction of the Arts to Theology").

Well known is the celebrated formula in which tradition has fixed the relation of the other cultural elements to theology: "Philosophy and science are the handmaids of theology." This formula is not a creation of the Middle Ages. We find it in Philo, who uses it to express the effort of a first theological humanism trying to elaborate the *sacra pagina* of the Jewish Old Testament. The Greek Fathers, however, used it in the same sense, for example, Clement of Alexandria, Gregory Nazianzen, and John Damascene. The medieval authors used it so much that we will not attempt to recount their texts.

3. IMPORTANCE OF "TEXT" AND COMMENTATORS. Reflection generally completely saves the serious historian from the impression that the Middle Ages were a long quiet lethargy of the spirit between two great creative epochs: Antiquity and Modern Times. Nevertheless it is undeniable that from the standpoint of religious thought and especially from that of theology, the Middle Ages considered itself as having received a heritage and so was obliged to safeguard and assimilate it. As to the High Middle Ages, historians have observed a certain passivity in the use of sources, the scarcity of new translations from ancient works, a kind of closed world. Still later, even when they make effective proof of greater initiative, the thinkers of the Middle Ages cover their personal production with homologous etiquette. The Middle Ages gives us a datum which must be taken as it is and which calls for nothing more than a commentary. This was their view of themselves. Intellectual work was simply

the assimilation of a text, the commentary on an accepted author. Teaching, in the schools, was essentially the explanation of a text. The essential act and the normal procedure of medieval pedagogy was reading, *lectio;* the teacher, the doctor, was called *lector.*

Simply read the prologue of Peter Lombard's *Sentences.* There it will be seen that this book which will serve as a "text" well up into the seventeenth century simply presents itself as a pure compilation of what the Fathers have said: "A short presentation of the thoughts of the Fathers, offering their doctrines and examples." In one place, asking himself, "What is original sin?" Lombard came up with this observation which tells us quite a bit about his habits of reflection and the spontaneous searchings of his spirit: "On this point the holy Doctors have spoken rather obscurely and the Scholastics have given us varying opinions."[5] So, in the mind of an important man of the Middle Ages, Christian thinkers divide themselves into two categories: on this side we have the "holy doctors" or, if you will, simply the "saints" who from here out represent authority; on the other side we have the "Scholastics," those who in the scholarly methods practiced then in the Church schools "read," that is commented on, the "saints." Even Abélard, in his prologue to *Sic et Non,* gives us insight to the general conviction of the Middle Ages that the Fathers must be *interpreted,* because *we* no longer have the inspiration of creative grace. In this context it should be noted that the works of the Fathers were often grouped with the *Scriptura Sacra,* which with the councils and the canons were the *lectio* and the object of commentary. Fortunately this assimilation did not deceive many and St. Thomas later straightened it out.[6]

The *auctores,* or *actores,* or *autores,* are the writers who in every case fashion authority, *auctoritas,* and serve as its model. Already in the classical tongue, *auctor* meant not

---

5. 1. II, dist. XXX, c. vi, p. 462.
6. *Sum. Theol.* 1ᵃ q. 1, a. 8, ad *2ᵘᵐ*.

merely the one who had drawn up a work of some sort, but he who had the juridical quality or dignity to do it. The Justinian Code opposed the *authentica et originalia rescripta* ("authentic and original texts") to the *exempla* ("copies or transcripts") and in ecclesiastical law Pope Gregory will employ this same terminology. By metonymy, the term "authority" will come no longer to mean the dignity which invests an author or his work but the cited text itself. "Authorities," this latter meaning was what the term had in the High Middle Ages when the sentence-compilers applied it to the patristic texts. The word implied both the idea of origin and of authority. The famous *Decretum de libris recipiendis et non recipiendis* ("Decree concerning books to be accepted and those not to be accepted") attributed to Pope Gelasius which reached into the ninth-century canonical collections officially brought a first distinction between the rejected books and what will be called the "account of authentic writings" (Hincmar de Reims), or the "authentic books admitted by the Church" (Yves de Chartres). Abélard will use them in composing his *Sic et Non*. The custom in a manner quite constant conferred the quality of "authorities" on the texts of the Fathers and a few other ecclesiastical authors. And these "authorities" were considered an undisputed "fact" which could indeed be interpreted but neither questioned nor denied.

The Middle Ages will resume a practice already used before its time. From these texts, handy and practical collections were gathered. Scholars undertook the *defloratio*, the gathering of the *flores* of the Father, of the "chains" and "florilegia," then the collections of *Sententiae*, presupposing a certain amount of harmonization. Many of the citations and "authorities" reproduced in the theological works of the Middle Ages come not from any direct reading of the original texts but from the florilegia and collections.

Whenever work is done on a datum considered mandatory, obviously its homogeneity must be affirmed and so the path of exegesis, more or less difficult, leads to the reduction of discord and the resolution of conflict. From the beginning, the Fathers had dedicated themselves to this work on the biblical text, especially in the hopes of setting up the concordance of the Old and the New Testaments. When the Fathers in turn were treated as a "text" an analogous labor was undertaken on them. Thus the Middle Ages generally ignored the historic point of view which, by situating a text in the circumstances of its origin, permits a judgment to be made regarding its meaning and scope and so reduce its apparent opposition to another text with different meaning and scope. Hence, beside interpretations of a historic sense and a critical sense, quite remarkable, there is a theological jurisprudence of textual interpretation. The good fortune of a second-rate author like Peter Lombard will derive in part at least from his success in establishing a kind of theological *via media* and graciously conciliating the authorities.

B. *The Philosophical Heritage*

There is no question here of my taking up the contents of the philosophical support furnished the Fathers or even the Middle Ages. Rather my point will be to note briefly the heritage received by the Middle Ages from Antiquity, especially from Aristotle, in the methodological structure of its theological work.

1. ARISTOTLE AND THE FATHERS. Aristotle had relatively little doctrinal influence on the Fathers. They suspected him rather of inspiring heresies. From the standpoint of method, however, his effect was quite considerable, although it was rather late. The Aristotelian method of *problema* and *aporia* came alive and influenced Neoplatonism of the first Christian centuries before it had any effect on the patristic Platonism properly so-called of the sixth and seventh centuries. From then on Aristotle contributes to the theological technique of the Oriental Fathers, notably with Leontius Byzantinus in whose writings we find not only the tech-

nique of the Aristotelian "question," but the use—by no means servile—of the Stagirite's philosophical categories in deepening his study of Christology.

However, it is especially with St. John Damascene that Aristotle's double influence of method and ideology is outstanding. Between John Damascene and the Scholastics it has been possible to establish a rapport which is not entirely external. His main work, *Fountain of Knowledge,* is a synthetic exposé of Christian doctrine. Moreover, as an introduction to dogma, he starts with κεφάλαια φιλοσοφκιά (philosophical chapters) which group philosophical definitions borrowed from pagan philosophers, particularly, from Aristotle, Porphyry, and Ammonius, as well as the Fathers of the Church. By this care for technical precision, by his use of Aristotle's philosophy in several theological questions, for example, in Christian ethics, by a certain elaboration of the methodological treatise *De Nominibus Dei,* John Damascene greatly influenced the development of theology. It was an influence, however, which was rather slow in reaching the West, since he was not known there before the middle of the twelfth century.

2. INTRODUCTION OF ARISTOTLE TO THE WEST BY BOETHIUS. It is not known for certain whether Boethius (d. c. 525) translated the entire corpus of Aristotle's writings. What is quite certain, however, is that the Middle Ages knew the philosopher's logical works thanks only to Boethius' translation. These were the *Categories* and the *Perihermenias,* to which must be added Porphyry's *Isagoge* in a revised translation by Boethius based on that of Marius Victorinus. Together these formed the *Logica Vetus.* They were to be followed, between 1120 and 1160, by translations of the *Prior* and *Posterior Analytics,* the *Topics* and the *Sophistici Elenchi* which made up the *Logica Nova.* It is then as a master of thought that Aristotle is received by the High Middle Ages. More precisely he comes first as a master of grammar, then as a master of reasoning and, finally in the thirteenth century, as a master in the knowledge of man and the world.

Beside the application of rational categories to Christian dogmas, Boethius introduced another radical factor to the development of the Middle Ages. This was the Aristotelian classification of the sciences which distinguishes in philosophy "three speculative parts, natural, mathematical, and theological."[7] This division was adopted by the twelfth century. It will be found in the works of Gerbert, Hugh of Saint-Victor, Raoul Ardent, Clarenbald d'Arras, etc. There, however, it is only a division of philosophy, and "theology" is by no means considered as a systematic elaboration of Revelation but as a part of philosophy enjoying a definite degree of abstraction and spirituality. Clarenbald d'Arras formally identifies "theologize" and "philosophize about God."

3. THE THREE "ENTRIES" OF ARISTOTLE. If it is true that a theology is characterized, at least on its speculative side, by the use it makes of reason in its construction of the Christian datum, then it must be admitted that theologizing is modified in its *modus operandi* by the different philosophical ferments which in turn may affect it. To the extent, then, that Aristotle was *par excellence* the philosophical ferment of medieval theology it may be said that the different aspects of him, which were successively known, determined for that theology different methodological regimes. But Aristotle's work was revealed to the theological thought of the West in three stages. This is why we may speak of the three "entries" of Aristotle.

The first "entry" is that of the *Logica Vetus* which presents in the *Categories* an analysis and classification of terms and in the *Perihermenias* an analysis of propositions. This, then, was a presentation of technical instruments for the textual analysis of statements. The High Middle Ages used it this way. With this approach to the Bible and the writings

---

7. Cf. *De Trinitate, Pl.,.*, t. LXIV, col. 1250; comp. *In Porphyr.*, t. LXIII, col. 11B.

of the Fathers, it naturally conceived theology as a knowledge of the Bible based on grammar. The example of St.
Augustine confirmed it in this approach. And if this Doctor
made little room in his writings for a "scientific" knowledge
of the nature of things, this part of his program was developed only after Aristotle's third "entry" through the efforts
of Albert the Great and St. Thomas. Theological study during this period up to St. Anselm rests in main under the
dominance of grammar.

Aristotle's second "entry," in the twelfth century, brought
to light the three other books of the *Organon*: the *Prior* and
Posterior Analytics, which present a scientific study of the
syllogism and different kinds of demonstration. At the same
time came the *Topics* and the *Sophistical Arguments.* These
are a scientific study of probably reasoning and its different stable principles. In short, a theory of knowledge and
demonstration. Growing out of this "entry" and noting the
growth of urban schools, a theology develops which formulates itself in "problems" or "questions." Obviously this
is the product of a reasoning mind which first consults the
text and then resorts to speculative problems as such, independently of the text. This may be called a theology under
the dominance of dialectics, understanding this term in the
general sense of the exercise of logical reasoning. It should
be clearly understood, however, that this classification in no
way denies the profoundly traditional character of theology
in the twelfth century and its continuity with the inherited
procedures of the patristic period and the schools of the
High Middle Ages.

Aristotle's third "entry," in the last quarter of the twelfth
century and the beginning of the thirteenth, brings to sacred
science a philosophical ferment which is no longer purely
formal but which deals with the very order of the objects
and the contents of thought. Aristotle now comes to Christian thought no longer as a master of reasoning but as a
master in the knowledge of man and the world. In short, he
brings with him a metaphysics, a psychology, and an ethics.

As a result, theology, at least with Albert the Great and St. Thomas, came under the regime of philosophy. Later on we will see what problems Aristotle's contribution could not fail to produce. For arriving with a philosophy of man, of natures, and of reality did he not imperil the exclusive sovereignty of Revelation in the very character of theological thought? The fear that this was a fact will inspire, as we shall see, a reactionary movement which was at the same time a vote of confidence for St. Augustine and the Fathers.

From Alcuin to the Twelfth Century

A. *Theology Under the Regime of Grammar*

Theological work in the High Middle Ages is mainly dependent on the resurrection of schools under the inspiration of Charlemagne and Alcuin's direction. This reform is explicitly inspired by St. Augustine, Cassiodorus, and, subsidiarily, by Isidore. It establishes in the Christian West the teaching of the seven arts, divided into the *trivium* and *quadrivium*, leading to the study of the "sacred text." This is the heritage of Greco-Roman culture transmitted by these men of the Church to Christians born among barbarians. The liberal arts consist of a first group, "literary" in tone, of grammar, dialectics, and rhetoric, called the *trivium,* and a second group, this time "scientific," of arithmetic, geometry, music, and astronomy, called the *quadrivium.* These arts were studied for themselves in the Carolingian schools and it was by no means prescribed that they terminate with the study of theology. Nevertheless, for that study it was thought that the arts had a propaedeutic value. For the Scriptures contain all wisdom and all truth but they make a very obscure book. If it is to be understood at all there is room for the service of human sciences. This is the tradition inherited from St. Augustine.

Alcuin speaks in general of the seven liberal arts. In his *De Fide S. Trinitatis,* however, he proclaims and practices the use of dialectics in the treatment of mysteries—better, he himself writes a *De Dialectica* where he shows an exact feeling for the role of that art. Dialectics is reasoning which concludes with necessity. Nevertheless, theological thought of the Carolingian epoch is indisputably characterized not so much by dialectics as by grammar, not so much by reasoning which proves as by the science of terms and statements which explain. The use of dialectics between Alcuin's day and Abélard's will at best be sporadic and occasional. St. Augustine, in his *De Doctrina Christiana*, had already noted the utility of *schemata* and *tropi* for a more precise understanding of the Scriptures. The Carolingian reform made an institution out of this conviction: "When figures of speech and the like are found in the Sacred Text, there is no doubt that anyone trained in literature will more quickly understand the textual meaning."[8]

As Fathers Paré, Brunet, and Tremblay have vigorously insisted in their *Renaissance du XXᵉ siècle*, every work of thought is tied to a "milieu": an economic, political, institutional, cultural milieu, which not only provides a framework, but also is a real condition of birth and growth. Now, first, as to the place of theological teaching: at that time these were the schools attached to the abbeys and the bishops' palaces—a milieu of tradition more than of progress and initiative. As long as theological teaching remained dispersed and under the immediate control of the bishops or abbots, the development of a theological science properly so-called was practically impossible. Next, the teaching personnel was composed of men of the Church who

---

8. *Capit.* "*De Litteris Colendis,*" in *Mon. Germ. Hist., Leges, Capitularia,* t. I, p. 79. Cf. Bede, *De Schematis et Tropis Sacrae Scripturae liber, P.L.,* vol. XC, col. 175; *Comm, in Pentateuchum,* Ex. viii, *P.L.,* vol. SCI, col. 302; *In Samuelem Prophetam allegorica expos.* col. 510 and 706; Raban Maur, *De. Cler. Instit., P.L.,* vol. CVIÏ, col. 395–96, which also has a chap. XX, *De Dialéctica,* col. 397–98, where dialectics is abundantly praised but from a rather defensive and apologetic viewpoint.

assumed the role of teacher though they were not real scholars. Theological science to develop must suppose a certain detachment from the hierarchical schools and a process of urban centralization together with the growth of a community of scholars. To sum up, theology of the Carolingian period is traditionalist in character. The works of that time tend toward reproduction and compilation. This is the age of *Catenae, Sententiae, Flores, Excerpta*, etc. Theology consists in a study of the Scriptures from a moral and allegorizing standpoint. This is achieved, on the one hand, by extracts from the Fathers, on the other, from the resources of the liberal arts, but particularly grammar. (Men like Raban Maur or his disciple, Godescale, are sufficiently representative of a theology nourished by a knowledge of the Bible, the Fathers, and grammar.)

It is generally agreed that the only thinker truly original by the contents of his doctrine was John Scotus Erigena (d. c. 870). However, from the methodological standpoint, he contributes very little. Having first confounded philosophy with religion, he assigns it the task of interpreting the symbols under which God is revealed in the Scriptures and then in nature. In this interesting concept we find an amalgam of an Augustinian tradition, the influence of Denis and Maximus the Confessor and we find a view of God and the world unified by the notion of exemplarism or symbolism.

B. *Dialecticians and Antidialecticians*

Dialectics, proclaimed by the Carolingian renaissance but not put to work, slowly gains support in the process of time. The eleventh century from the standpoint of its notion of theology is plagued by a fight between dialecticians and antidialecticians. Quite naturally this had the effect of promoting the need of reasoning. The dialectic champions wanted to apply dialectic principles in a stiff, abstract manner to Christian doctrine. The result was catastrophic. An intemperate application of the dialectical method to the Eucharistic dogma by Bérenger of Tours ended in a position which has been held to be negative heresy with regard to transubstantiation. Bérenger puts evidence above everything, above authority, even in matters of theology.[9] Hence, the controversy which ensues is one which every theology, holding any pretense to being a theology and not a pure transcription of faith, must endure. We shall watch it develop. The radical question is: Can Christian doctrines be understood in terms of reason's categories? If not, what status should be given to human reason which is God's creation and man's honor, since, as Bérenger himself says, "He is thus made known in his own image and as he is known to God."[10] If, on the other hand, the answer is "yes," does this not make Christian realities merely a matter of general laws which the human reason can attain, and, in that case, where is the mystery, where is the supreme, unique, and sovereign character of Christian realities?

This, then, is the stake at issue between the dialecticians and the antidialecticians. Some among these latter take an extreme position. They strongly assert with St. Peter Damien[11] that reason has no teaching authority in Christianity; that, hence, it must comport itself according to its station as a simple servant. They consider any encroachment of dialectics on the sacred text to be a sacrilege. They affirm very forcefully the transcendence, the character of unique truth of the Christian faith, which has been given us not for the purpose of fashioning it into a science but as a mode of living in penance and avoidance of the world. This is the ascetico-monastic solution which we will soon find again in St. Bernard and later in Pascal. It is an attitude inalienably Christian. But another attitude is still possible. In fact there is one which later the Church will strongly favor, namely, that all the data are in a hierarchical order. This is what gripped a man like Lanfranc, Bérenger's adversary and the founder

---

9. Cf. *De Sacra Coena*, Berlin, 1834, pp. 100–1.
10. *Ibid.*, p. 101.
11. *De Divina Omnipotentia*, P.L., vol. CXLV, col. 603.

of that Abbey du Bec where St. Anselm's important ideas will soon flourish. Lanfranc is a "convert," in the sense that having first been addicted to dialectics he is now entirely devoted to the study of Scripture. However, he is a moderate man and looking closely at the question, he follows the footsteps of St. Paul. Rejecting the possible excess of dialectics, he preserves its legitimate use. The use of dialectics would be perverse if it ended in belittling or dominating the Christian datum and thus emptying the mystery of faith.

C. *St. Anselm*

St. Anselm of Canterbury in this debate holds a somewhat similar position to that of Lanfranc. With Anselm we enter into a conception of theology which has a very high quality. Anselm unites the monastic Augustinian current, favorable to the self-sufficiency of the faith, and the current of speculative thought, degraded by the extreme dialecticians. "No Christian should openly discuss why the Catholic Church Fully believes and orally confesses a certain doctrine to be true. However, while simply believing and heartily living according to it he may patiently seek its rational basis. If he understands it, let him give thanks to God. If not, it is stupid to protest. Let him bow his head in submission."[12] "O Lord, I do not try to penetrate Your depth . . . but I hope in a small measure to understand Your truth, which my heart believes and loves. For I do not seek to understand that I may believe; rather I believe that I may understand. . . . Hence, O Lord, Who gives understanding to faith, give me, as far as You know to be expedient, to understand why You are as we believe and that You are what we believe." So begins the *Proslogion*. We have here an *intellectus fidei*, a *ratio fidei*, let us say an intelligibility of the faith whereby he who believes and he who loves can find delight. Anselm explains himself on the term *intellec-*

---

12. *De Fide Trinit. et de Incam. Verbi*, *P.L.*, vol. CLVIII, col. 263.

tus, this knowledge or this understanding, which a loving faith desires. It is intermediary, between faith and vision. He supposes the faith, more precisely, the loving faith, and proceeds from there. It is the fruit of an effort of penetration where the spirit uses all the resources at its disposal: analogies of the created world, principles of metaphysics and dialectics. He has for his goal a joyous perception, which in its inchoative and more or less precarious state is, nevertheless, in the genre of the beatific joy. In his theological works Anselm shows himself to be a true theologian or—if you will—a true metaphysician of dogma. But he is a metaphysician who has not read the *Metaphysics* of Aristotle. And if he is a metaphysician it is not by the application of a philosophy to the Christian datum, but rather because of what the pressure of faith itself, directly and without mediation, properly rational, contains of intelligibility.

Considered thus, this theological method poses no difficulty and it can be considered as giving its charter to scholastic speculation. Indeed Anselm has been called "the Father of Scholasticism." But Anselm goes much further, He makes more precise certain uses of the *intelligere* based on the *credere*. From this approach we want to discuss his famous argument in the *Proslogion* proving the existence of God and the *rationes necessariae* by which Anselm thought to prove the truth of the mysteries of the Incarnation and the Trinity. The commentators generally have smoothed over Anselm's position so that he can be freed of any accusation of rationalism. The problem which Anselm's method presents has been considered most frankly in the twist of his proof in the *Proslogion,* c. II and III. Karl Barth maintains that his position is purely theological, namely, he does not try to *prove* that God exists, but rather, maintaining by faith the fact of His existence, he tries to show why and how this is so. It is not a proof but a recognition of the existence of God.

Étienne Gilson insists on the demonstrative value which Anselm attributes to reasoning and also on the epistemology which his use of reason would suppose: namely, that a logical necessity must have a corresponding reality. He who *receives* into his spirit the *idea quo maius cogitali nequit* ("greater than which cannot be thought") cannot fail to admit the existence of such a Being. Anselm's argument, then, not only includes a working epistemology according to which a reality must correspond to every true object in the mind (Gilson), but also a psychology of the Augustinian persuasion according to which the soul's disposition intervenes to the extent that, thanks to God's illumination, it can perceive or not perceive, because it accepts or does not accept light from the interior Master. The objective value of the argument is hard to determine. Cf. Thonnart, Beckaert, and Poucet. In general, we think it unfair to read a post-Thomistic distinction of reason and faith into the writings of Anselm and Bee. Certainly Anselm well distinguished the two *types of knowledge* just as he distinguished the two *powers* in Christian society. But this distinction does not equal, either in the first or the second instance, the objective distinction of two *domains*. Rather there are two types of unequal capacities in one and the same domain, namely that of truth. Anselm put reason to work, but not as a philosopher. For him, reason could function in two ways. First, as the faculty of a man without wisdom either outside the faith or before its arrival. In this case the faculty does not attain its *rectitude* or fullness. Secondly, as the faculty of a believing and religious man on his way to celestial beatitude. The intellect in such a man is an organ or perception beyond pure faith but this side of vision. It is not necessary to give this procedure an epistemological title taken from a distinction of domains, while wondering whether it is philosophy or theology. All that is necessary is to say that Anselm's approach utilizes the power of reason such as is exercised in faith, rather in a life of loving faith, of prayer, of conversion of the entire man to the *Rectitudo* of God, whereby he realizes his own *rectitudo* or truth. It is a process of rational perception of the rationality *of that which is believed.* Quite characteristic is this statement of a disciple of St. Anselm, Aimer, monk of Canterbury: "Although we believe whatever the Scriptures direct us to believe (about Christ) . . ., it is, nevertheless, sweeter for us if in some manner we come to grasp by reason that the very object of our faith must be so and cannot be other than my faith teaches us. God is the supreme *ratio* and in Him resides the certain source of all rational argumentation."

Chapter Three
The Renaissance of the Twelfth Century

Theology Under the Regime of Dialectics

A. *The School of Laon and Abélard*

Recent studies have cast-better light on the role of the School of Laon in the theological movement. Many of the masters who were to write large on the pages of the twelfth century received their formation in the school of Anselm of Laon, himself a disciple of St. Anselm at the Abbey du Bec. From the viewpoint of the notion and structure of theology, Anselm of Laon has a twofold importance. First because in his *Sententiae*, partially edited in 1919 by Fr. Bliemetzrieder, *Beiträge*, t. XVIII, fasc. 2–3, an effort is made in the direction of systematization. Moreover the term *Sententiae* from his day forward will represent less a sort of florilegium or a work constructed along the lines of the *Sentences* of Lombard, but a foreshadowing of the great *Summae*. Thus theology takes more complete possession of its object. If in this systematic work Anselm does not seem to be a real pioneer from the methodological viewpoint, since he is content to give an explanation of the texts by means of glosses and commentaries, nevertheless we do find in his work the beginning of the *quaestio* procedure, that is of dialectical debate.

It is still a timid try and one which will not satisfy Abélard. After having studied and taught philosophy and secular subjects, Abélard came to the abbey school of Laon where he was to become a man "very strong for those who come only to hear him, but next to nothing in the sight of those who ask him questions." The scene which decided the method of Abélard is well known. Questioned by the master as to what he thought "about the reading of holy books" he, who heretofore studied nothing but physics and philosophy, replied that such a study could indeed be most salutary, but that he did not see why there was need of a commentary and of lectures to comprehend the writings and glosses of the Fathers. And so Abélard, called upon to explain the sacred texts without the help of commentaries and masters, began at Laon, by means of his own *ingenuity*, a procedure which he was to continue at Paris. Such is the way Abélard began theology. Although up till then he had only glossed the Scriptures, he undertook this task with all the resources of his spirit. Some six years later, at Saint-Denys, he pushed still further his innovation and the use of natural reason. "It happened then," he tells us, "that I applied myself to discourse on the foundations of our faith with the help of comparisons furnished by human reason, and that I composed on the Divine Unity and Trinity a theological treatise for the use of my disciples. They, as a matter of fact, demanded human and philosophical reasons, and required intelligible explanations rather than mere affirmations. They said it is useless to talk if one does not give an understanding of his remarks, that they cannot believe if they do not first comprehend and that it is ridiculous to teach others something of which neither they nor those who teach have an understanding."[1]

I. ABÉLARD'S THEOLOGY. For some time there has been an awareness of Abélard's "rationalism," but our idea of his position is even more exact since we have his logic texts, edited by B. Geyer.[2] Abélard is rather a dialectician and a logician than a philosopher. Therefore, it is in his position of logician that we comprehend his position as theologian,

---

1. *Hist. Calam.* C. IX, *P.L.*, vol. CLXXVIII, col. 140–43.
2. *Peter Abaelards philosophische Schriften*, in *Beiträge*, t. XXI, Münster, 1919–33.

and in his "nominalism" we get the true nature of his "ratio-nalism." We have seen Abélard requested by his students not to make statements which were unaccompanied by an *intelligentia:* The work of theology is precisely to conclude in that understanding. But in what does it consist? Must the mysteries be penetrated and demonstrated by reason alone, by a reason prior to faith and independent of it? By no means. At no stage of Abélard's thought will we find in it the affirmation that his theological work proceeds by the forces of reason alone and never falls back on Revelation. It is not to assemble the objects of faith that reason intervenes in the work of theology, but rather to set up a critical expla-nation of its statements. Abélard is less a philosopher inter-ested in the ultimates of reality, for example, in the reality or irreality of the universals, than a grammarian-logician interested in a critical study of propositions and their rela-tionships. He himself says that the "property of words and their correct distribution" are to be considered "rather than the essences of things."[3] His theology then must be inter-preted as a function of his logic. This is effectively what his pupil of 1136, John of Salisbury, suggests when he writes "Sermones intuetur" ("He understands the words.").[4] The most recent interpretations of Abélard follow the same line; B. Geyer speaks of "Sprachlogik"; J. G. Sikes, who tells us "Abailard's logic was essentially a logic of diction based upon a philosophical understanding of grammar."[5] Hence, when Abélard, in his *Tractatus de Untiate et de Trinitate Divina,* gives to theology the task of "assigning the causes of the Divine Names," it must clearly be seen that there is no question of attempting a perfect and complete under-standing of the mysteries, but simply of offering a logical explanation and justification of the announcements of Rev-

---

3. *Dialectica,* pars III.
4. *Metalogicus, P.L.,* vol. CIC, col. 874.
5. *Peter Abailard,* 1932, p. 97.

elation, of showing that the dogmatic propositions are in conformity with the laws of predicability.

Abélard, however, was not content to confine himself merely to a critico-logical commentary on the doctrinal statements; he also dug out reasons in favor of the very objects of faith, of the Trinitarian mystery in particular. In his opinion what was the value of these reasons? That of likelihood, "something similar and neighborly to human reason but not contrary to our holy faith." He might aim at an apologetic use of reason, "against those who glory in opposing faith by human reasons"; or he might apply reason to a constructive theology, thereby forcing himself to define by reasons of probability and fitness whatever can arouse the questioning spirit. Whatever may have been Abélard's pretention in attempting a demonstration of the Trinity, this is where he consciously stopped his thought on the theological level.

2. The *Sic et Non*. From the time of the Carolingian period the need was felt to reconcile the important authoritative texts which, on the same question, came up discordant. The elaboration of rules for this work of interpretation and agreement had been the work of canonists since the early part of the eleventh century. Unfortunately we no longer have the treatise in which Hincmar of Rheims set down his standards of interpretation, but its substance seems to have been passed on to Bernold of Constance (d. 1110), who in his theologico-canonical writings lays out very precise rules. With him and with the canonists who follow him, Yves of Chartres in particular, there is simply a jurisprudence of interpretation of the "authorities" which is being formulated. Abélard, in his *Sic et* Non, introduces the problem of the agreement of authorities into the heart of the theological method and give it a technical form of great precision. The viewpoint of historical development remains, for the most part, foreign to the rules of interpretation which he sets down. But he has a feeling for the

authentic meaning of a text and, in general, his standards are orientated toward the determination of that genuine meaning.

In Abélard's opinion, not only does the problem of the agreement of opposed authorities become a properly theological problem, but it becomes a technical part of the method. *Sic et Non is* built into a system working toward the dialectical process which from now on we are going to see taking shape in the *quaestio* and becoming the equipment proper to Scholasticism's theological work. "For by doubt we come to inquiry and from inquiry we come to truth," says Abélard in the Prologue.

Abélard occupies a respectable place in the development of theology and its method. In the three books, *Introductio, Theologia Christiana,* and *Epitome,* he has exemplified a theological elaboration which is no longer the commentary on a text, but a construction systematically spaced out. Under his aegis we have moved forward from the *Sacra Pagina* to *Theologia,* which latter now in turn gets under way for its truly scientific construction. As a matter of fact, the third book of the *Introductio,* unfortunately not developed, approaches the style which will later be that of St. Thomas, the method of the *quaestio,* founded on Aristotle's *Analytics.* Incidentally, Aristotle is there called *"dialecticorum princeps"* ("prince of dialecticians"). Abélard begins to introduce into his textual commentaries themselves, these *quaestiones.* This is a remarkable innovation and one with far-reaching consequences.

Let us see now if we can isolate Aristotle's influence and define its limits. The Abélardian proposal of a theology which would supply "human and philosophical reasons" came forth at a time when the second half of Aristotle's *Organon* was being broadcast in the West, that is, between 1120 and 1160. This comprises, of course, the *Prior* and *Posterior Analytics,* the *Topics* and the *Sophistical Arguments.* Abélard's first writings show little Aristotelian influence; in them Plato is rather the philosopher par excellence. But while

Abélard's *Dialectica* (c. 1120 sq.) still practically ignores the second part of the *Organon*, Adam du Petit-Pont makes use of the *Prior Analytics* in 1132, Robert of Melun comments on the *Topics* about 1140 and from then on a steady current of the new logic flows into the sacred sciences. Now this *logica nova* no longer contributes a mere table of predicables and a technique of analyzing propositions, but a theory of syllogism and of probable and scientific demonstration. Hence Aristotle is about to enter into theology itself, which thereby becomes a truly systematized knowledge and no longer a simple commentary. Nevertheless he still enters only as a master of logical thought and not yet as a master of thought as such or as a doctor of anthropological, psychological, moral, and metaphysical truths. This will be the work of the first years of the thirteenth century and, as far as the notion of theology is concerned, it will constitute a new step forward as well as the occasion of a crisis.

B. *St. Bernard*

Reaction set in at once. St. Bernard's opposition to Abélard is well known. He represents the old ascetico-monastic conception in which the monk has only to guard the common tradition and meditate on it so that he can live by it while doing penance. "The seven arts of the monk are his psalter," says the Blessed William of Hirschau,[6] St. Bernard admits that the arts and philosophy can be used only as something purely for the edification of oneself or of others. He wants no science but that of the saints, no disposition before God but that of admiration—none of this curious research: "which is a sort of admiration but not a scrutiny."

This reaction will continue and all through the course of the twelfth century we will hear a formal protestation against the introduction of dialectics and logic, not indeed

---

6. *Praef. in Astronomica,* ed. Pez, in *Thesarus anecdotorum,* t. VI, p. 261.

into the pedagogy of the clerics, but into the fabric of theological weaving.[7]

These reactions are produced in the name of what is called monastic theology. This is a nondialectical type of reflection, contemplative, nurtured in prayer based on communion with the celebrated mysteries which have become a part of one's life. There is no purely intellectual or reasoning collaboration. If the example of St. Anselm shows that this type of meditation can be rigorous, it is still true that it spontaneously develops into a symbolic expression favorable to a total but simple perception. Cf. St. Bernard, *In Cant.* 74, 2. This procedure has its consequences in the treatment of the sacred text. Obviously the spiritual meaning, accommodated to the life of the soul and religious experience, takes over. St. Bernard went so far as to elaborate a theory of this type of exegesis.[8] The mystical exegesis he gave to the famous passage "Lord, there are two swords here now" (Luke 22:38) is well known.[9] With such an exegesis practically anything could be found in the Bible. It is worthy of note here and now that Albert the Great and St. Thomas plainly affirm the scientific worthlessness to theology of a purely mystical interpretation of the Scriptures.

C. The Victorines and Peter Lombard

Was there, then, no possible agreement between the traditional mystic current and the logical or new philosophical current? Yes, and it will finally come to fruition in St. Thomas, who will tell us: "One should rely on reasons which search out the foundation of truth and make known how

---

7. Cf. among others, Gauthier of Saint-Victor, *Contra quatuor labyrinthos Franciae*, P.L., vol. CXCIX, col. 1129-72; Manegold of Lautenbach, *Opuse, contra Wolfelmum*, P.L., vol. CLV, col. 149–76; Étienne of Tournai, Abbot of Sainte-Geneviève, *Epist. ad Alexandrum III*, P.L., vol. CCXI, col. 517; The Benedictine Prior of Worcester, Senatus, *Against the Sent. of Peter of Poitiers*, T. E. Holland, *Collectanea II, Oxford Hist. Soc.*, vol. XVI, 1890, p. 181 sq.
8. Cf. *In Vigilia Nativitatis*, P.L., vol. CLXXXIII, col. 94.
9. Cf. *De Consideratione*, P.L., vol. CLXXXII, col. 776.

what is said is true. Otherwise, if the Master determines
the question on mere authority, the student will indeed be
assured that the thing is so, but he will acquire no knowledge or understanding and will leave empty-handed."[10]
However, St Thomas did not follow Abélard without intervening development. Between the two it was plainly necessary that, resuming Anselm's effort, philosophical reason
should be caught up again in the spiritual tradition stem-
ming from St. Augustine. This will be the work of the Victorines and Peter Lombard.

It has been said of Peter Lombard that he was "Abélard
who had found a fortune and become a bishop." As a matter
of fact, it is far from amusing that Abélard's effort, which
presented all the danger and intemperance of a work altogether too personal, should be mixed in the framework of
fervent monastic and mystical life, into the thought of a
man of the Church, of a man of government even, entirely
devoted to the *via media*. "Moderation was exercised in
both cases," says Peter Lombard of his own position with
regard to the use or rejection of dialectics.[11] The great inno-
vations are not fully serviceable until they have been baptized by ecclesiastical institutions and tradition.

Hugh of Saint-Victor will come to know how Abélard's
uniquely dialectical process is inadequate for theological
work. Certainly there is place for grammar, logic, and dialectics and they have their uses in the sacred science. But a
profound penetration into the Scriptures is another matter and for that it is not sufficient to be merely a philosopher. "In other writings the philosopher need only know
the meaning of words; but in Sacred Scripture a knowledge
of the meaning of things is very much more important than
that of words."[12] To build up a theology it does not suffice
to treat the Sacred Scriptures absolutely as another text and

---

10. *Quodlibetales*, IV, a. 18.
11. *Sent.* prol. Quaracchi, t. I, p. 3.
12. *De Scripturis*, P.L., vol. CLXXV, col. 20.

approach it merely with the resources of philosophy as Abélard boasted he could do. On the other hand, even if Hugh
returns theological work to its proper religious setting, he is
aware how much he needs the various resources of human
ingenuity. With magnificent prodigality he refurnishes the
Augustinian tradition on the formation of the theologian
by the liberal arts. But this *philosophic* of the seven arts, as
far as its contents are concerned, is no longer what it had
been from the fifth to the end of the eleventh century. It
has been enriched by Aristotle's methodologico-scientific
contribution. Instead of the seven arts, the Victorine now
piles up a rational classification of twenty-one disciplines,
thereby outlining a new program of education, which has
room for an ample conception of human knowledge.

The Abélardian effort to establish a body of logically
systematized Christian doctrine is reviewed in its turn
and eventually inspires those classical works known as the
Summa Sententiarum, the *De Sacramentis* of Hugh of Saint-
Victor and the *Sententiae* of Peter Lombard. The same term
Summa, which Abélard had already used in defining his
Introductio as "a sum of sacred erudition," reappears here to
designate a coordinated whole, a body of doctrine—no longer a lecture on the *sacra pagina*, but truly a work of "theology." What Hugh had thus realized in his *De Sacramentis*,
he explained and justified in his *Didascalion*. He adds to a
simple reading of the text (domain of *historia)*, a systematic
explanation which derives from it, which leans on it, yet is
at the same time its elaboration and an ordering of its disar-
ray. "I compiled this brief summa into one series so that the
mind would have something certain where it could center
and establish its attention, lest it be led astray without order
and direction by the various volumes of Scripture and manifold readings."[13] It would almost seem we are reading the
prologue to St. Thomas' *Summa*.

---

13. *De Sacr., P.L.,* vol. CLXXVI, col. 183.

We will not spend much time on Peter Lombard, because the general traits of his theology and the approach of his great work *Sententiae* are well known. In Peter Lombard it is not merely the Abélardian proposal to systematize which bears fruit, but notable citations from the *Sic et Non,* thanks to which the *Sentences* will represent for later theology a great synthesis of positive theology. His *Sentences* will become a textbook which, as a companion to the Bible, will give excellent matter for a display of the dialectical method. If this method has delivered all its benefits in the theology of the thirteenth century, the reason is, that beside the "questions of Sacred Scripture," it was able to develop most freely on the basis of a second "textbook," for which, as Fishacre will later say, "to read and dispute did not differ." And so, the importance of Peter Lombard's *Sentences* will greatly exceed that of his personal support to the elaboration of the theological method.

D. *Gilbert de La Porrée and Alain of Lille*

The need of method and classification is remarkable in the second and last third of the twelfth century. (A typical example is the prologue to the *Sententiae* of Robert of Melun.) The pedagogic need urged on the construction of methodical works that would organize material which elsewhere was found, dispersed and occasional. For example, this was the epoch when an attempt was made to set up an organic and systematic theology with texts drawn from St. Anselm. Hugh of Saint-Victor had also composed a work of this kind as he tells in the prologue to his *De Sacramentis,* and about 1165–70, Peter the Eater (Pierre le Mangeur) at the request of his *socii* drew up his famous *Historia Scolastica,* which applies to the historical narrative of the Scriptures the need to group and classify what is found in the sacred text. But, in addition to these pedagogic accommodations, theology in this second half of the twelfth century truly gains consciousness of itself and of its place in the different branches of science. For some time already under the term "faculties" a distinction had been made of the various disciplines which made up the contemporary education. Gilbert de La Porrée says, for example, "This is proper, since the faculties are diverse in accord with the kinds of things in question, thus, they are natural, mathematical, theological, civil, rational . . ."[14]

From that it is rather easy to determine with precision the proper method and regime of each of these "faculties" (= disciplines). Indeed we see the same Gilbert outline the first idea of a methodology.[15] His notion is that in every discipline recourse must be had to initial rules which are proper to it and correspond to its object: properly worded rules in grammar, common sources in rhetoric, theorems or axioms in mathematics, general statements in dialectics, indemonstrable principles in philosophy. The same in theology. And Gilbert tried in his commentary to isolate these rules which are rather of metaphysics or of theology in the Aristotelian sense of the term.

Gilbert's idea will not fade without an echo. John of Salisbury will soon take it up in his *Polycraticus*. But it is notably Alain of Lille (d. 1202) who will give it its most perfect realization. It is the prime concern of his *Rules of Sacred Theology*, where he states in the prologue: "This supercelestial science, which is theology, is not defrauded by its rules; for it has very suitable rules, which excel others in keeping with its obscurity and subtlety; and although the total necessity of the other rules is inclined to waver, because it is built solely on the customary modes of natural processes, the necessity of theological maxims is absolute and unbreakable, because these produce faith which the things of nature cannot do."[16] This text points out very well the considerable novelty of the idea: to assimilate theology to a "science" of

---

14. *Commentarium in libros Boetii de Trinitate, P.L.*, vol. LXIV, col. 1281A.
15. *Ibid.*, col. 1315.
16. *Regulae*, prol., *P.L.*, vol. CCX, col. 621 sq.

the same structure as the other human sciences. "I only did what had been done in all the other human sciences," Gilbert modestly wrote,[17] Alain's text highlights the difference in certitude and sources which distinguishes theology from the other sciences. But it must be admitted that his work on this point, like that of Gilbert, leaves much to be desired. The *regulae* which he explains in his book are quite philosophical and Fr. Chenu was able to remark in this regard and apropos of Gilbert: "The specific characters of the *regula* in theology are not distinguished from the common function of axioms; and under this vague notion are blended generalized observations, first principles, particular theses, common opinions, articles of faith, all things quite distinct in their origins, in their value of evidence, in their quality of certitude and hence in their scientific function."[18]

Another work by Alain of Lille merits to be noted here, his *Distinctiones dictionum theologicalium*. It is a kind of dictionary of theological terms. In a sense the work could be characterized as Preabélardian or Preanselmian, since it is practically exclusively devoted to a verbal or textual explanation of the sacred text. But his bent for defining terms and distinguishing the significations of words is quite characteristic of theology at the end of the twelfth century.

E. *The development of the Quaestio*

The method of *aporiae*, practiced by the philosophers of antiquity and specially by Aristotle, is found in the works of a number of Christian authors: Origen, Eusebius of Caesarea, the Ambrosiaster, St. Jerome, St. Augustine. This kind of writing was not specially devoted to scriptural matters and, in any case, it had built-in limitations. It was weak on moral, ascetic, or even grammatical considerations. It attempted to reply to scriptural and exegetical *difficulties* somewhat after the manner that Abélard replied to the

---

17. *P.L.*, vol. LXIV, col. 1316C.
18. *Revue des sciences philos. et théol.*, 1935, p. 265.

problemata. Heloissae, and St. Thomas will draw up his *Responsio de XXXVII articulis, Responsio de XLII articulis,* etc. Here we are not dealing with any systematic arrangement between the dialectic method and theological work.

From the patristic age, however, scriptural commentary often left room for "questions." If, for example, we carefully survey the twelve books of St. Augustine's *De Genesi ad Litteram,* we find that the commentary as such is repeatedly interrupted by a line of theological *quaestiones* which while they are directly concerned with the sacred text discuss marginally and quite naturally a point of doctrine. Still it must be noted that these *quaestiones* are often introduced for apologetic reasons or to satisfy a subtle curiosity, and not for a systematic elaboration of science.

Augustine's practice was still observed by the twelfth-century authors. But with them, the "questions" which interrupted the commentaries began to occupy a larger and larger place. Today it is quite easy to follow the history of this change. The methodic dispute or use of the *quaestio* was born in the framework of the textual explanation or *lectio.* Necessarily difficulties occurred in the explanation which gave rise to a discussion. Without doubt such discussions have always been practiced. We can find distinguished examples in the school of Anselm of Laon and William of Champeaux. But we feel it is with Abélard that the methodic (and methodological) use of the *quaestio* begins. Indeed not only did Abélard use the process in his commentary on St. Paul, but he made it the theme of his great *Sic et Non.* A "question" is born from an opposition of propositions whereby the mind is placed in a state of doubt. To escape that condition it must find a motive which swings it in favor of one of the alternatives, destroys the power of the opposing argument, or acknowledges to each of the two positions its portion of truth and so grants its consequential assent. So concludes Abélard: "By doubting we proceed to inquiry; by inquiry we perceive truth."[19] In his commentary on Boethius' *De Trinitate,* Gilbert de La Porrée gives us a more philosophical and precise formula of the role of the *quaestio:* "By affirmation and its contradictory negation a *question* is established."[20] But farther on[21] he adds: "But not every contradiction gives rise to a question. For when one side seems to have no truthful arguments at all . . . or when we can supply neither side with arguments to show its truth or falsity, then a contradiction does not become a question. But when both sides seem to have arguments supporting their truth, then we have a *question.*" A *quaestio* arises when two contradictory or contrary theses are both supported by arguments and a problem follows which the mind wishes to clarify.

From now on in the teaching of theology two processes, which at first blended together, will be clearly distinguished, the commentary and the discussion or *quaestio:* "The teaching of Sacred Scripture consists of three factors," Peter the Chorister (Pierre le Chantre) will tell us toward the end of the century, "reading, discussion, and commentary."[22] Only the master of theology has the right to do all three. It would seem that Simon of Tournai (who was teaching about 1165) will be one of the first to make a special exercise of the discussion, which, though born of the *lectio,* now becomes separate from it. The school of Saint-Victor is quite cool toward the dialectical process and Hugh hardly mentions it. William of Saint-Thierry, in his commentary on the *Epistle to the Romans,* will try to suppress the *quaestionum molestiae.* But in general the *quaestio* continues its steady gain. And this not only in the explanation of the Scriptures, but soon in the *Sentences* of Peter Lombard. In both places the *quaestiones* at first attached to the text tend to multiply rapidly, then to take on a certain independence and become organized

19. *P.L.,* vol. CLXXVIII, col. 1349.
20. *P.L.,* vol. LXIV, col. 1253.
21. *Ibid.,* col. 1258.
22. *Verbum Abbreviatum, P.L.,* vol. CCV, col. 25.

into a separate system, thereby reducing the commentary properly so called to a secondary role. We can follow this progress of the *quaestio* in Lombard's explanation as well as that of the Bible.

Thanks to Odon of Soissons (or of Ourscamp), about 1164, discussion comes again into the framework of the *lectio*. His *Quaestiones* are probably a collection of *quaestiones* originally asked on the occasion of textual explanations or *lectiones*. The Fathers of Quaracchi, editors of Peter Lombard's *Sentences,* drew up a list of the "questions" raised by the Master in his scriptural commentaries. Robert of Melun compiled a volume of *Quaestiones de Divina Pagina* and another entitled *Quaestiones de Epistolis Pauli,* whose contents and very title show that the *quaestiones* have arisen from a text and on the occasion of a commentary on that text. Indeed it is quite possible, even probable, that in their origin rather highly systematized works were nothing but an orderly outlay of questions asked in the teaching of the *lectio.*

A similar process of detachment and systematization takes over with the *quaestiones* to be found in commentaries on Lombard's *Sentences,* which along with the Bible became the textbook in theology. For example, in Peter of Poitiers and Odon of Ourscamp, the great Master's closest disciples, we find that the questions become part of the text like most elaborate glosses. We see in Hugh of Saint-Cher (d. 1263), that the commentary becomes almost uniquely an *Expositio textus.* In St. Thomas, on the other hand, the part of the commentary proper devoted to *Divisio* and *Expositio textus* is relatively small, and the treatise is composed of logically distributed *quaestiones* which are an original scientific construction. The same is true of Kilwardby, St. Bonaventure, and the great Scholastics. Moreover, it is very instructive to compare the questions raised by each author. With a disciple and friend of St. Thomas, Annibald de Annibaldis, there is no longer any *Divisio* or *Expositio textus,* but only *quaestiones.* With others, there is one volume of commentary by *Divisio* and *Expositio textus* and another of *quaestiones.*

So in the last third of the twelfth century an evolution has come about in the teaching and conception of theology. Instead of relying principally on textual commentary, theology now, like any other science, consists in research initiated by a "question." It has taken the road opened by Abélard which consists in treating theological matter by the same epistemological procedure as any other object of truly scientific knowledge.

Opposition is not slow in showing its sturdy neck. At the end of the twelfth century, Étienne of Tournai, Abbot of Sainte-Geneviève, denounces the peril in terms which it could be believed were borrowed from Luther in 1517: "Indiscriminately they compose new summulas and commentaries on theology . . . as though the opuscula of the Holy Fathers were not sufficient."[23] Another author, who belongs to the line of Saint-Victor and is quoted by Landgraf in *Scholastik,* 1928, p. 36, requests that the *auctoritates* be upheld or whatever is closest to them. Later Robert Grosseteste and Roger Bacon will protest against the fact that the Bible which is *the* text of the theological faculty has been supplanted by commentaries on the book of the *Sentences,* which is only a *Summa magistralis.*

But the movement is a fact. The *quaestio* procedure will take such a hold in the thirteenth century that it can be found in John of Meung's *Roman de la Rose.* St. Thomas' *Summa* will bring about the ultimate triumph of the *quaestio.* It is obvious that this work is essentially based on "questions." Each of its parts is called an "article," but it would be better named a "question," for it is built on the Aristotelian *problema* and the whole is organized, divided, and articulated in a systematic and rational manner. Teaching according to *lectio,* which St. Thomas does daily and which has given us scriptural commentaries is not discussed here for pedagogic reasons.

---

23. *Epist. ad Papam,* in *Chartul. univ. Paris,* 1.I, pp. 47–48.

Chapter Four
The Golden Age of Scholasticism

Theology Under the Regime of Metaphysics

This new period is extremely fruitful from theology's viewpoint, and the various positions with regard to its object and method are discussed in detail. Is theology a science? Is it speculative or practical? What exactly is its "subject matter?" But in addition to these technical discussions, a very important dispute dominated this entire period. This was the dash between Aristotelianism and Augustinianism.

A. *Aristotle, the Master of Rational Thought*

Aristotle's third "entry"—The new reality which dominated theology in the thirteenth century was Aristotle's overall philosophy. This philosophy at first was limited to the *Organon* which deals with the instruments and ways of thought. It is true that in the course of the twelfth century some elements of Aristotle's philosophy as such began to penetrate a few theological works. Simon of Tournai put him above, Plato. Beside the *Organon,* he knew the *De Anima,* probably some fragments of the *Metaphysics* and began to use the Aristotelian categories in the classification of notions, especially in ethics. At the end of the century a certain Peter of Poitiers will give like prominence to Aristotle's *Metaphysics.* Étienne Langton does the same for *Ethics,* while the Stagirite will already have received from John of Salisbury the title by which he will henceforth be known: "the Philosopher." But even so, these were only sporadic uses of Aristotle.

The change which begins in good measure with William of Auxerre and Philip the Chancellor at the beginning of the thirteenth century will be the work of Albert the Great and St. Thomas. It will suppose, moreover, a much more complete knowledge of Aristotle's works than what was possible in the twelfth century. But this material entry of Aristotle with the completed translation of his works was but the condition and means of the spiritual and ideological "entry" of the pagan Philosopher into the *Sacra Doctrina*. It is this latter entry which we will now try to outline.

As we have already pointed out, theology is human discourse on the things of God and under this formality, logic, grammar, and dialectics had been employed to fashion it properly. But the use of these tools did not introduce into the sacred domain any proper content or any foreign object. The novelty of Aristotle's "entry," which takes place at the turn of the twelfth and in the thirteenth century, is the application to theology of his physics, his metaphysics, his psychology and ethics. Moreover, this application involved a definite contribution of content and object into the very fabric of the sacred science. From then on, Aristotle will furnish not merely a certain external organization of revealed objects but also in the very domain, of the objects of theological science he will supply ideological matter which will concern not only the external approaches but the term and content of the thought itself.

The first characteristic effects of this new rational view of the world may be noted in the writings of Philip the Chancellor (d. 1236) and William of Auxerre (d. 1231). They will be found to a less degree in Simon of Tournai, Peter of Poitiers, and even Gilbert of La Porrée. Aristotle has three principal contributions to make to sacred science: (1) principles of rational interpretation and elaboration of the theological datum; (2) the possibility of rational systematic organization; (3) a scientific structure.

1. PRINCIPLES OF RATIONAL INTERPRETATION AND ELABORATION OF THE THEOLOGICAL DATUM. This can best

be seen in those parts of theology which require a psychology or an anthropology, where, for example, there are interrelations of nature and grace or the supernatural organism of grace and the virtues. A simple reference to the studies published by A. Landgraf and Dom O. Lottin shows that the very questions confusedly posed by the twelfth-century theologians were readily resolved in the writings of Philip the Chancellor or William of Auxerre by the application of an Aristotelian category which at once set up and organized the datum in a rigorous and clear manner. Thus up until the end of the twelfth century sanctifying grace was generally confused with faith and charity, while ordinarily the possibility of virtues, which did not manifestly operate, was not admitted. But serious difficulties followed. Where there was no exercise of virtue, could there nevertheless be virtue, and hence grace? If not, what then was the condition of infants who were baptized but still incapable of exercising any virtuous act? Beyond a timid try by Alain of Lille, it is to the Chancellor Philip we must look for the distinction of the three states of virtue: nature, habit, and act (*natura, habitus* and *actus).* In him also we find the distinction between the virtues and the supernatural life of the soul working out its justification, after the fashion of the Aristotelian distinction between the essence of the soul and its potencies. Thus it is found to be an analytic principle of the supernatural ontology of the soul which will permit a scientific construction of Christian anthropology. It is found, moreover, in the categories of Aristotle's natural anthropology under the guidance of this general principle that between nature and supernature there is a profound structural similitude. Philip of Greve brings us immediately to St. Thomas.[1]

It will be understood, of course, that such progress in the question we have been discussing presupposed a firm distinction between nature and supernature. Here once again

---

1.   *Sum. Theol.,* I^a-II^{ae}, q. cx, a. 3 and 4; Q. *Disp. de virt. in communi,* a. 1.

it is Philip the Chancellor who leads the way. Resuming the distinction between the natural and supernatural virtues, first projected by Gilbert of La Porrée and admitted by William of Auxerre and appealing to Aristotle's doctrine on elicited love he distinguished a natural love consequent on the natural knowledge we can have of God and a supernatural love consequent to the knowledge of faith. One of the first, if not the first to do so, he thus grounded in a philosophy of virtues specified by objects the idea of an ontological distinction between nature and supernature and that of ordination to the revealed God as essential foundation for supernatural ontology.

2. THE POSSIBILITY OF RATIONAL SYSTEMATIC ORGANIZATION. When we compare the order introduced in the theological datum by the great medieval syntheses, it is striking to see how, on the one hand, a passage works its way up from a more or less arbitrary collection of questions to a truly rational sequence and how, on the other hand, theology benefits from philosophical contributions in its attempts to set its house in order. Reflect, for example, on the question of the virtues. Peter Lombard obliquely introduced it in his Christology by the query: Did Christ have the virtues of faith, hope, etc.? And besides in the treatise on faith he finds no occasion to talk of heresy, but takes this up under his treatment of the Eucharist. Similarly, his consideration of sin in general must await his treatise on original sin. It is Prévostin and specially William of Auxerre who first form the virtues into a distinct treatise. Finally in St. Thomas we find the system astonishingly shaped and molded with at once a simplicity of line and a variety of subdivisions where nothing is arbitrary in the least. Aristotle, either by himself or accompanied by St. John Damascene has passed that way. Fr. Merkelbach has compared as to plan, perfection of analysis, and rational order, St. Thomas' treatise on the morality of human actions with those of the

principal theologians of the Middle Ages. The progress is evident and it is due principally to Aristotle's *Ethics*.

3. A SCIENTIFIC STRUCTURE. The growth of Aristotle's influence attains maturity when theology adopts epistemological stature. Of course this evolution does not take place at once. It will be truly consummated only in the writings of St. Thomas' commentators.

Up to this point, theology was conceived as a product of a special use of reason applied to the things of faith within the faith itself. It was the statements of faith which formed its object. Hence the question of the use of reason in theology was framed in the following terms: Can reason furnish proofs for faith? Can it convey arguments which prove the statements of faith?

Something of an affirmative position was taken by William of Auxerre at the beginning of his *Summa Aurea*. There theology was conceived as something promoted by faith, "faith making reason," and presented as a supernatural gift of light, which, under God of course, had in itself its justification and opened to the faithful a new world of knowledges. This notion of faith prompted William to parallel faith with the natural light of first principles which are self-evident or *per se nota* and open up for the intellect the entire order of natural knowledges. "Theology, therefore, has principles, or articles of faith, which, however, are principles only for the faithful and are known *per se* to the faithful and hence, need no proof."[2] But in the cited passages taken from questions concerning the faith, William had only one concern: to account for the immediacy of the faith, relying on nothing else which might be superior to it. He states: "If there were no principles in theology, it would neither be an art nor a science,"[3] and, he declares: "As other sciences have

---

2. *Summa Aurea*, ed. Pigouchet, Paris, 1500. L. Ill, tract. Ill, c. 1, q. 1, fol. 131^d; cf. also tract. VIII, cap. *de sapientia*, q. 1, fol. 189^e and 1. IV tract. *de baptismo. cap. de bapt. parvul.*, q. 1, fol. 254^e.

3. *Ibid.*, fol. 131^d.

their own principles and conclusions, so too has theology."[4] He did not think to develop the parallel between faith and the first principles in this sense that theology would spring from the principles of faith, as science from the principles of reason thereafter to devote itself to a deductive operation and draw from these principles new conclusions which would be the proper object of the science. This parallel, in which he has always spoken of the *principia per se nota* ("principles known of their very nature") and not of the *principia scientiae* ("principles of science"), was invoked in favor of the faith and was not developed in favor of theology whose "reasons" seemed to him to have the simple role of "proving faith, of revealing faith."

In this treatment of the "natural reasons," William emphasized very strongly the primacy of the datum of faith. Heresies, said William, have sprung from an undue application of natural principles and categories to the things of God. There are concepts which are valid in philosophy but which have no application to theology: "That rule of Aristotle, viz., that whatever is so by its nature, is more so than that which is not so by its nature, is true for the things of nature, where natural things are engaged with natural things. But where natural things are engaged with the First Cause, it is not true."[5] Thus William faced the problem of rational theology which from now on we are going to encounter in all its force. He gave it a clear solution. We will see throughout the thirteenth century and up to Luther's time the idea developing that philosophy and theology represent two self-sufficient disciplines whose exigencies and specificity must be respected.

The parallel, launched by William, between faith and the principles *per se nota* will be caught up and developed in a sense which will try to conceive theology as a kind of Aristotelian science. Fr. Cuervo has perhaps somewhat exag-

---

4.　*Ibid.,* fol. 254[e].
5.　*Ibid.,* L. II, tract. V, q. 1, fol. 46[d].

gerated the trend of some texts of Albert the Great in that direction. However, if the whole of his *Commentarium in I Sententiarum, distinctio prima,* is hardly explicitly favorable to a theory of theology-science, several passages of the *Summa Theologiae,* edited later, are most formal and rigorous in this regard.[6] However, Albert did not arrive at the idea of a subaltern science. We will not pursue further his notion of theology, which was not, from a technical standpoint, very original. On the other hand, Albert began the revolution which St. Thomas carried to completion, in favor of a sharp distinction between philosophy and theology and especially in favor of the consistency of created natures and of the rational knowledge which reveals them.

The parallelism suggested by William of Auxerre is perhaps more clearly noted in the *Quaestiones* of some Franciscan authors writing prior to Albert's *Summa* and the *Summa* of St. Thomas. Either in the *Quaestiones* of Odon Rigaud around 1241–50, or those of William of Meliton about 1245–50, or those of the *Codex Vaticanus Latinus 782,* we find Aristotle's idea of science applied to theology and the characteristic objection, drawn from theology's *singular* objects, abundantly developed.

B. *Theology according to St. Thomas Aquinas*

Without entering into great detail, we will pause for a moment on St. Thomas' notion of theology, for it marks a decisive orientation despite the diverging interpretations that the commentators have given his thought.

St. Thomas explicitly treated the question of theological method three times: in the prologue to his *Commentary on the Sentences* (1254), in his commentary on the *De Trinitate* of Boethius, q. II, and finally in the *Summa Theologica,* 1ᵃ q. I (about 1265). To these major texts others are sometimes

---

6. Cf. 1ᵃ pars, tract. 1, q. IV, sol.; q. V, memb. 2, ad aᵘᵐ; memb. 3, especially contr. 3, ed Borgnet, t. XXXI, p. 20, 24–26.

added, in particular the *Contra Gentiles* 1. I, c. III–IX; x. II, c. II–IV; 1. IV, c. 1 (1259); *Sum Theol.*, 1ª, q. XXXII, a. 1, ad 2^{nm}; IIª-IIªᵉ, q. I, a. 5, ad 2um; *Quodl.* IV, a. 18 (1270. or 1271).

Here, in short, are our conclusions: (1) St. Thomas did not change the traditional manner, received from St. Anselm, Abélard, and William of Auxerre, of conceiving the relation between theological work and revelation. For him theology was the rational construction of Christian doctrine itself. (2) But he did change the output and contribution of reason to this work, because, thanks to Aristotle, reason with him was quite different from what it had been before him. It knew the nature of things and could formulate a philosophy. (3) This view, however, rested on presuppositions and posed problems which for theology were at once a novelty and an occasion of crisis.

1. St. Thomas did not change the relation of theological labor to Revelation. This we will see in the theological theory he proposed; also in his development of that theory; and, by way of confirmation, in what his immediate disciples had to say on the matter.

(a) *St. Thomas' theory.* The first *question* of the *Summa* begins with an *article* in which St. Thomas establishes that it is necessary (by a hypothetical but absolute necessity) that man, raised to the supernatural order, receive communication of knowledge other than merely natural knowledge. This communication is Revelation, that is, "the doctrine of faith" or "sacred doctrine" or "Sacred Scripture." All these expressions taken univocally throughout the first *question* are on the whole equivalent. In fact St. Thomas does not hesitate to use one for the other in the course of an argument. Cf. for example a. 3. *Sacra doctrina* is revealed doctrine, a. 1, in all its breadth and whose object is "whatever pertains to the Christian religion," *prol.*; it is contrasted to the "philosophical (or physical) disciplines," a. 1 and *Cont. Gent.*, 1. II, c. IV; it also comprises the Sacred Scriptures,

Scriptura sacra hujus doctrinae, says the prologue of the first question, as well as the catechesis, Christian preaching, and theology in its scientific form.

We have a hint then as to the meaning of the question in article 2, "Whether sacred doctrine is a science?" In posing this question St. Thomas takes *sacra doctrina* in the sense of article 1, namely, Christian doctrine, and effectively asks: is Christian doctrine such that it has the form and verifies the quality of a science? This is not a matter of simply identifying Christian doctrine and science, for revealed doctrine involves many aspects and acts which do not belong to the scientific order. But it is a question of knowing whether Christian doctrine at least in one of its functions, one of its activities or one of its acts, can verify the quality and merit the name of science. To this question St. Thomas replies affirmatively and, in the *Summa* at least, he is satisfied to say that the *sacra doctrina* verifies the quality of science in the category, studied and defined by Aristotle, of "sub-alternate" sciences.

In his commentary on the *De Trinitate* of Boethius, q. II, a. 2, however, he tells us more explicitly what he means by claiming for *sacra doctrina* the quality of science. When certain less known truths are made manifest to the human intellect by their connection with better known truths, that, he says, is science. God has a perfect scientific knowledge of all things, for He sees the foundation of effects in their causes, of properties in their essences and finally of all things in Himself, of Whom they are a participation. By grace, faith in us is a divine knowing, a definite communication of God's knowledge. But this communication is rather imperfect and the human spirit naturally desires a fuller grasp of the objects revealed. This grasp can be sought either by supernatural activity in a vital manner and tending to imitate the mode of apprehension of God Himself, or by a properly intellectual activity which follows our human mode and is, on the whole, the work of theology. So, starting from faith and under its positive direction, we have an activity according to our human mode of operation, which is reasoning. Does this mean that the truths of faith will be in us like principles from which we shall deduce new truths, thereby leaving the realm of faith to enter that of theology? Undoubtedly there is no reason to exclude from St. Thomas' design these theological ("properly so-called") conclusions, which terminate in truths not enunciated in the revealed doctrine. But this is not what St. Thomas had in mind. Quite simply, *sacra doctrina* takes on the form of science and so merits the title, when it links up certain truths of Christian doctrine, which are less known or less intelligible in themselves, with other truths, also contained in Christian doctrine, better known or more intelligible in themselves. This, we say, is like linking up conclusions with principles and is the proper mode of human understanding. It makes little difference whether or not the truth-conclusions are expressly revealed. What is important from the human standpoint is that "from some known things, others less known are understood." Whereas God knows all things in Himself, "in His own manner, which is simple intuition, not discursive reasoning" and so has intuitive knowledge, we know the same things according to our human mode, "which is a discursive approach from principles to conclusions." So it is that in the sacred doctrine certain truths play the role of principles and others, which we attach to the first as effects to their cause or properties to their essence, have the role of conclusions.

Thus sacred doctrine verifies the quality of science when it develops in a strictly discursive manner, where the less known or the less intelligible is joined to the better known or the more intelligible. And so we link up with article 8 of the *Summa* where St. Thomas defines what it is that sacred doctrine demonstrates and how it fashions arguments. And he there adds, as in other similar places, the example of St. Paul who in his First Epistle to the Corinthians, c. 15, established our own resurrection by arguing from Christ's resurrection, better known and certainly the cause and foundation of ours. The scientific quality of sacred doctrine consists then in the fact that starting with the truths of faith taken as principles we can, by reasoning, establish other truths which will appear certain through the certitude of the first.

By this intellectual effort *sacra doctrina* will reproduce, as far as it can, God's *science,* that is to say, the order according to which God, in His wisdom, links all things together, each according to its degree of intelligibility and being, and finally brings all things to Himself. We are here at the heart of the Thomist notion of theology and we are no longer dealing merely with article 2 and article 8 of the *Summa* but with article 7 together with St. Thomas' assertions on the *articuli* and the *per se credibilia* (recently brought to light by Bonnefoy and Charlier). It is the theologian's task, then, to discover and reconstruct in a human science the lines, sequences, and order of God's science. In his sacred doctrine, therefore, the wise Christian will strive to link up secondary things, which in themselves have less being and less clarity, with primary realities which have more.

This linkage of conclusion-truths to principle-truths, St. Thomas worked out according to the following scheme. The principles are the *articuli fidei* (articles of faith), which are *per se et directe* (of themselves and directly) objects of Revelation and hence of faith. These are essentially the articles of the Symbol or the Apostles' Creed promulgated by the Church. These articles of the Creed are only the first presentation (by way of Revelation and not by way of theological science) of two *credibilia* (truths accepted on faith) which are absolutely prime and implicitly contain the entire substance of the Christian faith. These first two *credibilia* convey the mystery of *God Himself.* First, His necessary mystery, namely, His existence as a Being Triune and One. Secondly, His free mystery, that is, the Incarnation which redeemed and deified men. Because of their content these two *credibilia* form a criterion for the entire economy of Revelation. Indeed, a thing is revealed and proposed by the Church for our faith in so far as it bears a relation to these two prime truths. Hence it seems to us that these two prime objects furnish a principle for defining *revelabilia* and the objects of sacred science. *Revelabilia*, then, would be anything, bearing a relation to the two mysteries of God and Christ the Savior, which falls under the Revelation of which these two mysteries are the essential object.

Therefore the sacred doctrine inasmuch as it is a science reproduces as far as possible (but in an order of ascent to the principle) the vision of God's science. Its goal is to bind everything to God Himself in His mystery both necessary and free. The subject of *sacra doctrina* is God, for it is in virtue of their relation to God Himself that all things have theological significance.

From this it also follows that sacred doctrine is wisdom, in fact, supreme wisdom. But, as St. Thomas observes,[7] it is acquired wisdom, of intellectual mode, and it is also the supreme science. It must be distinguished, he continues, from infused wisdom which is mystical in nature.

It seems proper to complete this exposé of theology-science by briefly stating what St. Thomas has to say about the different roles played by reason in the formation of sacred doctrine.[8] According to the texts cited, reason, in addition to a preliminary role, has four functions in theology:

(1) *Preliminary Role.* To establish by a rigorous philosophical demonstration the *praeambula fidei*: the existence and unity of God, the immortality of the soul, etc.

(2) *Role defending the articles of faith.* It is not to prove the truth of these articles—for this is impossible—but to show that they necessarily follow from parts of Revelation

---

7. *Sum. Theol.*, I^a, q. I, a. 6, ad 3um.
8. Cf. *In I^{um} Sent.* prol., a 3, sol. 2 and a. 5, sol. and ad 4um; *In Boet. de Trin.*, q. II, a 2 and 3; *Cont. Gent.*, 1. I, c. IX and X; *Sum. Theol.*, I^a, q. 1, a. 2 and 8; q. XXXII, a. 1, ad 2um; *Quodl.*, IV, a. 18.

admitted by the adversary, if he admits any. If not, then its role on this level is to show that the objections offered by the contradictor are invalid.

(3) *Deductive Role.* This is reason's main function in theology, whereby an unknown or poorly known truth is brought to light through its connection with a better known truth. As we have seen, these truths face each other as conclusion and principle, respectively. St. Thomas describes this function in these terms: "The search for truth in these investigations begins with the principles of faith."[9] And again: "It proceeds from principles to prove something else"[10]; "from articles of faith, this discipline argues to other truths."[11] This type of argument can start from two principles of faith and end in a truth which is not found in the formal facts of Revelation. Indeed it appears we must admit that St. Thomas sanctions the use of rational principles and philosophical premises in this discursive formulation of sacred doctrine: "This doctrine has for its first principles the articles of faith, and from these principles (but by no means rejecting the common principles) this science proceeds."[12] From this it is clear that St. Thomas' form of argumentation must not be restricted to the combination of a secondary revealed truth with an article of faith. Despite the texts some have tried to do this. For example, In *III*[um] *Sent.*, dist. XXIII, q. II, a. 1, ad 4[um], St. Thomas distinguishes the disclosure of an article of faith by another article from the case of a reasoning process whereby "from articles of faith certain other truths in theology are syllogistically derived."

(4) *Explicative and Declarative Role.* This is practiced with regard to the principles themselves, that is, the articles of faith, and strives to penetrate them and, as far as possible, make them comprehensible to the human spirit. This is mainly done by offering analogies and congruent reasons.

---

9. *In I*[um] *Sent.*, prol., a. 5, ad 2[um].
10. *Sum. Theol.*, I[a], q. I, a. 8.
11. *Ibid.*, ad 1[um].
12. *In I*[um] *Sent.*, prol., a. 3, q. 2, ad 1[um].

Here St. Thomas' position is very clear: the assistance of reason is aimed "at a greater revelation of the truths which are handed down in this science."[13] Recapturing the expression of analogous and moral arguments for which Abélard was so often reproached, St. Thomas speaks of a validation of the truth for which "some probable arguments have been adduced."[14] He intends "to collect probable truths."[15] Elsewhere, he illustrates this mode of argumentation by the example of St. Augustine who tried to clarify the mystery of the *Three* Persons by numerous analogies borrowed from the natural order. Let us add that while such arguments do not constitute proofs, nevertheless they have real apologetic value and aid the faith.

(b) *The practice of St. Thomas.* A problem arises when we try to consider the theological method which St. Thomas really practiced. As a matter of fact, he never taught the *Summa,* for each morning he gave his theological lecture in the form of a commentary on some biblical text of the Old or the New Testament. These commentaries, to which we may join the Prologues from the *Sentences* and two inaugural discourses, form a Christo-centered synthesis which is practically a New Testament theology. In the *Summa* and the *Disputed Questions* St. Thomas assumes the history of salvation centered on Christ and displays a strong eschatological sense, but he reduces these data to their elements or formal structures which he situates in a nonhistoric plan. Here we briefly inspect this systematized theology and we do not take up the question of documentation or St. Thomas' method of referring to Revelation or treating its documents and, in particular, the Fathers. But we do wish to review rapidly the four headings of reason's intervention distinguished above and see how St. Thomas made use of them.

---

13. *Sum. Theol.* I[a], q. I, a. 5, ad 2[um]; *In Boet. de Trin.*, q. II, a. *2*, ad 4[um].
14. *Cont. Gent.*, 1.I, c. X.
15. *Ibid.*, c. IX.

(1) *The Preambles of Faith*. It is well known that where transcendent truths can be proved, St. Thomas there uses a rigor never surpassed—for example, when treating of the existence of God (in Sum. Theol., Iᵃ, q. II, a. 1); of the creative power reserved to God alone (in q. XLV, a. 5); of the immortality of the soul (in q. LXXV, a. 6); and of the impossibility for man to find beatitude in a created good (in Iᵃ-IIᵃᵉ, q. II, a. 8).

(2) *The function of defense*. St. Thomas' abundant argumentation against the *Gentiles* is well known. But it is well to underline even in his speculative work the importance of defense. The protection of doctrinal purity, the pursuit and refutation of heresies always appeared to him to be the forefront duty of a Christian doctor. In numerous articles, his speculative elaboration tried to show from what misunderstandings of the subject errors have proceeded and how the mystery must be intellectually outlined if these errors are to be avoided.

(3) *Role of Inference and Demonstration*. St. Thomas seems not to have employed this function of theology very much, that is, in the sense of obtaining theological conclusions which are objectively new with regard to the revealed datum. However, we would have to put into this category certain theses on moral theology and Christology where the introduction of ethical and anthropological principles brought about a new development. So we have the distinction of the virtues and gifts, the system of virtues, the affirmation of the unity of being in Christ, of the exercise of an active intellect in Him, etc.

But in practice St. Thomas generally bases a truth of sacred doctrine on a better known truth of the same doctrine. In this way he adds to the knowledge of a pure fact the knowledge of reason, "on account of which a thing is true," and so by a rational examination of the dogmas the pure adherences of faith are doubled by a scientific knowledge established in the very interior of these adherences. Such is evidently the case for the truths accessible to reason which belong in the "Preambles of Faith" and which St. Thomas does not establish "whether they are" without giving the reason "why they are." But such is also the case of the pure truths of faith and first of all of that one which he himself gives as an example: our resurrection affirmed not only as a fact, but founded in Christ's as in its principle. It is truly "to investigate the root and make known why it is true" in the theological construction to link up our resurrection with that of Christ. To seek the reason for certain facts in other facts is the function of theology. When St. Thomas, for example, connects the *fact* of Christ's perfections and weaknesses to His mission as Redeemer, he thereby assigns its reason and renders it intelligible.

Thus theological labor establishes a sort of scientific double for the statements of faith. Not certainly by proving through reason the fact of revealed truths, but by finding in the interior of faith and under its guidance the foundation of secondary truths in principal truths. In this way, what was at first only believed becomes at once believed and known. As a revealed fact, it is always believed and not known. As attached to another revealed truth and explained by theological reason, it becomes, in rather imperfect conditions, the object of a science and of a scientific approach.

(4) *Explicative and Declarative Role.* This is an extremely fertile function in theology. It goes from the simple explanation, thanks to analogies and congruent arguments, to the essential explanation. There are first of all explanations of the statements of faith. These consist in interpreting the unsystematized statements of Christian doctrine in terms of justified categories in human science, whether we are dealing with the preliminary notions of a treatise, or an integral mystery whose intellectual construction will spread over an entire work. It is thus that the categories of scientific anthropology constantly serve in the treastise on Christ to interpret and rationally organize the revealed datum, or, the categories of cause and sign in the treatise on

the sacraments. As to the first case (systematic interpretation of notions), the *Summa* presents numerous examples, particularly in the Second Part, where the majority of the treatises begin with the definition of the virtue to be considered. Cf. Iª-IIªᵉ, q. LV, a. 4; q. LXXI, a. 6; q. XC, a. 1; IIª-IIªᵉ, q. IV, a. 1; q. XXIII, a. 1; q. LVIII, a. 1; q. LXXXI, a. 1.

The arguments of convenience of fittingness, which strive to gain admission and comprehension for a Christian mystery by analogy with things known in the universe, are frequent in St. Thomas' work. They constitute one of the principal features of his theology, perhaps the principal one. St. Thomas excels in pointing out these harmonies between the supernatural world and the natural world and inserting a particular fact into a universal law overflowing the moral order itself and ruling everything that is. Examples: Sum. *Theol.*, IIª-IIªᵉ, q. II, a. 3, for the question: "Whether to believe something above natural reason is necessary for salvation?" q. CIV, a. 1, for the question: "Whether man ought to obey man?" IIIª, q. VII, a. 9, for the question: "Whether in Christ there was the plenitude of grace?" etc.

Indeed he knew very well that the general law invoked was not that which accounted for the existence of the Christian fact. When he invoked the principle that the closer a receiver is to an inflowing cause the more he partakes of this influx (IIIª, q. VII; a. 9), he knew very well that it was not for this reason that Christ had the plenitude of grace, but he thought that this might help someone who already knew by faith that Christ was "full of grace" to construct intellectually and to comprehend in some measure this mystery. And again when he asked[16] whether Christ had by His passion merited to be exalted: it was not in virtue of the principle of justice (according to which he who has been treated worse than he deserved must be exalted beyond his strict due) that he affirmed the mystery, but in virtue of the text from *Phil.*, II, 8, cited in the *sed contra*. The Christian

---

16. *Sum. Theol.*, IIIª, q. XLIX, a. 6.

fact was not a case of the general law invoked and it was not because of this law that it was true. But the general law helped to interpret it intellectually and, to a certain extent, made its reasons comprehensible. So "reason does not sufficiently prove the basis, but to the basis once established it points out appropriate and consequent effects."[17]

It must be noted nevertheless that in numerous cases the argument from fittingness comes close to being a veritable explanation and joining those "reasons which search out the foundations of truth and let it be known how. what is said is true."[18] To the degree in which the analogy invoked is rigorous, it really becomes an indirect analysis of structure and truly reveals the profound nature of things. So theology abstracts connections which, founded in the nature of things, have the necessity of that nature. Thus when St. Thomas questions whether Adam's sin is transmitted to posterity by way of generation and argues from this fact that humanity is like a single man of whom we are members, he gives us an analogy which is very close to an explanation of structure. However, it must be noted that this explanation in no way pretends rationally to prove the *fact*, which is held by faith. Its only purpose is to render the fact as intelligible as possible. The very *article*, which we have just referred to above, illustrates this remark very well. Its introduction states: "According to the Catholic Faith the following is to be maintained. . . . However, as for investigating how this is so . . ."

To sum up, theology, as St. Thomas understood and practiced it, appears to us as a rational and scientific consideration of the revealed datum, striving to procure for the believing human spirit a certain understanding of the datum. It is, if you will, a scientifically elaborated copy of the faith. What objects of simple adherence the faith delivers, theology develops in a line of humanly constructed

17. *Sum. Theol.,* I^a, q. XXXII, a. 1.
18. *Quodl.* IV, a. 18.

knowledge, seeking the reason for facts; in short, reconstructing and elaborating in the forms of human science the data received by faith from the science of God Who created all things. Thus through his spirit directed by faith, man arrives at a strictly *human* understanding of the mysteries, utilizing their connection or their harmony with his world of natural knowledge. He must radiate the revealed doctrine by his human psychology replete with all its legitimate and authentic acquisitions which, after all, are also a gift of God.

(c) *The Disciples of St. Thomas.* Of the above interpretation of St. Thomas' thought we find a confirmation in the writings of his immediate disciples.

Annibald de Annibaldis, disciple and friend of St. Thomas, in his commentary on the Prologue to the *Sentences,* develops a notion of *theologia* or *sacra doctrina* exactly along the lines we have stated above.

Remi de Girolamo (d. 1319) was another immediate disciple of St. Thomas. As far as we can judge from the exposé of his thought made by Msgr. Grabmann, he is in the same line as De Annibaldis.

Clearer still is the position of another disciple of St. Thomas, Bombolognus of Bologna, who repeats word for word certain texts from the *Sentences* of his Master.

Again, although without doubt he is not an immediate disciple, the author of *Correctorium Corruptorii "Quare"* is certainly one of the first Thomists. We think it fitting then to add his testimony here.

Finally, even though he shows other influences than that of St. Thomas, I still want to add to this list Ulrich of Strasbourg and his *Summa de Bono.*

2. St. Thomas transformed the output of reasoning in theology. For St. Thomas, human reason could attain a knowledge of the nature of things. It had a philosophy. It cannot be denied that Albert the Great and Thomas Aquinas appeared as innovators in the thirteenth century. What set them apart was the fact they had a philosophy,

that is, a rational system of the world, which in its order was consistent and self-sufficient. The first writings of the young Dominican were on *De Ente* and *De Principiis Ndturae*. And, whereas Bonaventure, according to his own testimony, had Aristotle introduced to him as a master of errors, St. Thomas met Aristotle as a master in the rational knowledge of the world.

What then did Albert and Thomas Aquinas do? What was the point of the dispute which arose between them and the Augustinians? When Bonaventure, Kilwardby, Peckham, and others opposed Albert the Great and St. Thomas what did they want and why did they act? We must look at this closely and carefully. On the one hand, these opponents were far from rejecting philosophy. They were philosophers as enthusiastically as those they fought. On the other hand, it is clear that neither Thomas nor Albert refused to subordinate philosophy to theology. The formula *ancilla theologiae* (handmaid of theology) was common to the two schools. And still there were two schools. Why?

Following Augustine, the Augustinians considered all things in their relation to the last goal. A purely speculative knowledge of things had no interest for the Christian. To know things was to know them in reference to God, Who was their end. Truly to know things was to refer them to God by charity. So, in the Augustinian perspective, things will be considered not in their pure essence, but in their reference to the last goal, in their concrete state, in the use man made of them in his return to God. In this way, nature was not distinguished from its concrete state of impotence with regard to the good and of incertitude with regard to the true, which Christians had experienced. Again, if "to know things, is to determine the intention of their first agent, who is God," then things were to be considered in their relation to the Will of God, Who made them as He wanted and used them how He willed. From this viewpoint and looking at the world this way, a miracle was as true and as normal as the natural order, for in a sense, every-thing was a sign and everything was a miracle. Along this line, the nominalistic Augustinians developed the notion of the "absolute potency" which played a role in their critique of St. Thomas' theology. (It is interesting to note that this viewpoint returned in a magnified form with the Reform-ers of the sixteenth century.)

On the other hand, for St. Thomas and for Albert the Great, his master, if it was true to say that everything had a relation to the last goal, i.e., God, this, however, was under the formality of the final cause and the exemplary cause, the latter, a kind of extrinsic formal cause. It was not under the relation of the form itself, whereby a being is properly said to exist. Things had their own nature which did not consist in their reference or their order to God. So, con-centrating merely on what things were in themselves, we could see in them the nature, the *quid,* by distinguishing this form from the mode or the concrete state or from the reference to an end. In this perspective, things, but par-ticularly human nature, remained the same under the different states in which they were cloaked and, most sig-nificantly, human nature under the regimen of the Fall as in the Christian dispensation. *What* things were, answered to the Thomist distinction between the *principia naturae* and the *status.* This is not to say that some Augustinians like St. Bonaventure failed to recognize the distinction between nature and the state of nature, but they refused to consider pure nature in itself a valid concept and to the-ologize about pure forms, abstracted from their concrete state. St. Thomas, instead of looking at things more or less globally from the angle of a first cause and the final end, had a formal view from the standpoint of the things them-selves. It was in light of this view of the nature of things that the miracle was defined. This approach excluded the miraculous use of beings created by God and made quite pointless the dialectic of interventions between God and the *potentia absoluta.*

In the Augustinian school, true knowledge of spiritual things is also love and union. Moreover, the truth of the true knowledge does not come from experience and sensible cognition, which attains only reflections, but from a direct reception of light coming from the spiritual world, that is, from God. This is the illumination theory. Now, this is very important for the notion of theology, for the distinction between philosophy and theology and for the use of "natural" knowledge in a sacred science. In this perspective, between the illumination of natural knowledge and that of the faith there is a deepening of God's gifts and the necessary aid but also a certain continuity. The theory invites the suppression of practically all barriers between philosophy and theology and wants the first only as a preparation relative to the second. This link between the two disciplines is maintained throughout the history of the relations between reason and faith.

St. Thomas maintained the strictly Aristotelian distinction between the order of exercise and that of specification. For him, things were the legitimate object of a purely speculative knowledge. This knowledge aimed at things in themselves, each one for what it was. It was from the senses that he received its content, being capable of wheedling whatever intelligible elements things presented of themselves. This abstracting action was successful thanks to a light which, though given by God, did not cease to be truly ours but remained in us as a permanent potency.[19] The relevant text is famous. But it has not yet been remarked that the treatise on methodology from *In Boet. de Trinitate* begins with an article in which St. Thomas met the question of illumination head on by laying down precisely the different conditions of the infused light of faith and the natu-

---

19. Cf. St. Thomas, *Quaest. disp. de spiritualibus creaturis,* a. 10, ad 8^{am}.

ral light and the manner in which each must be referred to God. So, in the Albertino-Thomist perspective, natural and supernatural light were not considered simply from the standpoint of their unique source, but in relation to a defined *nature*. From this angle, their distinction was much firmer and much more effective.

Finally, if we consider the utilization of sciences and philosophy in theology, we see that in the Augustinian school their status follows the status of things themselves. As these have validity or meaning only in their relation to God, so the sciences will not convey to Christian wisdom a knowledge of the nature of things in itself but only examples and illustrations. These have a symbolic value to assist the understanding of true Revelation, which comes from on high and is spiritual. We also see in what sense the Augustinians will talk of philosophy as "the handmaid of theology." The sciences exist only to serve and they may be asked only for that. Certainly they are not expected to impart any truth of their own. Such is very likely the meaning of the expression in the letters of Gregory IX and Alexander IV to the university of Paris.

For Albert the Great and St. Thomas the sciences represent a genuine knowledge of the world and of the nature of things. For things have their own consistence and intelligibility and this knowledge in valid even in the Christian economy. Therefore, the sciences in their order have a veritable autonomy of object and method, just as in their order they convey their own truth. In this perspective the expression "handmaid of theology," which St. Thomas also uses,[20] has a very different meaning from the primitive Augustinian sense, for "the better to assure the services of her slave, theology begins by freeing her."

Now we understand better why Albert and St. Thomas followed the thought of Aristotle. They were looking not only for a master of reasoning but a master in the knowl-

---

20. *Sum. Theol.*, I^a, q. 1, a. 5, ad 2um.

edge of the nature of things, of the world and of man himself. Certainly St. Thomas was not ignorant any more than St. Bonaventure that all things must be referred to God. But alongside that reference to God in the order of use or exercise, he recognized an unconditioned bounty to the speculative intellect in the nature or specification of things, which was a work of God's wisdom. There was question of speculatively reconstructing the order of forms, of *rationes,* put into things and into the very mysteries of salvation by the wisdom of God. Such a program could be realized only by a knowledge of forms and natures in themselves. This is why St. Thomas' Aristotelianism is not external to his theological wisdom or to the very conception he has fashioned of it.

And here is how reason's usage in theology is transformed by theology. The elements of theological labor are furnished by Aristotle's philosophy, but not without some correction and purification. All the notions of cause, essence, substance, potency, movement, and habit come from Aristotle. And not only in the order of natural sciences but in those of anthropology and ethics, as well, he gave us notions such as: the agent intellect, free will, goal, virtue, justice, etc. Certainly, others than St. Thomas, in fact, the "Augustinians" themselves, used and quoted Aristotle. In the second half of the thirteenth century, with perhaps one or two exceptions, all of them thought in Aristotelian terms. But we must beware and not believe that under this terminology we will really find Aristotle's thought and his conception of things. Under a literary and perhaps psychological unity the schools preserved a profound diversity in their philosophical thought and their systems of the world. And this in the interior of the same religious Order which would generally be considered a single school of thought. The categories of matter and form, of hylomorphic composition, for example, in these different authors cover very different notions and examples could be multiplied. On the contrary, as to St. Thomas, outside of a purely formal mode of thought, Aristotle gave him a rational view of the world which in the mature work of the Christian doctor became the elaborate means of producing a human copy of God's science, which we know to be the ideal of his theology. Aristotle brought to the thirteenth century and particularly to St. Thomas, the idea of nature and the science of an order of natures. And without modifying in its formal structure the relation between reason and faith, he did modify the output of reason and transformed theology. Thanks to St. Thomas we really have a theological system.

3. PRESUPPOSITIONS AND QUESTIONS IMPLIED BY THIS POSITION. (a) The theology which took this position was forced to justify its stand by a theory of analogy and nomina divina (divine names). In the course of history, as the application of a rational and philosophical technique to theological problems increased, the need became more urgent to establish the legitimacy of attributing our created concepts and terms to the uncreated God. With the theologians at the end of the twelfth and the beginning of the thirteenth century, this urgency was obvious.

St. Thomas takes this position of the propriety of rational propositions in theology with a perfectly clear conscience. His judgment is based on a concept of nature and grace which may be considered classic in Catholic speculation. We have an important expression of this concept:

> The gifts of grace are added to nature in such a way that they do not blot it out but rather perfect it . . . and even though the human intellect is incapable of discovering what is revealed to it by faith, nevertheless it is impossible that what is divinely given us by faith should be contrary to that which has been given us by nature. This latter view must be false, for otherwise, since both are given us by God, God Himself would be the author of falsity, which is impossible.[21]

Theology's justification as an expression of the mystery of God quite obviously calls for a theory of analogy and a crit-

---

21. In *Boetium de Trin.*, q. II, ad 3um.

ical study of the "divine names." St. Thomas reverted to the question many times.[22]

(b) If the theology presented by St. Thomas implied certain suppositions, which, in passing, are the same for all theology, this fact posed some very serious questions of so grave a nature that theology in the thirteenth century seemed headed straight for a crisis.

The process, which consists in abstracting something "formal" and disengaging this from its modes and then applying this "formality" to the mysteries of faith by the use of analogy, rests entirely on the distinction between a *ratio* and its mode and on the conviction that a *ratio* does not change its essential laws when it is expressed under these different modes. In short, a rational theology rests entirely on the conviction that in the transposition of an idea to the level of transcendent realities, whose positive mode escapes us, the *eminenter* does not destroy the *formaliter*. For example, it is quite well known that the manner in which Christ influences and acts on men is something eminent and unique; or again that the procession of the Word in God is accomplished in a manner which is eminent, unique, and inaccessible to the mind of man. But it is also known that, provided these ideas are purified and attain the perfection of pure formal *rationes*, it is possible and legitimate to apply the metaphysics of causality to Christ's actions and the philosophy of generation and intellection to the procession of the Word.

But, such a procedure presents a serious question. Does it not incline the theologian (and his disciples) to regard Christian things merely from the point they have in common with natural things and thereby set up the simple solution of general laws which would embrace the things of Revelation as mere varieties of a given kind or class? And does it

---

22. It may help to cite him in chronological order. *In I^um Sent.*, dist. XXII; *Cont. Gent.*, 1. I, c. XXIX sq.; In I^um *Sent.*, dist. II, a. 3, which presents a question disputed at Rome and finally inserted here; Q. *disp. de potentia*, q. VII; *Sum. Theol.*, I^a, q. XIII.

not risk persuading the theologian to forget the character of a unique and original "whole" which belongs to the order of faith, and transfer this character to metaphysics or to a rational explanation of things of which the Christian order would only be another example? If, for example, I construe that part of theology which talks about man according to the anthropological categories of philosophy, in terms of matter and form, essence and faculties, etc., do I not run the risk of falsifying the revealed anthropology which the Bible has given me; the characteristic anthropology of St. Paul, for example, with its categories of an interior and an exterior man, of the flesh and of the spirit, etc. And, if the anthropological categories I use are not even those of Plato, but are Aristotle's . . .

To understand the real danger it is helpful to study St. Thomas' method of procedure. He had so much confidence in the categories of philosophical sciences and in rational sequences that not only did he introduce them into the elaboration of the object of faith but in a definite fashion used them to direct that elaboration. Here are two examples of his method: (1) *Sum. Theol.*, Iᵃ-IIᵃᵉ, q. LXXIII, a. 1, where St. Thomas asks if sins and vices are connected. Now, Holy Scripture gives us a text which seems to deal with this subject: "And whosoever shall keep the whole law, but offend in one point, is become guilty of all," James, II, 10. It would seem that in such a question the theologian had only to comment on this text and draw his conclusions. Not so St. Thomas. He constructed his reply on a psychological analysis of the condition of a virtuous man and a sinner, that is, on anthropology. After that he reconsidered St. James' text as posed in the first objection and confined himself to a critical gloss in view of his general theological doctrine on sin. (2) Asking himself in *Sum. Theol.*, IIIᵃ, q. XIII, a. 2, whether Christ had omnipotence relating to changes which could affect creatures, St. Thomas found himself faced with St. Matthew's text, 28, 18: "All power has been given to me in heaven and on earth." Once again, it would be expected that St. Thomas would make this text the pivot of his article. Rather, he cites it in the first objection and builds up the theology of the question by applying in three conclusions two fundamental distinctions whose categories are borrowed from his general philosophy.

Does it not seem probable that such confidence in reason may endanger the unique, original, and transcendent character of Christian realities? The question is to know whether in keeping with the distinction introduced by St. Thomas, which would apply, for example, between the carnal act *in se,* which is good, and its sinful modality as found in the state of fallen nature, we might not find ourselves asserting the goodness of the carnal act just as it is concretely. By giving a definite status to natures, even in the order of second causes, are we not risking the loss of our sense of the novelty of Christianity, of its originality, and especially of its sovereignty over nature itself? Against the naturalism of the Aristotelians this will always be the fear and the objection of the Augustinians, especially of St. Bernard, St. Bonaventure, Pascal, and even Luther.

As a matter of record Martin Luther gives us a highly significant text on this problem. In his commentary on the *Epistle to the Romans* (1515–16) he glosses on the words *expectatio credturae:*

> The Apostle philosophizes and thinks about things in a manner quite different from philosophers and metaphysicians. For the philosopher's eye is so focused on the presence of things that all he sees are their quiddities and qualities, whereas the Apostle lifts up our eyes from the presence of things, from their essences and accidents, and directs them toward the future of these things. For he does not talk about the "essence" or the "operation" of a creature or about its "action" and "passion" and "motion" but in a new and

wonderful theological vocabulary he speaks of
the "expectation of creatures," so that when the
reader sees this he is no longer idling with the
poor creature but looking forward, intending and
seeking. But alas! how profoundly and harmfully
we adhere to predicaments and quiddities . . .[23]

In our opinion St. Thomas really surmounted the danger we
have just pointed out. He held that it was not Aristotle but
the datum of faith which had the commanding position.
Moreover, long before Luther he noted that with regard to
the sacred doctrine an undue amount of attention can be
given to philosophy. First, and obviously, if the philosophy
is false.. Secondly, if faith and its revelations are subjected
to a philosophical measurement, whereas it is philosophy
which should submit itself to the measurements of faith.
Aristotle's unique role was to furnish faith with the means
of constructing a rational bridge to man's normal circle
of knowledge. When we apply the philosophy of man to
Christ or the philosophical analysis of the human act and
elements of morality to vice and sin, it is clear that it is the
Christian datum which commands attention and which
"leads," while the philosophical contribution comes along
merely as helpful support. If we look carefully and closely
at this support we will see that in every case Aristotle is
either surpassed or corrected. What would have been quite
serious, would be to have left Aristotle out of the elaborations of faith. Supposing, as is just, that he represents philosophy, this omission would have produced on one side of
Christianity a block of reason and culture and on the other
a most dangerous isolation. Cf. Charlier, Essai *sur le problème théologique,* p. 86.

The theological thought of St. Thomas, as of the Middle
Ages, at least up to his time, was based essentially on the
Bible and tradition. We can never stress too much the fact

---

23. *Romerbrief,* ed. Ficker, II, pp. 198–99; also Weimar t. LVI, pp. 371–
72.

that in those days theological teaching was profoundly biblical. The ordinary lecture of the master was a commentary
on Sacred Scripture. This is why the scriptural commentaries of St, Thomas represent his ordinary public teaching as
a master.

The Augustinian Line

A. *The Augustinian tradition of the "Churchmen"*

In the life of the Church there is probably no period when
a difference of attitude can be more clearly recognized
between the men of science, who represent the initiatives
of thought, and the "Churchmen," who represent tradition
and retain certain positions calculated to edify the faithful. In the thirteenth century, tradition and the positions of
"Churchmen" are of an inspiration distinctly Augustinian.
These can be summed up in a phrase: Reason is competent
for terrestrial things, whose possession does not interest
the Christian; but it is incompetent for spiritual and eternal
things. Hence there must be a constant distinction between
two levels, two orientations, two spiritual powers, and two
manners of thinking.

Hence, with the advent of Aristotle into Christian
thought, the Augustinian "Churchmen" got busy. They
could not permit either that the Faculty of Arts treat topics not within their competence, that is, topics which even
if they were within the view of reason certainly exceeded
its forces; or that the Faculty of Theology borrow from the
science of created things a vocabulary and categories of
thought to conceive and express the things of God. Very
explicitly these are the two themes of the Augustinian reaction to the rise of Aristotelianism.

That reaction first took to task the theologians who
introduced the thought categories and the philosophical
vocabulary into sacred doctrine. This for example is the
object of recriminations from John of Saint-Gilles (1231),

or from Odon of Chateauroux on various occasions. It is the object, above all, of the most vehement warnings of the Popes addressed to the Masters of the Faculty of Theology at the University of Paris. Gregory IX wrote on the 13th April 1231: "Nor shall they present themselves as philosophers . . . rather in their classes they will discuss only those questions which they can solve with the help of theological books and the treatises of the Holy Fathers."[24] Nevertheless, the Aristotelian flood continued to grow and protestations and warnings continued with equal vigor.

In the second half of the thirteenth century, the Masters of the Faculty of Arts, finding in Aristotle a purely rational interpretation of the world and of man himself, had the presumption to propose on these basic questions an independent and self-sufficient doctrine. They did this either because they wanted to treat theological questions by pure philosophy, or, making philosophy not only an independent but a sovereign science, they theoretically or practically declared its self-sufficiency and in its name issued dogmas on man's destiny, his rule of life, etc. This trend, already started by John of Meung and Andrew the Chaplain, reaches a paroxysm in the *De Vita Philosophi* of Boèce de Dacie. It was this dangerous current allied to Latin Averroism which prompted the condemnation delivered by Étienne Tempier in 1277. Its very first lines state: "Some students of the arts at Paris, exceeding the proper limits of their faculty . . ."[25]

When we reflect that this condemnation included the work of Albert the Great and St. Thomas, we are disposed to agree with Fr. Mandonnet that St. Thomas' canonization in 1323 was a factual consecration of his doctrinal hegemony and, especially, of his position in theological methodology. As a matter of fact, St. Thomas' position still inspires theological teaching in the modern Catholic Church and the

---

24. *Chartularia Universitatis Parisiensis*, t. I, n. 79.
25. *Ibid.*, n. 473.

division of that teaching into philosophy and theology has established his methodology as a sort of institution.

B. *General Position of the Augustinian Masters*

Outside of St. Bonaventure, the principal Augustinian Masters are Alexander of Hales, Fishacre, and Kilwardby, on the one hand, Robert Grosseteste and Roger Bacon, on the other.

Alexander of Hales (d. 1245), Fishacre, who wrote about 1236–48, and Kilwardby about 1248–61, are in basic agreement. For them theology is a knowledge of the affective and moral order, inspired by the Holy Spirit. It concerns the true simply under the aspect of the good. "It may indeed be called a science but not in Aristotle's sense. For it is a science which reaches intelligence only after it leaves faith."[26] And elsewhere he adds: "Only after it leaves a living faith, motivated by charity."[27] "Hence it is not a rational or demonstrative science, but one which is affective, moral, experimental, and religious."[28] "Finally it is a science whose certitude does not stem from a rational inference derived from evident principles, but from the light of the Holy Spirit which the truly spiritual man experiences internally."[29]

Kilwardby repeats the Augustinian idea that all science is in the Sacred Scriptures. Bacon and Grosseteste come up as the protagonists of a strictly scriptural theology. Theology, says Bacon, has, as every discipline, its text; and its task must consist in commenting on that text, which in the case of theology is the Bible. As a matter of fact, it is possible to find in the sacred text the occasion to treat any and all topics of theology. This, however, must be linked with the text, for it is not proper—as has been happening for the past fifty years—to isolate the "questions." As aids to this textual theology Bacon strongly advocated a knowledge of Greek

26. Alexander of Hales, *Summa Theologiae*, c. I, ad 3[um].
27. *Ibid.*, ad 4[um].
28. *Ibid.*, c. II, obj. f and resp. ad obj.
29. *Ibid.*, c. IV, a. 2.

and Hebrew as well as an acquaintance with the sciences or philosophy.[30] Scripture, indeed, which is the treasure of Revelation and hence the supreme source of illumination, embraces all truth. In it are contained both theology and philosophy. This latter, he says, is simply the content or the physical aspect of Revelation, while the former is the truth or the mystical dimension of scientific knowledge which embraces philosophy. Hence it follows that the two knowledges are not opposed to each other. Philosophy has all its truth finally "in the field of Scripture," just as Sacred Scripture has its plenary explanation only after an extensive knowledge of the sciences, which constitute the ensemble of philosophy. Hence Bacon's reformist program: the unity of Christian wisdom (Bacon omits the term "Christian"), whose foundation is the illumination theory.

This was good Augustinian tradition, which held that the sciences and philosophy participate in the theological elaboration merely as a propaedeutic. It sharpens and exercises the intellect. It also supplies examples to illustrate and explain the biblical symbols borrowed from the created world.

C. St. Bonaventure[31]

Just as in St. Thomas, it is not possible to point out a real evolution in St. Bonaventure's thought. Nevertheless, in the course of his life, it seems that he became progressively better acquainted with the true source of his own doctrine.

For St. Bonaventure, theology is a production of grace. It is to be considered a consequence of the communications which God gave us of Himself. Theology therefore is situ-

---

30. *Opus tertium*, c. xxiv, p. 82.
31. The main texts in which Bonaventure gives us his notion of theology are: In 1*um* *Sent.*, *Proem.*, ed. Quaracchi, t. I, pp. 1–15; *Breviloquium*, prol., t. V, pp. 201–8; *Itinerarium mentis in Deum*, t. V, pp. 295—313; *De reductione artium ad theologiam*, t. V, pp. 319–25; *Collat. de donis Spiritus Sancti*, esp. coll. iv and viii, t. V, p. 473 sq. and 493 sq.; *Collat. in Hexaemeron*, coll. i–iii and xix, t. V, pp. 329–48 and 420 sq.; *Sermo Christus unus omnium magister*, t. V, pp. 567–74.

ated for St. Bonaventure as for St. Anselm "between faith
and appearance." But then the Bonaventurian formula for
theology would not be "faith seeking understanding"—still
acceptable to St. Thomas—so much as a text like "But we
are transformed into the same image from glory to glory,
as by the Spirit of the Lord," II Cor., iii, 18. St. Bonaventure
does not make this text the slogan of his theology (which
he distinguishes from faith) but he does cite it repeatedly.

The first light received from God is reason. But when
Bonaventure considers reason's concrete possibilities, he
severely limits them, since he claims that man in his present
state cannot come to know superior truths simply by reason. Hence, in a most explicit manner Bonaventure denies
a "separated" philosophy as well as reason's efficacy with
regard to spiritual truths. This was the reason for his opposition to the "naturalism of Albert" and of Thomas Aquinas.
However this does not mean that philosophy is not the first
step toward wisdom. The desire for wisdom which gives it
a start will be satisfied only by grace and faith. Nevertheless
man must not fail to comply with that desire and go as far
as possible in its natural pursuit.

In the order of grace and Christian wisdom, progress
toward the perfect possession of wisdom, which is peace
and perfect union with God, is marked by three stages or
grades. First, the grade of virtues, in which faith opens our
eyes to help us find God in everything, next, the grade of
gifts and, third, the grade of beatitudes. Now the acts of
virtues, gifts, and beatitudes are respectively defined as:
credere (believing); *intelligere credita* (understanding the
things believed); *videre intellecta* (seeing the things understood). There is then an activity of understanding (*intelligere*), based on faith and tending toward a state of union
and knowledge of that which is perfect. This understanding
is derived from the illumination of gifts, especially from the
gifts of science and knowledge.

Hence, this knowledge of mysteries, which is the object
of theology, is for Bonaventure an intermediary stage

between the simple assent to faith and the Vision. It concerns, of course, the objects of faith, but it adds something to those objects. *"The credible passes into the realm of the intelligible by the addition of reason."*[32] So, this knowledge of mysteries, fruit of the *gift* of knowledge and, subsidiarily, of the *gift* of science, follows a rational pattern or mode, *cognitio collativa.*

Bonaventure says that the *gift* of knowledge *multis laboribus habetur* ("is achieved by much labor.")[33] Moreover, he asserts that man must prepare himself for this *gift* and that nature and experience collaborate with divine illumination to fashion it. But if nature collaborates, the development of this *gift* will not proceed according to the laws of the other sciences. For this is a knowledge which is the fruit of supernatural illumination: *"Theology, as a science founded on faith and revealed by the Holy Spirit . . ."*[34] *"Philosophical and theological science is a gift of God."*[35] Theology, for St. Bonaventure, is a gift of God, a gift of light descending from the Father of lights. Hence it is not a purely intellectual *gift*. It presupposes not a dead faith, but a living faith of prayer, the exercise of virtues and the yearning for a union of charity with God.

Here we arrive at an essential point, where the theology of Bonaventure and Thomas Aquinas are clearly distinguished. For the latter, theology is the growth of the convictions of faith and the construction of these convictions into a body of knowledge consonant with human reason. Like all things, it develops under God's providence and is rooted in supernatural faith, but it is strictly a rational construction. The wisdom of theology is distinguished from the infused gift of wisdom, which develops as an experimental and affective body of knowledge. On the other hand, theol-

---

32. *Sent.,* proem., q. 1, sol., t. i, p. 7.
33. *In Hexaem.,* coll. iii, n. 1, t. v, p. 343.
34. *Breviloquium,* prol.
35. *De donis Spir. Sancti,* coll. iv, n. 4, t. v, p. 474.

ogy is an intellectual wisdom, acquired by personal effort, which tries intellectually to comprehend and reconstruct the order of the works and the mysteries of God by tying them up with the mystery of God Himself.

As for Bonaventure, the material of this wisdom can very well be the same. But the direction of its construction is different. Theology certainly implies a dynamic synthesis of faith and reason. But rather than an expression of faith in terms of reason, or of revealed light in the human intellect, it is a progressive reintegration of the intelligent man and of the entire universe known by him in the unity of God, by love and for love. It is a realization, more perfect than those which precede, less perfect than that to which the soul still aspires, namely, of the light and the grace of God. Without eliminating man's activity and effort, it is identical with the infused gifts of the Holy Spirit. There is no longer question of reconstructing the order of God's wisdom so much as there is of recognizing that order by the human spirit, so that it may be used to mount to God, not so much to know Him as to realize Him in oneself.

From this we can readily expect that the knowledge of creatures which enters into the constitution of theology will not be considered and required in the same way by Bonaventure and Thomas Aquinas. For the latter, it is the scientific and philosophic knowledge of the laws and the nature of things, based on sensible experience, which enter into the objective construction of theology. For Bonaventure, the source of our knowledge of God is not dependent on a knowledge of creatures, derived from the senses. In his view we have need for creature-knowledge simply as an occasion to recall God and a means to realize better the intricacies of revelation. This is why, although theology is constructed thanks to the two *gifts* of science and knowledge, it resides principally in the *gift* of knowledge, which looks above, and less in the *gift* of science which looks below to sensible creatures. The proper domain of theology is not the knowledge of spiritual things which can be gained from an acquaintance with sensible things, which are mere symbols of the spiritual. Nor from the nature of things, which is the object of philosophy and to which the *gift* of science is dedicated. Its proper domain is the understanding of the things of God, which can be achieved by using the intelligibles, which are the object of the *gift* of understanding.

Hence for Bonaventure the use of philosophy is basically extrinsic to the transformation of revealed objects into knowledgeable objects. This is the work of theology. We rediscover here what we have already found above as characteristic of Augustinianism: a theoretic manner of considering creatures which the Seraphic Doctor expounded in *De reductione artium ad theologiam,* which he worked up in the *Itinerarium.* This consists in arousing a spiritual knowledge of God in ourselves by seeking both occasion and matter in everything creatures offer us as images and mirrors of God. Certainly the profane sciences will serve theology but it will use them quite extrinsically. In fact it receives nothing intrinsic except from Revelation nor does it learn anything worth while from the "book of creatures." For it is not the knowledge of natures which enables it to understand something of the mysteries of God, rather it is the inspired Scriptures which reveal the true symbolic value of creatures with regard to God. However, theology must read the book of creation to realize its finality, to refer back to God the light He has spread over the garment of creation to its ultimate edges. *Sic Scriptura sacra, per Spiritum Sanctum data, assumit librum creaturae, referendo in finem,*[36]

As in the case of St. Thomas, we can find St. Bonaventure's notion of theology repeated by his disciples: Eustace of Arras, Gauthier of Bruges, Matthew of Aquasparta, John Peckham, Roger Marston, and lastly—although he is not an immediate disciple and crediting him with his own originality—by Raymond Lullus. Matthew of Aquasparta follows

---

36. *Brevil.*, proem., § 4, t. v.

St. Bonaventure closely, and, beyond him, St. Augustine, St. Anselm, and the Victorines. If Matthew may be said to represent St. Bonaventure's positive side, then Peckham represents the side of Augustinian reaction to the philosophic naturalism of St. Thomas and his Dominican disciples. It was this latter who in 1286 charged Richard Clapwell with heresy in several of his theses, of which the eleventh (at least in the original listing; the definitive text has only eight theses) was: "He maintains that in those things which are of faith he is bound to assent to no authority, either of Augustine or Gregory or the Pope or to any *magisterium* whatsoever, except to the authority of the canon of Sacred Scripture and to necessary reason." *Revue thomiste*, 1927, p. 279.

Various Positions and Discussions

It would be futile to devote a kind of monograph—however brief—to the theological methodology of each theologian of the thirteenth and the beginning of the fourteenth century. However, before entering the partly new world inaugurated by Scotus and the Nominalists, we would like to assemble some information here on the most disputed points regarding the notion of theology. Following the lead of the authors themselves, we will present their ideas under the headings of the four causes.

A. *The Efficient Cause*

This is the Holy Spirit, whenever there is question of the Sacred Scriptures. As to each particular book, he who wrote it raises no particular problem, as Hervé Nédellec and Alphonsus Vargas explicitly point out.

B. *The Formal Cause and the Proper Mode*

This means the internal structure of a given theology, from which would spring its specification. In the thirteenth century the great discussion centered about the question: Is theology a science? St. Thomas gave an affirmative reply to this question. Not that he thought it necessary for theology, beginning with faith, to demonstrate objectively new conclusions. Rather it was his view that theology should devote itself to a rational and scientific construction of everything that fell under the light of Revelation. In this way, theology verifies the quality of a scientifically acquired *habitus,* and so enters into the category, foreseen and defined by Aristotle, of the *subaltern* sciences.

Much discussion took place on this question, whether or not theology was truly a science in the Aristotelian sense. No, said many, because it supplies no evidence. To this the partisans of theology-science replied, theology supplies no evidence for the mysteries it talks about, but, faith being supposed, it supplies formal evidence of the connection of its conclusions to their principles: "It is not a science of consequence but of consequences."

These discussions did not fail to draw attention to theological conclusions. As a matter of fact, writers at the beginning of the fourteenth century began to give to the notion and expression of "theological conclusion" a new twist. Actually, the majority of Masters gave the title of *science* to theology, but understood it in many different ways. Very few purely and simply denied it the quality of science. An example of this latter group is Alphonsus Vargas, an Augustinian evidently influenced by Durand de Saint-Pourçain. But the majority held that theology is a science, either in a broad sense, or in a proper but imperfect sense.

It is clear that unless they wished to make theology a purely formal dialectic and go so far as to admit—as will be done later—that there can be theology without faith, theology's scientific quality can be maintained only by forcefully noting its union with the science of God and the Blessed. This simply means to affirm its character as a subalternate science. Later Cajetan will underline this need of union so that the science of theologians will not be reduced to a mere science of logical deductions.[37] This quality of subalternate science, attacked by Duns Scotus, was criticized by many theologians at the beginning of the fourteenth century and was admitted by them only in a broad and improper sense.

Among the doctors at the end of the thirteenth century, Henry of Ghent is practically unique in his position regarding the formal cause of theology and more precisely regarding its inspiration. He maintains that between faith and vision there is a special intermediary light, infused by God, *illustratio specialis, lumen supernaturale,* which becomes the proper reality of the theological science.

C. Material Cause

This obviously involves the *subject* matter of theology and is a particularly agitated topic. The question is based on the classifications of Aristotle given in the *Posterior Analytics.* Here we can only group the opinions in a documentary manner. After considerable study, it seems to us there are seven groups which we can enumerate without concerning ourselves with their chronological order or value.

1. TOTAL OR INTEGRAL CHRIST. This position is attributed to Cassiodorus; it could also be claimed as St. Augustine's. It was shared by Robert of Melun, Roland of Cremona, Kilwardby, Odon Rigaud, William of Méliton, Robert Grosseteste, and finally by Gabriel Biel and Pierre d'Ailly.

2. REALITY AND SYMBOLS. This is the technically Augustinian division revived by Peter Lombard.

3. WORKS OF CONDITION AND REPARATION. This is the division of Hugh of Saint-Victor, of Peter the Eater and their respective disciples.

4. GOD IN SO FAR AS HE IS THE ALPHA AND OMEGA; THE PRINCIPLE AND END. This is the opinion of Albert the Great and his disciple Ulrich of Strasbourg. Albert in his *Summa*

---

37. *Com. in* I^{um}, q. i, a. 2, n. 12.

seems clearly to criticize St. Thomas' position on the unity of theology found in the *revelabile* (the revealed fact).

5. God; Everything with Relation to God. This is the simple forthright position of St. Thomas. At the end of the thirteenth century and the beginning of the fourteenth century this position was shared by Duns Scotus and his disciple, John de Basoliis, by Hervé Nédellec, Henry of Ghent, and Godfry of Fontaines, and others.

6. A position which at best must be called *synthetic*. Despite their undeniable Christological tendencies it is shared by Alexander of Hales, St. Bonaventure, Odon Rigaud, and Peckham. Alexander gathers together the *Works of Reparation, Christ,* and *Cod or the Divine Substance.* He sums up his own position in these words: "The doctrine of theology is about the Substance of God effecting through Christ the work of human reparation."[38] Bonaventure proposes a synthetic view still more complete. He distinguishes the subject to which everything be referred *as to their principle,* namely *God.* Then the subject to which everything be referred *as to their integral total* and this is the *total Christ.* And lastly the subject to which everything be referred *as to a universal total* and this is *reality and symbols,* or *the credible as it passes into the realm of the intelligible by the addition of reason.*[39]

7. Finally, we have the view of Olieu, which presents another way of getting everybody to agree. He tells us there is no point in looking for unity in the subject of a sublime topic, *which entirely transcends both matter and genus.**

---

38. *Sum. Theol.,* 1.I, trac. intr., q. i, c. iii, p. 13.
39. *In 1ᵘᵐ Sent.,* proem., q. 1, t. 1, p. 7; *Brevil.,* prol., 4, t. v, p. 205.
* *Editor's Note.* This is an interesting opinion which recalls Anaxagoras' position and forecasts that of Teilhard de Chardin and Bertrand Russell. What was obviously not understood is that unity is an *analogous* concept. Its perfection depends upon the elevation of an intelligence. This elevation does not depend on the increasing multiplication of time and space. It depends rather on an integration

d. *The Final Cause*

This can be approached from two viewpoints. We have the example of Hervé Nédellec. He gives us the viewpoint of the *necessity* of a supernatural science. To this view, obviously there can be no objection as Hervé observed. Then there is the viewpoint of the *finality* of this science. And this brings up the much disputed point as to whether theology is speculative or practical. Moreover, it is quite interesting to note that despite their systematically different positions—and the difference is by no means superficial—all these theologians feel constrained to agree on a character of theology so original that it cannot be univocally classed under any of Aristotle's categories. There are only a few who straightforwardly admit that theology is a practical science. These are Odon Rigaud, William of Méliton, Auriol, and finally Scotus, who broadens the Aristotelian notion of practical science by the idea of *praxis circa finem* ("the speculatively practical").

The majority of medieval theologians considered theology as a special type of science, viz., at once speculative and practical and mainly directed toward enabling us to achieve our goal, which they termed "affective." Better than the others, Albert the Great formulated this original quality of theology, thus: "This science is properly affective, that is, of truth which has not been secluded from the concept of the good; hence it perfects both the understanding and affection."[40]

---

with itself. In simple terms, going back to Anaxagoras, we ask ourselves the question is the "mind" *source* or *end*. If *end*, then, let us buy ourselves a boat in the flow of evolution. If *source*, then, sit quietly and someday get acquainted with your intellect. St. Thomas tells us this identification takes a long time to achieve; and I say, the natural dispersion of matter in man tends him toward division and multiplicity. Hence, he is a rare specimen who understands unity and its analogous variations.

40. *In I^um Sent.*, dist. I, a. 4.

In the thirteenth century St. Thomas was practically the only one who maintained that theology was primarily speculative. At the same time he insisted that under the formality of a divinely communicated wisdom, it at once comprised and surpassed the practical and the speculative.[41] The majority of the Dominican theologians at the end of the thirteenth and the beginning of the fourteenth century were faithful to the Common Doctor's position.

The Fourteenth Century. The Theological Critique

A. *Duns Scotus*

Scotus gave us his most explicit views on theology in his *Opus Oxoniense* (before 1302) and in the *Reportata Parisiensia.*

The originality of Scotus' position is derived from the accent he puts on a critique of our natural and supernatural knowledge of God and on the conditions and limits of that knowledge. This critique seems inspired by his reaction to the Albertino-Thomistic philosophical "naturalism" and the absolute naturalism of the "channels" of Averroistic inspiration. In this way Scotus continues the line of Bonaventure, Matthew of Aquasparta, and John Peckham and resumes the direction which had just been affirmed in the condemnations of 1270 and 1277. On the other hand, he outlines a defense against naissant Nominalism. For this reason he is anxious to determine the realm of metaphysical certitudes. But this cannot be done, however resolutely realistic he may be, without himself entering into that critical current which is soon going to undermine theology.

Very early, the Franciscan School had felt and affirmed the radical difference between the God of the philosophers and That of the Christians. This sentiment was expressed in a choice, not only in favor of Augustine against Aristotle and philosophy, but also, among the commentators on

---

41. *Sum. Theol.* I^a, q. i, a. 4 and 6.

Aristotle, in the choice of Avicenna against Averroes. This is particularly true in the question of the intelligence's object and the object of metaphysics. It is remarkable that about the year 1245 Odon Rigaud had already pointed out that perhaps the object (*subjectum*) of metaphysics was not God but *being.* Scotus resumes this idea. For him metaphysics has as its object *being* determined by the categories and classified by the transcendentals. Hence it does not bear directly on God Whom it attains only vaguely in His general idea of Being. And when it wishes to predicate some affirmations about God, it can only reveal its own impotence.

Theology alone speaks directly of God. But a distinction is still necessary. What there is question of here, is to know God in Himself, in His own individuality. That is, no longer to know God *confuse,* but *ut hic.* But such a knowledge can be truly had only from an intuition of the Divine Essence. God alone, Whose essence and intellect are one, has such an intuition by His very Nature. Hence, to consider what may be called *theologia in se,* we must admit that God alone is a theologian. However, by Revelation, we can attain its object, *Deus ut hic,* not indeed intuitively but under the formality of infinite being, which is the most elevated idea we can formulate of God. Such is the status of human theology.[42] Not truly reaching *Deus ut hic* and so being a theology only by Revelation, it will necessarily be positive and scriptural. Moreover it will be able to predicate a valid affirmation about God depending totally on what is revealed to us *by the will of the Revealing God.* (Whence the notion of *objectum voluntarium.*) Scotus strongly accentuates the singular character of everything that concerns God Himself, *essentia ut haec.* About all this, he tells us, metaphysics, Which knows nothing of this singular Being or His particular Will, can give us no information. Much better are Sacred Scripture and the tradition which completes it. These are

---

42. *Op. Oxon.,* prol., q. ii lat., n. 4 and 12, t. viii, p. 123 and 150 sq.

given to us in and by the Church. Hence our theology will necessarily be ecclesiastical, dependent on that Church.

But even though Scotus had plainly been influenced by the positivistic atmosphere of Oxford and though he develops the theological critique we will not go along with him as far as fideism which will be the consequence of that same critique and especially of Nominalism. Powerless to found a science bearing on God, when left to its own forces, reason nevertheless becomes an effective purveyor of *rationes necessariae,* when put into the capable hands of a theologian. This does not mean that Scotus believes the truths of faith can be strictly demonstrated by reason even when fortified by faith. A distinction is necessary. *Rationes necessariae* can very well be proposed without their conveying any evidence of the necessity on which they are grounded. "Be it said against the authority of Richard and Anselm that like the other Doctors they themselves propose necessary reasons (*rationes necessaries)* which are not evidently necessary; for not every necessity is evident necessity."[43] In human theology there can be no demonstration by an *evidently* necessary reason, for such a demonstration must be made *ex aliquibus necessariis per se notis mediate vel immediate* ("from some mediately or immediately evident necessities"). Therefore, our ability consists in coming as close as possible to the substance of these necessary reasons, in pushing upward as far as possible from the less probable to the more probable and even to the nearly evident but never reaching evidence. God alone is the true theologian. It seems that in the best cases, according to Scotus, these reasons can normally lead us to a possibility—not, therefore, to the fact of a mystery but simply to its possibility. This lack of evidence in theology's arguments radically prevents it from being a science, at least in the proper sense of the term. This is Scotus' opinion.[44] The scientific quality of

---

43. *Rep. Paris.,* prol., q. ii, n. 18, t. xxii, p. 43.
44. *Op. Oxon.,* prol., q. iii and iv lat., n. 26, t. viii, p. 183; 1. III, dist. XXIV, q. unic., n. 13.

our theology cannot be saved by the idea of a subalternate science. Frankly, it is not clear that Scotus fully understands the term.

And so theology is not a science in the proper and rigorous sense of the term. But, if God is truly *scibilis* (knowable) only to Himself in the intuitive vision of His singular Essence, He is *operabilis* (operable or practicable) and *attingibili* (attainable) by us in this life. "We however (in opposition to the Philosopher) make the cognoscible operable, that is attainable by operation, which is the true meaning of praxis, and *in se* highly cognoscible."[45] The Christian knows that love is the end or purpose of everything, that even God knows Himself only to love Himself and that *our* theology, whether it has for its object the necessary mysteries of God or His contingent volitions, is none the less a practical science.

Such in brief is the Scotist notion of theology. If we compare it with that of St. Thomas we may note the following points. On St. Thomas' side, our knowledge of things is conceived in such a manner (analogy) that the notions, purified and disengaged from their mode, can be validly applied to the things of God. There is at one and the same time perfect distinction between philosophy and theology and yet a certain continuity between our knowledge of the world and our knowledge, even supernatural, of God. On Scotus' side, metaphysics has for its object the being of the categories and hence cannot raise a valid affirmation on the singular reality of God. To be sure, the theologian grants philosophy the possibility of furnishing proofs but this can be done only by transferring that possibility to a new order. In a word, there is no continuity.

From another standpoint, Scotus' theology appears much more systematic and dialectic than that of St. Thomas. The continual critique of arguments, the constant intervention of disjunctions between order *in se* and the order of fact, and the incessant overthrow of positions give to Sco-

---

45. *Op. Oxon.*, prol., q. iv, n. 42, t. viii, p. 286.

tus' theology an overtone which is extremely philosophical and dialectic. Moreover, it is astonishing to see how much of the vocabulary of current theology, of the actual "Scholastic" theology of different Schools, is found in his works. In some cases, of course, the terms go beyond him, to Henry of Ghent, for example. It is also surprising to see how Scotus' critical viewpoint invariably introduces a systematic interpretation of a given fact which before him had been received more or less as it stood. His theology, which he wanted to be as positive and scriptural as possible, gives at first glance the impression of being constructed to the maximum by a "subtle" dialectic taking its principles from some systematic order.

B. *The Nominalists*

Whether or not to group Durand de Saint-Pourçain (d. 1334) with the Nominalists and to what degree are still mooted questions. Relative to theology's object he distinguishes three *habitus* ("habits" or intellectual levels of approach). "First, the *habitus* by which alone or principally we assent to those things which are revealed in Sacred Scripture and as they are revealed . . . next the *habitus* by which faith and whatever is revealed in Sacred Scripture are defended and proclaimed from certain principles more evident to us . . . theology is accepted as the third *habitus* of those truths, deduced from the articles of faith and the statements of Sacred Scripture, as conclusions from principles . . ."[46] Judging from the third *habitus,* theology cannot be said to be a science except in a very broad sense of the term. In q. vii, fol. xiii C sq. Durand rejects the idea of a-subalternate science. Moreover, in this third division which is deductive, he maintains that theology can deduce only practical conclusions, since speculative truths are only the object of defense and explanation, which pertain to the second *habitus.* To these three *habitus* correspond three subjects. To the

---

46. *In Sent.,* prol., q. i, Paris, 1508, fol. ii E–G.

first, which is really identified with faith, we have the *actus meritorius vel salutaris* ("the meritorious or salutary act"). To the second, corresponds God "under the formality of Savior" (and this includes the Trinity), while God "under absolute formality" is the subject of philosophy. Finally to the third, for speculative truths, we again have God "under the formality of Savior" and for practical truths we have the meritorious works. From this it is evident that for Durand theology in the first and third sense is simply practical and, only in the second sense, speculative. (Note carefully above that the speculative truths of the third *habitus* are possible only under the formality of the second.) This obviously deprives theology of any possibility of unity or homogeneity. "Theology is not one science, but several."[47]

We will simply mention Peter Auriol (d. 1322) and pass on immediately to William of Ockham (d. 1349), head of the Nominalist school.

Ockham's theological thought springs from the conjunction or better the juxtaposition of two elements. First, his religious faith and, secondly, his general idea of philosophy. This is essentially a philosophy of knowledge and demonstration, which is radically a critical examination of our manner of stating things.

Ockham is first of all a believer and for him God is omnipotently Absolute and sovereignly free. In recent years the religious value of the Nominalist attitude has been strongly underlined. In a sense, this may be interpreted as a reaction to Scotus and his distinctions between the knowledge and the will of God. Ockham's thinking as did that of Scotus went along with the reaction of thought following the condemnation of 1277 against the philosophical treatment of mysteries. While Ockham's philosophy and its relation to faith are different from those of Scotus, the God of Ockham and the Nominalists is the same as that of Scotus (and Durand de Saint-Pourçain), viz., a sovereignly

---

47. *Ibid.*, q. iv, fol. viii 1.

free Omnipotence, a pure, creative Liberality. However, Ockham's notion of a sovereignly powerful and free God is developed in a special sense which has immediate effects on theological methodology. God can do whatever can be done without implication of contradiction, hence He can do directly whatever can be done by the secondary causes. This fact, if fact it be, obviously eliminates any useful or valid consideration of the nature of things as well as the notion of analogy as St. Thomas conceived it.

However, in formulating the status of theology, Ockham's critical and nominalistic epistermology is going to interfere with this otherwise simple notion of God. It comes down to this: that in using our reason our distinctions and affirmations have no validity beyond our concepts and our words and apply in no way to the Divine Reality. This is entirely simple and whatever is attributal to It is truly identified with that Simple Reality. From such a standpoint there can be no question of a theology which, beginning with a knowledge of things and Revelation, would attempt to reconstruct the forms of a science of God. The Divine Simplicity is opposed to such a project and before it human reason is impotent. It is for this reason that Ockham considers any attempt to solve the mystery of predestination as illusory. Like creation, all that can be said about it, is that it is, viz., an absolutely gratuitous fact. In like manner, human reason can come up with no answer to the contradiction it sees in the following propositions: "The Essence is the Son," "The Father is not the Son," but nevertheless "The Father is the Essence." Before this mystery the spirit stands arrested either in negation or in pure and simple faith.

From now on what will be the status of theology which tradition in the wake of St. Augustine and St. Anselm set "between faith and vision" in a "faith seeking understanding"? Of theology understood in this sense we find nothing in the works of Ockham. For him, there is, of course, faith on the one side and scientific knowledges or dialectics on the other. There is a certain give-and-take between the two, which is precisely theology. But in this give-and-take the extremes remain juxtaposed, heterogene, and exterior to each other. There is never that organic and vital conjunction which in the eyes of a Thomist is precisely theology. Ockham states his position quite clearly. In the believer there is nothing supernatural except faith, and there is no other *habitus* in him having any reference to the *credibilia* except this faith. What then is the *habitus* of theology and what does the theologian acquire beyond the faith? Two things: 1. A deepening of his acquired faith, that is, his human faith, which is neither infused nor salutary and is proper to the believing theologian. 2. Many scientific *habitus* which he finds in and by the study of theology, but—to speak truthfully—which he could have acquired by an independent study of these sciences and which even an infidel could also have procured.

As R. Draguet has remarked in the *Revue cathol. des idées et des faits,* the Nominalists defend the diverse origins and the different values of the elements which enter into the theological structure. But behind this pleasant attention given to the original revealed fact and behind this happy feeling for the unequal values of the elements which make up the theological structure, is there not a serious loss of the profound meaning of that structure itself and of its fundamental unity? In short, does not this theory amount to the juxtaposition of a pure scholar, who is also a logician, over against a simple believer in the Word of God? Does it not forget, at least in part, the Augustinian tradition of religious contemplation which had up until then reigned in the Occident and which had combined "understanding the faith" with "nourishing the faith"? For Ockham, the *rationes probabiles* are no longer the nourishment of the salutary faith which links us with Christ, but only that of the faith acquired by investigation.

Certainly, we must not exaggerate. Man's need for speculation is imprescriptible or absolute and hence it appears, as it should, with Ockham and his disciples, Peter d'Ailly (1420), and later Gabriel Biel (1495). Ockham, Peter d'Ailly, and especially Biel want to find some understanding of the truths of faith, however obscure that understanding may be and however poor may be its rational means of support. It remains true that if the need of speculation is not henceforth dead, the possibilities of theological speculation are considerably reduced or modified.

Serious consequences follow which will continue to develop until the sixteenth century.

1. There is a definite rupture between philosophy and theology and even between philosophy or rational knowledge and religion. And hence a disjunction between two orders of things which tend to distribute themselves thus: on one side, a purely religious reality, a spirituality of faith, a mysticism of internal experience, which is no longer nourished by an activity properly speculative or theological. On the other a purely dialectic and formal speculation, which produces a very critical logic that simply applies itself to School questions which are reasonably systematic. In the first line above, we find Gerson, who is first nourished by St. Bonaventure and then by the mystics of the *devotio moderna* where Luther will find some spiritual consolation. In the second line, the treatises of the Nominalists themselves, of Ockham, for example, for despite the religious inspiration of their critical attitude, their theological works appear as a logical, dialectic, and critical treatment of School questions. The effect of this critique will be to transform many questions such as infused grace, the sacramental character, transubstantiation and several phases of penance into empty diagrams.

The distrust regarding reason or, at least, regarding its excessive use in the form of dialectics in the fourteenth century will lead to a reform of theology primarily toward the spiritual needs of souls, and this will be inspired by a religious sense much more than by any scientific exigencies. Thus Gerson, Nicholas of Clemanges, the Carthusian Nicholas of Strasbourg, etc. Others, for example, Nicholas of Cusa and William Durand the Younger, will demand a return to the sources as the only possible remedy to the then current state of theology, of which they had a very poor opinion. Indeed they will seek to transform theology into authoritative decisions based on Scripture and the canons, which would nullify so many vain controversies.

2. A necessary consequence of the devaluation of rational knowledge is the fideistic attitude. These two positions follow each other in rigorous symmetry or proportion. Not that it is just to accuse all the Nominalists of total fideism, but, in general, fideism is an attitude widespread among them.

3. A great development in questions of critical methodology, where we can discover three principal points of application: (a) The relation of rational certitudes and natural logic to the certitudes and logic of faith. In short, the question of knowing whether logic *(logica naturalis)* is valid in theology and in accord with the "logic of faith" *(logica fidei)*. This was a question already loaded with certain Lutheran positions, (b) The systematic application of a critique to the heart of the data and problems which are properly theological. Generally this critique draws its inspiration from the principle of divine Omnipotence and the distinction between *potentia absoluta* and *potentia ordinata*. For example: from the standpoint of *absolute potency* is it possible for sin and grace to co-exist or for the sinner to be justified without receiving grace, etc.? Under this heading the certitudes and possibilities of theological speculation are considerably reduced. .(c) The critical viewpoint could not fail to extend to the very sources of theology since the fideistic attitude stressed theology's dependence on these and on the *magisterium*. We have already noted in the fourteenth century a certain development of questions critical both of sources and method. Later this will become the treatise on theological *loci* or sources.

An Evaluation of Theology in the Scholastic Period

What characterizes the theology of this epoch is confidence in speculation and, first of all, in human knowledge. Whether that knowledge had meaning by itself, as St. Thomas taught, or whether it received validity only under the aegis of faith and theology, as Scotus taught, the fact remains that it always has value *in itself*. The work of speculation is also considered as self-justifying, even when it is intrinsically coupled with the life of charity. By that we mean to say that theological speculation is pursued for itself, for the intrinsic value of true knowledge, even if it has a necessary relation to charity. It is, however, not subordinated to the direct needs of the Church, to the defense of doctrine, instruction of the faithful, or evangelization in general. The theology of the great Scholastic era is the product of an activity which was developed for itself. It is not our purpose to justify this point of view. But much to our purpose are the questions, what *de facto* was the value of this effort, and is it true that certain signs of current theological decadence come from a logical development of dangers and excess borne by Scholastic theology? In this regard, three points appear specially noteworthy.

A. *The excessive domination of a method too exclusively rational and logical*

We have seen that the introduction of dialectics, with the *quaestio* as a technical instrument, determined the use of two parallel methods for theology: commentary and disputation. From the beginning, at each step of the process a reaction takes place, so that we can stake out the development of the dialectical method by marking the reactions it arouses. Robert of Melun (d. 1167) complains of those who neglect the text for the commentaries. The commentary of

Peter of Poitiers on the *Sentences* arouses the indignation of the Benedictine prior at Worcester. The first *Summa*, that of Alexander of Hales, stirs up Roger Bacon to lengthy criticism. And so it goes. The object of these anxious thoughts was always the same and it took the following two forms. Were theologians going to debase the mystery of God to a merely human curiosity? Were they going to supplant the word of God, the Bible text, by more rational writings or exercises which sometimes were not even commentaries?

The thirteenth century had felt the poignancy of these problems and gave them a methodological and pedagogic solution. This consisted in firmly maintaining a course in biblical studies side by side with the rational and dialectic treatment of theology. Not only was the Master's ordinary lecture—poorly attended by the way—a "reading" of some book of Scripture, but to remedy the fragmentary character of this study of the Bible, a course in rapid reading of the text was instituted which covered the entire Bible, *legere Bibliam biblice* or *according to the Parisian mode of study*. However, it seems that with the passage of time these arrangements were changed or repealed. In the rules of the University of Paris for 1387 we come across an authorization for the Scripture bachelors to exchange the study of two books of the Bible for two disputations.[48] At the same time, that is to say, in the course of the fourteenth and fifteenth centuries, the reading of the original texts of the Fathers decreases steadily, so that, as Fr. de Ghellinck notes, "the place in the Church left open for the Fathers diminishes because of the expansion of the works of Aristotle and the Scholastics."[49] Fr. Denifle likewise remarks that in the fifteenth century the great works of the Fathers are hardly ever consulted, since theology had become a work of logic. Apparently only some extracts and purely moral works are in use.

---

48. *Chartularia Universitatis Parisienas*, t. II, n. 28.
49. "Patristique et argument de tradition au bas Moyen Age," in *Aus der Geisteswelt des Mittelalters, Festig. Grabmann*, t. I, p. 421 sq.

This hastening retreat from the textual datum in the face of logical construction and system is seconded by a definite debility in the proceedings by which theology should make use of and incorporate its datum. The great weakness of Scholastic theology is its lack of a historical sense. This consists of being able to read a text or comprehend a fact not in one's personal intellectual perspective but according to the perspective in which a given text or fact is really found. This means to seek out the proper context of each fact. The absence of a historic sense consists in locating everything in one's present personal context. Only rarely did the Middle Ages have this historic sense. It was interested in objectivity, the absolute character of the object, the equating of the intellect to a kind of knowing endowed with perfect certitude.

Certainly the Middle Ages had a marvelous knowledge of Sacred Scripture and its culture could rightly be called a biblical culture. Without doubt, the great theologians, and in particular St. Thomas in his commentaries on St. John and St. Paul, are good exegetes. But the absence of a historic sense many times has pushed the medieval Masters into interpreting the terms and statements of the Bible, not as a part of the Bible itself but as ideas of their time and their milieu or again as theoretic ideas sometimes foreign to the literal and historic sense of the text. On the extreme side we will have the most unlikely use of texts; as for example, *Spirituals judicat omnia* ("the spiritual judges all things") and *Sunt duo gladii hic* ("we have two swords") are thought to express the relations of spiritual and temporal power. But even without going to the extreme of these dangerous aberrations we will have the danger of interpreting the words of Scripture, not by an investigation into the genuine sense of the biblical categories, but by finding out what the same word means to other authors, Aristotle, for example, or what it stands for in a medieval Latin context. Examples: St. Thomas from the sixth book of the *Nichomachean Ethics* applies Aristotle's analyses directly to the intellectual gifts of wisdom, Science, and intelligence spoken of in the Scriptures. In the question of Christ's "capital grace," he interprets the word *caput* not by an exegetical study of its use, but by a systematic analysis of the idea of "head." Does the systematic interpretation rejoin the exegetical interpretation? In substance, yes, and it is certain that the great Scholastics have not deviated doctrinally. But it must be granted that we have here all the elements of a false method, the danger of developing theology in a purely dialectical and deductive manner, using the biblical texts in an accidental manner simply for decorative purposes.

Similar observations can be made with regard to the writings of the Fathers. Whereas the great Scholastics of the twelfth and thirteenth centuries often read the Fathers in the original text or a Latin translation, those of the fourteenth and fifteenth centuries confined themselves to extracts and a regime of excerpts and collected quotations. Whence the regrettable development of a method from which the best Scholasticism was not totally exempt and from which even the Scholasticism of our day has not yet completely recovered. This consists in citing to support a thesis systematically developed for itself and by purely logical processes, one or two fragmentary texts, extracts of extracts, borrowed from authors of widely different historic context. These texts, treated thus, present merely a caricature of the positive datum.

It is well to recall how the theologians at the end of the thirteenth century established the scientific character of theology by declaring it to be a *scientia consequentiarum* and not a *scientia consequentium,* that is, a perception of the truth not of things themselves but of the demonstration of conclusions. This, of course, is an irreproachable position provided the Master preserves faithful and fruitful contact with the scriptural and patristic datum. During the fourteenth and fifteenth centuries when this contact becomes increasingly more sterile, theological structure grows proportionally more systematic and its apparel more dialectic.

The awareness of mysteries whence springs our faith is no longer paramount. Hence the object of *sacra doctrina* risks becoming no longer things essentially religious but more or less rational propositions. It is absolutely against this that humanism will react and so will Martin Luther. Hence it can rightly be said that this defect or deviation we have just pointed out constitutes Scholasticism's responsibility for the doctrinal tragedies of the sixteenth century.

B. *The Danger of Useless Subtlety*

The dialectic method of the *quaestio* was without doubt a great step forward. Nevertheless it presented the risk of being developed for its own sake and thereby invading the whole field of theological endeavor. As a matter of fact, *everything* can be called into "question" and even a "solved question" can in turn stir up a quantity of questions regarding each of its elements and so on *ad infinitum*. If we succeed in analyzing all the aspects and facing all the difficulties of a given subject by the dialectical method of the *quaestio,* that is fine. But there is a risk that the method will continue to function for itself. Historically, this occurred after each forward step made by the dialectical method. Thus in the twelfth century John of Salisbury gives a very sound diagnosis of the evil. But the "Cornificians" have survived and renew themselves from age to age. The humanists in their turn will react strongly against them, as will some theologians who are anxious to justify their complaints. If an excess of the historic sense has its drawbacks, mediocre erudition and historicism or the absence of a historical sense very definitely have theirs. In medieval Scholasticism, the difficulties raised by texts, particularly those of the "authorities," have been too often solved, not by recourse to the "context," with the relativism this loyal method implies, but by distinctions setting up an ideological scheme completely cut off from time.

The great medieval theologians generally avoided any excessive application of the dialectical method or the *quaestio* procedure. Nevertheless the danger of vain curiosity and dialectical subtlety was not imaginary, as the following warning clearly demonstrates. This was formulated by the general chapter of the Friars Preachers in 1280: "We admonish that Lectors and Masters and other Brothers must apply their minds to theological and moral questions rather than to the philosophical and curious."[50]

C. Danger of crystallization into petrified systems

This danger flows from the preceding one. With the great Scholastics, the system lives by their creative intuitions and they put the dialectic mechanism at the service of real problems. But the Masters teach and there are those among their students who are aggressive and twist and turn and defend their conclusions at any cost. "Scholastic" has two meanings. There is a strict and a pejorative sense of the term. This latter is true especially when we fail to feel the profound meaning of problems and treat them in a purely academic manner. Or when, instead of living by principles for his own sake, a person argues for someone else's conclusions, or for the conclusions held by a group with the rudeness and narrowness, the formalism and the inability to assimilate which are generally the signs of an *esprit de corps*. It is not by chance that the term "Scholastic" is linked with that of "school." It has been justly remarked that while developing the schools and becoming a tool of the "teachers," theology lost contact with the life of the Church and became an instrument of specialists. And since, as a matter of fact, the diocesan clergy always have had trouble in training theologians, since the schools of theology for the most part were staffed by the religious Orders, theology for all practical purposes grouped itself into schools which were identified with the great religious organizations: the Dominicans, Franciscans, Augustinians, etc. Toward the middle of the fifteenth century, theology had become an affair of mon-

---

50. *Acta capituli generalis*, ed. Reichert, t. I, p. 209.

asteries and specialized houses of study, a question of rival schools and disputes between systems. It is of schools of this nature and precisely while talking of Thomism and Scotism that M. Gilson was able to write: "On both sides they committed the fault of philosophizing on philosophies instead of philosophizing on problems . . ."[51]

The imperfections which we have just pointed out are not the product of the great Scholasticism but of its decadence. Nevertheless, any decadence of an institution denounces in that institution something which constitutes a risk or hazard, quite independent of the dangers which can come from the outside. This risk or hazard it runs of its very nature and the danger is, so to speak, essential to the institution. Scholasticism, sprung from the confident promotion of reason in the science of faith, involved a problem very much its own. By thoroughly exploiting the resources of natural reason, the better to understand mysteries, how can it preserve for Christian beliefs their dominant character and their "total" value? By introducing the play of dialectics into the *sacra doctrina* how can it preserve the effective primacy of the "datum"? By using a knowledge of the realities of our world to give an intellectual structure to the revealed mysteries, how can it retain for these mysteries their sublimity, their character of uniqueness and revelation of *another* world? The problem of Scholasticism is basically the problem of all theology.

---

51. *L'esprit de la philosophie médiévale*, Paris, 1932, t. II, p. 267.

Chapter Five
The Reformation and the Counter-Reformation

New Problems and Goals of Modern Theology

The era we now enter is characterized in its notion of theology as in everything else by (1) the growth of problems and new intellectual needs; (2) the collapse of the synthesis and unity characteristic of the Middle Ages in all domains; (3) the birth of new forms of activity and research. These changes, begun in the fifteenth century, will continue to operate effectively until the middle of the nineteenth century, when general attempts at a new synthesis will begin.

After a brief outline of the new problems which arose we will list the replies offered. These can be put into five groups: Humanist, Lutheran, traditional Scholastic, Mystic, and progressive Scholastic.

A. *The Problems and the Needs*

It is a fact that for many at the end of the fifteenth century the ancient forms of the medieval synthesis no longer seemed satisfactory. A definite need was felt to renew or to find new forms for life and thought. A "modern mentality" was bom which considered the past outmoded and sought entry into a new era.

This period, marked as it was by a general need of renovation, seems to pose three interrelated problems in which classical theology was called into question even to its internal structure. (1) A spiritual and vital need; (2) the recent critical approach to the texts and the consequent historical sense; (3) a new cultural and anthropological orientation.

1. A SPIRITUAL AND VITAL NEED. Nominalism and the excessively dialectical and subtle Scholasticism of the late Middle Ages finally succeeded, each in its own fashion, in separating the intellectual from the religious. Nominalism, although it professed a profound religious attitude, separated the object of religion and the order of human understanding and thereby made itself incapable of presenting the believer with an intellectual, religious outlook. Decadent Scholasticism developed excessively and almost exclusively in the realm of systematic conclusions and so it blotted out all religious intuitions which are indispensable to theology. It is astonishing to notice that at the end of the fifteenth century speculation as a form of discussion between schools was almost solely on a philosophical level. For example, Thomism and Scotism were treated as the philosophical positions of St. Thomas and Scotus much more than as presentations of their theological syntheses. Hence, when a need was felt to rise above the level of the *ratio* ("reason") to attain that of the *intellectus* ("understanding"), together with the *intuitions*, which no discursive thinking can dispense with, the temptation was to have recourse not to theology but to mysticism. This was the decision of the Alexandrians, of Raymond Lullus, Nicholas of Cusa, Denys the Areopagite, and even Albert the Great. Aristotle was still considered the Master of conceptual and dialectical technique. But others were turned to and the elements of a superior knowledge were looked for elsewhere than in theology. Everywhere we can sense the search for a more direct and simple contact with the religious object, the desire to turn that object over to souls in a state of certitude, i.e., doctrinal purity, and under a form no longer philosophical or intellectual, but religious, warm and consoling.

2. THE NOVELTY OF CRITICAL CONTACT WITH THE TEXTS AND HISTORICAL SENSE. A. Humbert has described the return movement to the sources, especially to the texts and above all to the Bible text, which took place rather

widely at this time. This begins in the first works of philology and critical erudition with Pico della Mirandola
and Ficino in Italy. From them it proceeds more or less
directly to John Colet in England, Lefèvre and J. Clichtoue
in France, Reuchlin in Germany, and finally to Erasmus
himself. From these scholars came an extensive editing of
texts, the famous edition of the New Testament in Greek by
Erasmus, 1516, and countless publications of the writings
of the Fathers which were then printed generally at Basel.

Certainly the texts, Bible and Fathers, were far from being
ignored by Scholasticism. It has been unkindly remarked
that the Humanists did nothing but print medieval manu-
scripts. But in this recourse to the text, in this frequent con-
sultation of the authors, the generation of 1500 brings us a
new viewpoint. It inaugurates a reading of texts done from
a standpoint no longer intemporal and unconditioned but
historical. In other words, no longer from the standpoint of
an acquired tradition, but critical and heuristic. And, first
of all, it is necessary to be sure of the text and sure that this
text is from this author. Hence a mountain of textual and
literary criticism, of editing, of critical interpretation, with
recourse to the historical and philological context, etc. This
it is which marks the difference of approach to the same
biblical text, say between Nicholas of Lyre, solicitous only
about the theological meaning, and Laurent Valla, or better
still J. Colet and Erasmus. This latter in particular objects
to the theologians who borrow a few words from Scripture
and accommodate them to their doctrine without bother-
ing to look up the context of these words and their meaning
in that context.[1]

3. A New Cultural and Anthropological Orientation. W. Dilthey, E. Cassirer, and after them K. Esch-
weiler have written on the new man of the Renaissance,
characterized by the subjective viewpoint. Here we will

---

1. *Encomium Morias,* c. LXIV.

call attention only to a few traits which directly interest the concept of theological work. Man is conceived less willingly according to what there is in him of the speculative and rational. There is less confidence in the logical proof and a tendency to replace the deductive and speculative spirit by one that is more intuitive and vital. In the course of the seventeenth century and later this tendancy will reappear as the need not only to distinguish in the order of objects between the realm of the truths of faith and that of the truths of reason, but, in the subjective conditions, between the mode proper to religious knowledge and that proper to rational activities.

This is very important and involves theology not from the outside but structurally. For theology, by definition, implies at its root the act of faith and in its elaboration a use of the human spirit. Now, the pressure which we are pointing out tends to modify more or less the notion of these two elements: the act of faith and the acts of the human spirit. The new approaches undeveloped in the religion of the countries which remained Catholic, will grow in the Germanic and Anglo-Saxon countries, which in great part had turned to Protestantism, and they will return toward the end of the nineteenth century under the form of problems and solution tentatives which, poorly formulated in the devious terms of "pragmatism" and "modernism," still beat on the threshold of our theology.

B. *The Solutions*

1. HUMANISM. Humanism involves a very marked reaction against the external form of Scholasticism. This it considers less than elegant and quite poverty-stricken in its literary modes. Often, the term "Scholastic" will be given to the theology which remains in the "barbarous" form of the Middle Ages. But beyond the question of style is the investigation of the dialectical method, of the *quaestio* and the *disputatio* which Humanism inaugurates. For the "questions" are barbarous, excessively and uselessly subtle; they

have added nothing to human knowledge or rather they have added only division and incertitude. Moreover, these questions present a dryly intellectual attitude of the human mind. They open the gates of theology to the invasion of philosophy and purely philosophical problems, whereas theology should speak only of Christ, lead to Christ, and open the profound meaning of the Scriptures to man's interiorly illuminated soul.[2]

The Humanists assail a thing only for the sake of replacing it. In place of the *disputatio* and the dialectical method, they want to see the texts and the exegetical method cultivated, the Bible text first of all and next the ancient authors. The *sincera theologia*, the *philosophia Christi* is the Sacred Scripture read for itself in its original Greek or Hebrew text and, in second place, the writings of those who being closer to the origins had a purer, simpler meaning of the Gospel. For the theologian it is simply a question of understanding them and proposing them to others. So to name their Christian doctrine without further qualification, it is not astonishing to see the Humanists recapture the phrase by which the Fathers, especially the Greek Fathers, had already designated the Gospel: *Philosophia Christi* or *Philosophia Christiana*. Thus, after his *Epistola de Philosophiae Christiana*, 1518, Erasmus will publish an *Exhortatio ad Philosophiae Christianae studium*, 1519–20, which in less than twenty years will go through thirty-five editions.

In the Humanist program there was first of all a positive side corresponding to the appearance of a new resource for the human spirit which theology owed it to itself to assimilate. As a new viewpoint and a historical method, as a recall to theology's sources and a provider of texts, Humanism represented a normal and fecund movement. Moreover the

---

2. See especially the typical treatise of Leonardo Bruni, *Libellus de disputationum exercitationisque studiorum usu*, of 1401; Erasmus, *Encomium Morias*, and the Preface to his edition of the New Testament, 1516, which was published separately in 1518 under the title of *Ratio seu methodus compendio perveniendi ad veram theologiam*.

progress realized by Erasmus—or thanks to his influence—in biblical studies was canonized in part at least in the fifth session of the Council of Trent.

However, the Erasmian program was not content to reform or complement Scholasticism. It was to replace it and, in short, to suppress it. Indeed in Erasmus' opinion there was no longer any place for the intellectual construction of Christian doctrine under a scientific form corresponding to the exigencies of speculative reason. There was room only for a detailed knowledge of the texts which would inspire a moral way of life. There was no place for a speculation attempting to elaborate a scientific knowledge of the nature of Christian things. So A. Humbert has said quite justly of John Colet and his rivals that Catholics in intention and position no longer grasped the doctrinal ensemble of the faith.

It is true that in its early stages, especially in the work of Ficino and Pico della Mirandola, Humanism had represented a union of Christian Revelation and pagan philosophical thought. But this union was fashioned in a manner quite different from that prevailing in Scholasticism. In Scholastic thought Plato and Aristotle intervened simply by the content of speculative truth which their writings revealed. Thus their thought could enter into the very constitution of a properly theological doctrine. But for the humanists, even when he is joined to the Gospel, Plato remains himself, Aristotle remains Aristotle. They are not reduced to a statement of speculative truth which is neither Plato nor Aristotle as such nor even objective truth acquired by the spirit. Hence the character of juxtaposition which the Humanist treatises present, hence their composite character, their apologetic aspect. In them the pagan philosophers seem mere illustrations or external props rather than an internal ferment of thought in the process of construction.

But in Erasmus' works, there is not even question of that. He is not only anti-Scholastic, he is anti-speculative and, while he might not be able to be described as anti-dog-matic, he certainly would have been content with a mere fideism together with a tendency to reduce religion to its moral elements.[3] By this anti-theological attitude, despite their attachment to the Church, Erasmus and the Humanist movement prepared the way for a religion without dogmas, which, after Spinoza, will be that of modern deism and play a great role in the inspiration of present-day disbelief. The Humanist program, however, did not triumph over the ancient methods overnight.

2. LUTHER. We merely wish to outline the Reformer's position which represents an enraged Augustinianism shorn of its Catholic ties. Without schematizing to excess we can sum up Luther's position along these lines.

(a) Christianity is purely a question of salvation. Now, my salvation is in Christ alone. This supposes I am con-verted to Him. It is for this that His Word has been given to us in the Scriptures and that this Word has been preached to us in the Church. Neither the Sacred Scriptures nor the teaching of the Doctors have any other end than to convert us from that which is not Christ to that which is Christ and to put Christ the Savior, that is, Christ crucified, into our hearts. There is here a double affirmation: (i) Salva-tion, which is Christ, supposes that man is converted from everything that is not Christ, that is, from-the exterior, from all that St. Paul calls the "Law," which according to Luther embraces all work exterior to the Gospel; he is con-verted to a faith which consists essentially in a total dis-trust of self and an uninhibited confidence in Christ the merciful Savior. (2) The Sacred Scriptures and Christian doctrine, which are concerned solely with the salvation and conversion just mentioned, do not bring us a specula-tive knowledge of things but are purely orientated to pro-mote our conversion from sensible things and our world to Christ's world of salvation. There is then a radical differ-

---

3. See, for example, *De servo arbitrio, Opera,* t. IX, col. 1217.

ence between philosophy and theology. Philosophy is the science of our world, and theology, or Christian doctrine, is the science of salvation. They treat of two heterogeneous orders of thought, so that no application of our natural knowledges is valid in theology.

(b) This impossibility of applying our rational knowledge of natures and the law of things to the Christian order is all the more severe since human nature is sin-laden. Salvation is not achieved by an elevation of nature with the aid of grace but by a dislike of natures and through faith alone, *fide sola*. It is thus there develops in Luther's thought beside his anti-ecclesiastical and anti-institutional ideas, the anti-Scholastic, anti-rational reaction of which his famous *Disputatio contra scholasticam theologiam* of 1517 is one of his most characteristic expressions:

> Prop. 43: "It is an error to say: *without Aristotle the theologian is not made.*" Prop. 44: "Rather the theologian is not made unless he becomes so with Aristotle." Prop. 45: "*The illogical theologian is a monstrous heretic* is a monstrous and heretical statement." Prop. 47: "No syllogistic form is contained in the Divinity." Compare the *Disputatio Heidelbergae habita* (1518), Prop. 19: "He is not worthily called a theologian who *invisibilia Dei per ea quae facta sunt, intellecta conspicit.*" Prop. 20: "But rather he understands who has seen the visible and secondary things of God through sufferings and the Cross." Prop. 29: "He who wishes to philosophize in Aristotle without danger, must first be stultified in Christ."

We see that it is theology, as conceived by the Christian tradition especially since the days of St. Anselm, which is sapped at the base—its base being precisely the possibility of applying the concepts of reason to supernatural realities. Luther calls any theology which would retain some continuity and some relationship between the order of things or of natural knowledge and the order of Christian things and of faith, *theologia gloriae* ("theology of glory"). To this he opposes the *theologia crucis* ("theology of the cross"), characterized by the radical discontinuity of the two orders and the submission of the entire Christian order to the exclusive criterion of salvation under the Cross. The *theologia gloriae* which strives to comprehend the more by the less and the pure intelligibles of Christ by the sensible forms of philosophy, is in reality a theology of darkness, whereas the true Christian finds wisdom in the Cross.

(c) What does Luther advocate to replace a speculative theology intellectually construing the datum of Christian doctrine? A theology which would be a true Pietism, prepared from a mainly textual study.

A theology which would be a true Pietism, for there is no question of knowing the nature of things, even those that are Christian, but only of living with Christ. From 1509 he wanted to leave the study of philosophy for that of theology. So, what in his opinion was the marrow of theology? "If you take delight in reading pure, solid theology poured out in the German tongue, but like the ancient script, then get yourself Tauler's sermons . . ." he said in a letter to Spalatin on 14 December 1516. Luther's theology is a pious, heartfelt theology in which there is no question of dissecting objects by knowledge but simply of clinging to them in a warm, consoling faith. It is a theology of salvation which turns its back to our world and goes to Christ in a realization of one's faithlessness but with total confidence in our Savior. A theology ceaselessly referring to the interior experience of conversion from false realities to the sole Truth, a theology of salvation *sola fide*. Here is a text which Ritschl and Hamack have cited as typical: "Christ has two natures; how does that concern me? If He bears the magnificent and consoling name of Christ, it is because of the ministry and task He has undertaken. It is that which gives Him His Name. Be He by nature man and God, that is His affair. But that He has consecrated His ministry, that He has poured out His love to become my Saviour and my Redeemer, it is here I find my consolation and my good . . ."

This pious and salutary theology took form especially in religious acts of faith and prayer. It did not admit that the Bible should be read, as did the Scholastics, "for knowledge as from an historical document" but simply "for meditation."[4] But for its preparation and circulation it did admit of a small amount of study primarily devoted to the Scripture texts and secondarily to certain Fathers, notably St. Augustine. "Our theology and St. Augustine," writes Luther, 18 May 1517, "make great strides and reign in our university. Aristotle is going down bit by bit and is nearing his definitive ruin. There is a general disgust with the lectures on the *Sentences* and there is little hope of recruiting any auditors unless the real theology is taught, that is, the Scriptures or St. Augustine or some other Doctor."[5] To work out such a program, some literary studies are necessary, particularly a knowledge of ancient languages. This is the area in which Luther and the Reformation sympathize and collaborate with Reuchlin, Erasmus, and Humanism in general. Luther adds and to the end of his life will continue to add a minimum amount of logic, rhetoric, dialectics, and philosophy. But Luther both here and in his notion of theology remains an exasperated Augustinian. It was in the Augustinian tradition to treat the liberal arts and especially philosophy as propaedeutics preparing the human spirit for contemplation. Luther recaptures this viewpoint while pushing it to the extreme, so that his very texts which affirm the benefit of philosophy and logic, affirm still more forcefully that they can have no *place in* theology itself.

Luther will sire a double posterity. These two lines, opposed to each other, can nevertheless, it seems to us, legitimately lay claim to him as their author. In one of these

---

4. *Tischreden*, Weimar t. IV, n. 5135.
5. *Briefwechsel*, t. I, p. 99; cf. p. 139.

lines Luther interiorized the principle of Christianity, giving
to theology, as a twofold textual interior, a spiritual criterion
referring to salvation and to the experience of salvation.
This guaranteed for posterity the offspring of Schleiermacher and a "theology of experience" according to which the
"Dogmatics" has for its object to describe and systematize
religious experience. In the other line, however, adhering
to the objective datum of Sacred Scripture and symbols of
the ancient Church, he systematized theology according
to a dialectic of radical opposition between our world and
God, between the "Law" and the Gospel. In this way he can
be recognized as the father of "dialectical theology" animated by the rejection of the analogy of being and anything
"supernatural" which is not God, the Uncreated, Himself.

From the viewpoint of the further development of Catholic theology, Luther's rejection of any theological norm
other than the Scriptures challenged theological science
to its very foundations. We shall see that this was to lead
to the creation of a defense and a critical methodology of
those foundations: treatises on tradition, the theological
sources and apologetic justification of the faith as well as
the Church and its magisterium.

C. Continuation and Development of Medieval Scholaticism

Some theologians, several of whom must be numbered
among the very great, continue the theology of Medieval
Scholasticism, not only in its principles but in the problems
treated and method used. These are the commentators who,
attached to the doctrine of a Master, make it by that very
fact a "school tradition." Unquestionably, the authority of
St. Thomas after his canonization is affirmed and extended
in an exceptional manner. His progress can be measured in
the course of the fourteenth and fifteenth centuries. This
general approbation accorded St. Thomas will have great
influence on the very conception of theology. First, directly,
by the development of the tradition left by St. Thomas; then,

indirectly, by the elimination of another tradition from ecclesiastical circles, that is, the Augustinian line, especially after the Reformation and Jansenism. These were crises in which that tradition played a definite role.

Taking for granted this preeminence of the Thomistic tradition, we will keep to its line in mapping out the development of Medieval Scholasticism. This will take us up to the eighteenth century. The stages are staked out by the great names of Capreolus (d. 1444), Cajetan (d. 1534), Bañez (d. 1604), John of Saint-Thomas (d. 1644), the Carmelites of Salamanca (between 1637 and the beginning of the eighteenth century), finally, as types of a tradition henceforth determined, Gonet (d. 1681) and Billuart (d. 1757). The development of the Thomistic Scholastic tradition is characterized—as far as theology is concerned— by the increasingly strong application of the Aristotelian notion of science and by increasing precision in the definition of a theological conclusion.

As we have seen, discussion between the schools quickly settled on the question whether or not theology is a science. St. Thomas' disciples, who held for the affirmative, were led to define theology-science with reference to its *conclusions* as a science of conclusions, *scientia consequentiarum*. The expression *habitus conclusionum* is found in St. Thomas, but it has not the meaning there that it will acquire at the beginning of the fourteenth century. It means principally the argumentative structure of sacred doctrine, as we have pointed out above. Henceforth attention was directed almost exclusively to the conclusions of theological science. Capreolus defines the scientific quality of theology thus: "It is not a science of the articles of faith, but of the conclusions which follow from them."[6] After having defended the scientific quality of theology, he defends its speculative quality, then its unity as a science, finally the selection of *God* as its subject and its principal and direct *objectum formale quod*

---

6. Q. I, a. 1, 5ᵃ concl.

(precise formal object of investigation). Nevertheless, if he insists on conclusions as the object of theology-science, he does not define this latter as a *revelabile,* understood as something mediately or virtually revealed.

This precision is not yet found in Cajetan. According to him, theology is distinguished from faith inside the very same revealed teaching. Theology has for its object the conclusions, while faith has for its object the articles or dogmas, which are, after all, the principles. The principles or revealed truths contain the conclusions *virtualiter* ("virtually"). So, while the principles are the object of an immediate and simple adhesion of faith, the conclusions deduced from them are the object of a properly scientific adhesion. They are the object of a science which is certainly coming from a divine light, and in which the revealed light of the principles is communicated to the conclusions. But this light is only derived, for "we assent to the conclusions because of the articles." And the derivation is due to human reasoning. It seems to us that Cajetan reports St. Thomas' thought very well but in a more involved vocabulary. He clearly saw the meaning of *sacra doctrina,* and that, when St. Thomas asks himself if the *sacra doctrina* is a science, he is really asking if the revealed teaching, when it involves a deduction of conclusions, verifies the quality of a science. Again like St. Thomas, nowhere does he explicitly face up to the question whether or not the conclusions of theological science are *new* truths, that is to say non-revealed. It suffices that in the revealed teaching, they have a function and a value of truth deduced from principles. It seems indeed that for him theology did not formally have for its object the "virtually revealed," but simply the truths which in the Christian teaching are founded on other truths as in their principle. Finally Cajetan, like St. Thomas, does not expressly speak of the premises of reason concurring with a premise of faith to produce the theological conclusion. Again like St. Thomas, he does not exclude this concurrence as a possibility.

Cardinal Toletus (d. 1596) follows Cajetan on every point. On the other hand, the Dominican school of Salamanca, distinguishing faith from theology, defines this latter as that science which is rationally deduced from propositions of the former, *habitus conclusionum* ("a habit of conclusions").

Bañez is Melchior Cano's disciple. While defending the Scholastic method against the attacks of the Humanists, he wrote in polished Latin and developed his commentary on article eight of the first question into a neat little volume, De *locis theologicis: Scholastica commentaria in Ium partem Summae S. Thomae Aq.*[7] He is resolutely one of those Scholastic theologians "who succinctly and in a dialectical manner work out the sacred doctrine."[8] Bañez devotes considerable effort to defining the *lumen sub quo* or the *ratio formalis sub qua* of theology, that is to say, the light which makes any sort of object an object of theology. It is *divina revelatio*, says he. "Therefore, the formal reason under which we know God and what is of God, is a divinely infused light whereby whatever is in our intellect of the intelligible theological *esse* is formally illuminated."[9] The light which makes any object an object of theology is an infused light which, in the person, corresponds to supernatural revelation. What is it, then, which distinguishes theology from the faith? First of all it is essential to the "illumination" (this is our translation of the term *revelatio* as Bañez uses it here) of the faith to be obscure, while obscurity is accidental to theology, for this latter makes every attempt to line up its principles in full clarity. Next, infused illumination of the faith is the immediate motive of assent given directly to each and every assertion of the faith. These in turn will be the principles of theology. But theology is defined by its conclusions, for these alone are properly its object. Now, of

---

7. Ed. by L. Urbano in *Bibl. de Tomistas Espanoles*, t. VIII, Madrid and Valencia, 1934.
8. *De locis*, p. 82.
9. Cf. A. 3, a. 7, a. 8 and *Com. in II^{am}-II^{ae}*, q. I, a. 1, dub 2, Venice 1602, col. 15–17.

assent to conclusions—object of theology—infused illumination is the motive only "through the medium of a consequence evident to another light. And thus is acquired the
theological habitus and the theological light which is virtually from Divine Revelation. Hence the proper and formal object of theology is virtually revealed."[10] The *objectum
formale quo* ("the formal light under which a science proceeds") of theology then is not the same as that of the faith.
For it is the light of revelation but in so far as it is extended
by reasoning (and hence by an intervention of the natural
light of the human mind) to a conclusion deduced from the
truths of faith.

The homogeneity between theology and the faith evidently enjoys a plenary session when the conclusions are
drawn from two truths of faith. This is the case which Bañez
naturally prefers to study. But he also treats that of a conclusion proceeding "from one proposition which is certain
according to the Catholic faith and from another naturally
known by natural light either immediately or mediately,
either from natural philosophy or moral or metaphysics."[11]

The intervention of John of Saint-Thomas in the definitive determination of the Scholastic notion of theology may
be seen especially in two points: the definition of virtual
revelation and the value of a theological conclusion drawn
from one premise of faith and one of reason. The first point
is taken up *In Iam partem,* q. I, disp. II, a. 1, m. I and III.
The second is treated in numerous passages. It is obviously
a personal discovery especially dear to the author.[12]

The *ratio sub qua* of theology is virtual revelation, that
is to say, the light of revelation derived from a conclusion
of reasoning properly so-called. The theological conclusion
retains from this light a certain scientific quality, *scibilitas,*

10. *De locis,* p. 33; cf. *Com. in IIam-IIae, loc. cit.,* 3ª concl., col. 16.
11. A. 3, p. 33; cf. a. 2, p. 21.
12. See, among many others, *Logica,* IIª pars, q. XXV, a. 1, ad 3, Reiser
   ed., p. 777.

which permits it to be placed in the field of sciences hier-
archized according to its degree of abstraction. The term
virtualiter revelatum is defined exclusively as a truth not
formally revealed, but deduced from Revelation by a correct process of reasoning. There is then, with regard to St.
Thomas and his earliest commentators, certainly no infi-
delity, but a certain specialization, a precision, in the sense
in which this word implies a certain amount of elimination. Theology is no longer simply defined in the terms of
St. Thomas by the fact that it orders and constructs Christian teaching in its principles and conclusions, but by the
deduction of *new* conclusions. The second point, showing
John of Saint-Thomas' influence on Scholasticism is this:
while for Bañez the conclusions obtained from a premise of
faith and a premise of reason were not brightened by a light
as purely theological as the conclusions resulting from two
premises of faith, John of Saint-Thomas put the two cases
rigorously on thé same level. In fact we have the impression
that for him the more purely theological is perhaps the first.
On the one hand, his effort to maintain the unity of one
lumen sub quo in the two cases and, on the other, the fully
theological quality of this *lumen,* is excellent. To achieve
this, he has recourse to the idea of instrumentality and
shows that the truths of reason employed in a theological
argument are in that case no longer pure truths of reason.
For, although they are not intrinsically transformed, they
are, in the actual use to which they are subjected, assumed,
corrected, measured and approved by the principle of faith
with which they are constructed. Together with this principle, they make one sole *medium* of demonstration, which is
not something of faith and is no longer something of pure
reason, but very properly a theological medium, producing
a theological *scibilitas.* In this way John of Saint-Thomas
again takes up the line followed by Bañez. According to this
the most scientific theology is constructed *in the faith* and,
henceforth, despite the very marked intervention of philo-

sophical principles into its construction, the intervention objectively adds nothing to the datum of faith.

The position of John of Saint-Thomas is that which has passed on to later Thomists. Billuart, for example, defines theology as "The doctrine of divine things which draws its conclusions from the immediately revealed principles of faith.[13]

Neither Suárez nor the Carmelites of Salamanca commented on the first question of the *Summa*. Their idea of theology is to be found partly in the philosophical writings to which they refer and partly in their treatise on faith. Here they consider the notions of formally revealed and virtually revealed and the definibility of both. Charlier, in his *Essai sur le problème théologique*,[14] synopsizes their thought thus:

Suárez clearly distinguishes the *assensus theologiens* ("theological assent") from the *assensus fidei* ("the assent of faith"). The latter has for its object the formally revealed, the former the virtually revealed. The virtually revealed in the strict sense refers to a conclusion deduced from a proposition of faith "by virtue and assistance of some natural principle, as when a natural property is collected from a revealed one."[15] Virtual Revelation is similar to the concept "of property which in no manner is formally contained in the thing referred to, but only in its root, as in the example of risibility and the like."[16] In this case, the *assensus theologicus* is based on reasoning, properly so-called, as on its proper and formal cause. The strictly theological conclusion is not of its very nature an object of faith, since it rests on a formal motive distinct from the formal motive of faith. It becomes an object of faith only in the case of a definition by the Church, which then proposes it not as virtually revealed but as formally, immediately and *in se* revealed.

---

13. *Summa S. Thomae*, 1ª pars, *dissert. proemialis.*
14. Paris, 1938, p. 24.
15. *De fide*, disp. VI, sect. 4, n. X.
16. *Op. cit.,* disp. Ill, sect. 11, n. V.

The Salmanticenses in their turn will say that a conclusion deduced from a principle of faith and a principle of reason by way of demonstration is not a proposition of faith, but a theological conclusion. As to the truth rigorously deduced from two formally revealed premises, there is room for a distinction. This truth can be considered, (1) under the modality of a deduced truth and, as such, it is a theological conclusion; (2) it can be considered in itself from the specific and reduplicative standpoint of its being true and, as such, it is a proposition of faith.

It is pointless to pursue any further this inquiry into St. Thomas' commentators who in the sixteenth and seventeenth centuries prolonged the line of Medieval Scholasticism.

This Scholasticism, product of the schools, the creation, more often than not, of religious defending the tradition of their Order, and finally representing the speciality of a world apart, is much more polemic than it was in the thirteenth century. The division and development of questions demanded by the school controversies are infinitely more than in the days of St. Thomas or St. Bonaventure. Moreover this Scholasticism is exclusively endeavoring to develop the systematic side of the theological tradition in which it is inserted. It defines itself as "Scholastic" because of a dialectical and metaphysical treatment of the problems furnished by the tradition of the School. And it devotes itself to treating them part by part with the resources and according to the exigencies of dialectics and metaphysics. Apropos of Capreolus, Mgr. Grabmann remarks that of the three lines followed by St. Thomas, the speculative, the historico-positive, and the mystical line, he only continued the first. As a matter of fact this Scholasticism profited little from the new acquisitions brought in by Humanism. The contribution of the scriptural and patristic datum is often mediocre. Even in Cajetan's work, his exegetical effort is, in a word, extrinsic to his speculative activity. On the other hand, in his excellent speculative questions, which are abundantly

developed, the philosophical interpretations and constructions are extensively pursued. In the work of John of Saint-
Thomas, several great questions are preceded by rather
formidable philosophical pre-notes. Moreover in their
exposés of the notion of theology itself, these theologians,
as Gabriel Biel had done before them, quite readily referred
to various philosophical treatises. So it is that the effort of
Scholasticism has terminated in a very forceful elaboration
of philosophical notions pledged to speculative theology. It
is constituted as a Scholastic "Christian philosophy," whose
notions, so to speak, have been cut to measure for theological use. The result is that for its own problems, theology
has little to do but run to this arsenal it has collected. It is
the existence of a Scholastic "Christian philosophy" which
explains and justifies the extremely philosophical trend of
many of the treatises of Scholasticism in the sixteenth and
seventeenth centuries.

Obviously it will always be a temptation for Scholasticism to conceive the work of speculative theology as an
application to a special datum preserved by the philosophical categories. When John of Saint-Thomas, who certainly
was a contemplative of great profundity, expresses the function of the theology-science in these terms: "supernatural
things treated in the fashion of metaphysical science and
discussed in natural terms . . ."[17] he denounces any potential
deviation from this important and legitimate function. The
real danger exists of considering the role of faith in theology merely as preliminary, necessary to furnish the starting point, but truly border-line and extrinsic, while the real
theological work is then done by the simple application of
metaphysics to this datum held as true. How then, while
constructing a rational interpretation, can theology preserve for that Christian datum its specificity, its character
of a whole, and its original reality?

17. *De fide*, disp. II, a. 8, n. 6, p.386.

D. *New Form in Catholic Theology*

1. EFFORT TO INTEGRATE MODERN EXIGENCIES. MEL-
CHIOR CANO. The Humanist movement followed by the
Protestant controversy raised up in the Church a mass of
questions and an effort to create a fundamental theology in
which the sources, the condition, the certitude and method
of religious thought will be studied critically. This effort
first got under way at the school of Salamanca and particularly under Melchior Cano. The renewal of Scholasticism
which took place at Salamanca in the sixteenth century is
due to Francis of Vitoria, who at Paris had been under the
influence of Peter Crockaert and through him benefited
by the Humanist movement of Louvain. Together with the
two Soto's, Cano was his pupil and, becoming Master in his
turn, was the professor of Medina and Bañez. The Masters
of Salamanca spread all over Christian Europe and carried
with them the message of a renewed Scholasticism: Toletus
to Rome, Gregory of Valencia to Ingolstadt, Rodriguez of
Arriaga to Prague.

Cano is a theologian of Scholastic formation, but one
who wishes to take into account Humanism and its con-
quests: history, the editing and criticism of texts, etc. Cano
has from many angles a Humanistic sensibility and mentality. Psychologically, he is a modern and wishes to found a
theology "more up to date." It is this Humanistic mentality
which leads him to place in the foreground of his theological work a critical appreciation of the value of a determined
position and to determine this position by appealing to a
positive datum. This does not mean that Cano denies the
validity of reasoning. In his *De Locis Theologicis* (1563)
he severely judges any fideistic attitude, he criticizes those
who would like to stop with the letter of the Sacred Text, as
did Erasmus, and he justifies the use of reason in theology.
Classically, he assigns to Scholastic theology three goals:
deduction of conclusions, defense of the faith, illustration

and confirmation of dogma with the aid of human sciences. But like every student of Vitoria, he knows the abuses which have discredited rational theology and he denounces them. He advocates a profound reform: the *ratio* which deduces the conclusions is good, but we can know nothing more in the conclusions than what is given us by the principles, and nothing which exceeds in certitude and value, the certitude and value of the priciples; in short, rational theology draws its value only from the positive datum—that is to say, *auctoritas*. The theologian then will be a veritable scholar, worthy of the name, only if he critically appreciates the data from which he starts. Cano reacts against a theology which would be only a body of reasoning and he very forcefully affirms that theology, like any other science, thrives from a datum, from a positive starting point, which is a definite this or that and which no amount of reasoning can create. All his effort then is devoted to a systematical and critical study of the different sources from which the theologian should take his work material and which he calls *loci* or "sources." He devotes himself almost exclusively to determining the proper value, the criteria, the conditions of appreciation and utilization of these *loci*. We see this clearly when at the end of 1. XII of his *De Locis* he himself gives us three examples of his method.

It can be seriously questioned whether speculative theology, the *theologia scholae,* remains after Cano's day what it was in St. Thomas' time. Cano abandons the use of the *quaestio,* and the way he speaks of the *quaestio theologica*[18] leads one to believe that for him it is no longer an instrument of science, but a process of pedagogy and discussion. Likewise the way he talks either about the theological conclusion or the function of explanation and illustration (1. VIII, c. II) seems to refer only to the explanation of what is found as such in the principal *loci,* Scripture and tradition. In other words, theological argumentation would

18. *De Locis Theologicis,* 1. XII, c. V.

be only a type of explanation like any other and not that gathering of reason's authentic resources for the construction of Christian doctrine such as it was for St. Thomas. However, it would be unjust to render Cano responsible for the excesses or deviations which his initiative may have permitted to others. For a progeny of authentic disciples follows in his wake. He created the scientific and critical treatise of theological methodology and all the *De locis* are tributaries of his.

2. COLLAPSE OF THE ANCIENT UNITY OF THEOLOGY. NEW SPECIALIZATIONS. With many, the effort to keep abreast of the new demands works out not in the direction of preserving unity of thought but in that of specialization and division. The fact is general and characteristic of the modern epoch at the end of the sixteenth century. This is the collapse of the medieval synthesis. But not everything is "collapse" in the advance which we are going to analyze. And the fact of specialization, which is quite manifest, is in great part the normal and beneficial consequence of the new acquisitions which constitute progress.

Very soon, the theological work loses its unity and breaks down into specialties. Of course, the tradition of the School continues. *Cursus* are drawn up. No only the *Summa* of St. Thomas, but even well into the seventeenth century the *Sentences* are still the classics which teachers commented upon—for example, Estius (d. 1613). But most of the time, the treatises which are published bear miscellaneous epithets which indicate the specialization of the purposes or methods: biblical, Catholic, Christian, dogmatic, fundamental, moral, mystical, natural, polemic, positive, practical, Scholastic, speculative . . . etc. To take only one example, Fr. T. Lohner will publish in 1679 a work entitled *Institutiones quintuplicis theologiae*, and the *five theologies* will be: positive, ascetic, polemic, speculative, and moral.

We will confine ourselves to three divisions which may be regarded as characteristic of the new theology: Scholastic and mystic, dogmatic and moral, and especially, Scholastic and positive.

(a) *Scholastic Theology and Mystical Theology.* With a Thomas or a Bonaventure mysticism is integrated into theology, so that theology can fulfill all the obligations of its function of wisdom. From this plenary viewpoint, a separate mystical or spiritual theology had no purpose. Nevertheless in the fifteenth century a separation starts taking place. Toward the end of the sixteenth century, the *Exercises* of St. Ignatius will appear, then a little later, the writings of the reformed Carmel, then those of St. Francis de Sales. These spiritual works are masterpieces, but they do not stem from the classical speculative theology. Deploring the split between the two fields, Gerson would have wished them reunited: "Since up to now our study was to blend this mystical theology with our Scholastic theology . . "[19] Significant is the fact that in their *Tabulae fontium trdditionis christianae,* Frs. Creusen and Van Eyen, when they began work on the fifteenth century, were obliged to start a new column so they could classify writings under the rubric of *Theologia ascetica et mystica.* So a new specialty is being created in theology, or, I am tempted to say, is being separated from theology. Over against *Scholastic* theology there will be opposed from now on a *mystical* or *affective* theology, which will have its doctors, its works, its sources, and its style.

The term "mystical theology," favored by Denis, is of long and honorable usage, but its opposition to "Scholasticism" dates especially from Gerson, as we see, for example, in the *Lexicon theologicum* of Jean Altenstaig, Antwerp, 1576. The expressions *ascetic* theology or *spiritual* theology come later.

The Dominicans made an effort to satisfy the demands of the spiritual movement while at the same time preserving the unity of theology. Contenson makes a desperate attempt to avoid a cleavage between subtle but dried-up Scholastic speculation and pure spirituality. In his *Theologia*

---

19. *Cantica Sympsalma* I, 1, *Opera,* La Haye, 1728, t. IV, p. 39.

mentis et cordis he tries to return spiritual value to a theology from which people are turning because it fails to nourish their souls. Massoulie, who will complete Contenson's unfinished work, is still more strongly anxious to reinstate the matter of spiritual life into theology. A few years before Contenson, L. Bail published his *Théologie affective ou Saint Thomas en méditations* (1654), and some years before that (1647), Louis Chardon wrote his *Croix de Jesus*.

"Affective" theology is understood here not as a theology experimenting with the things of God but as a dogmatic theology treated in a spirit of piety and edification. In reality, in keeping with Chardon's masterpiece, we hold out for an intermediary type of theology. Certainly, for him there is question of drawing from a contemplative study of the mysteries an explanation and regulation for the things of the spiritual life. But the choice of the mysteries to be contemplated, the choice of the "themes" of contemplation and the orientation of the study, according to Chardon, come not from the theological datum as such, taken in its objectivity, *in se* and according to its pure verity as an object. Rather they come from the spiritual experience or the knowledge of souls acquired by the spiritual director. It is then a theology whose finally decisive "theological *locus*" is the experience of "holy souls" and not the pure, revealed truth, objectively contained in the classical, theological *loci*.

In a word or two let us point out the methodological position of Contenson in his *Theologia mentis et cordis*. He depends on the tradition of Salamanca and quotes Soto, Medina, and Cano. In keeping with that tradition he strongly underlines the linking of theology to its sources and its homogeneity with the faith. He stirs into his reasoning citations from the Scriptures and the Fathers. But his own intention is to reinstate spiritual elements and mystical values in Scholasticism, forming a unique theology. He defines the *objectum formale quo* of theology as the *revelatio virtualis*.[20] He so strongly underlines the

20. *Theologia mentis et cordis*, 1. I, diss. I, c. 1, specul. 3.

homogeneity of theology and faith that to him reasoning seems to be a mere condition of the application of the premises of faith. Hence, the final assent springs only from the truths of faith, as from its veritable cause. This position will be reasserted by Schaezler and, in his turn, by Fr. A. Gardeil. Finally, Contenson is of the opinion, alone in this, that theology is a *habitus entitative supernaturalis* ("a habit which is supernatural by its nature"), but nevertheless acquired. He is fatally led to this view by his strong belief in the objective continuity between theology and faith.

(b) *Dogmatic Theology and Moral Theology.* The rupture between dogma and moral in Post-Tridentine theology is often called to our attention in scholarly works. But it is not an easy matter to state when and how this break took place. The Middle Ages had known this distinction. Take, for example, Peter the Cantor in his famous *Summa Abel;* he writes: "Theology is two fold: the superior or celestial, which is devoted to a knowledge of divine things . . ., the inferior or subcelestial, which gives us information about *mores.*" We find a similar distinction in William of Auxerre, Robert de Courçon, John de la Rochelle, Peter of Poitiers, and, before all of these, in Yves de Chartres. Finally, we find the expression *theologia moralis* as early as 1160 in the *De virtutibus et vitiis* of Alain de Lille. Nevertheless in the Middle Ages this division was of a purely pragmatic nature. It was understood to be within the fold of one and the same discipline and it never occurred to anyone to separate them. On the other hand, in the last quarter of the sixteenth century in the works of a great number of authors, morality becomes a separate domain, free from the direct and constant influence of dogma.

What causes will explain this event? For lack of detailed studies of the times, it is difficult to say. Some suggest Protestant influence as a contributing factor but they offer no fact, no justification. This position, of course, is not impossible, for, as a matter of fact, the work of the Calvinist Lamber Daneau, *Ethicae christianae libri tres* (1577), is undoubtedly one of the first treatises of separated moral theology. Fr. Tillmann underlines the influence of the precepts of the Council of Trent. These had to do with the detailed confession of sins and obviously affected the flow of works on casuistry taking place at that time. Another final point perhaps is the fact that the authors of the works on separated moral theology are practically all Jesuits and Spaniards: J. Azor, *Institutiones morales;* H. Henriquez, *Theologiae moralis summa;* Th. Sánchez, *Opus morale in praecepta Decalogi;* L. Mendoza, *Summa totius theologiae moralis;* etc.—to cite only the principal works among the first specimens of a literature which became quite abundant. These volumes generally present a treatise on the final goal of man and the morality of human acts, a treatise on the sacraments, the natural and positive law (the Decalogue and laws of the Church), the sanctions of ecclesiastical law, and finally a treatise on eschatology.

These authors have neither the intention nor the awareness of innovating. Nevertheless, there is a great difference between this separated moral theology and the ancient moral section of theology. Previously, there was first a scientific study of human action terminating in a theological science capable of directing this action; next, there were practical manuals summarized for the use of confessors. The new moral theology captures the line of these manuals, but inserts into them the material of theological treatises. It also tries to set before the confessors not only a memorandum summarizing the scientific treatises of moral theology, but a complete self-sufficient manual in which the material of these treatises is integrated under the title of principles immediately applicable to practical decisions.

The ancient *Summae* or manuals for the confessors were simply lists, quite brief, essentially practical and most frequently arranged in alphabetical order. Henceforth there will be a systematic ensemble which will be self-sufficient. And so moral becomes a specialty among the disciplines which are taught and written up at length. It is a particular discipline which has its own method and its own data. There will be a treatise on the last goal separated from the treatise on God just as there will be a treatise on the sacraments separated from the treatise on Christ. So the new productions of moral theology will undergo the danger of being influenced by philosophy rather than dogma. Already Vásquez sees in the analysis of morality and the kinds of virtues and sins nothing but pure philosophy and, for this reason, considers the moral part of theology as subalternate to moral philosophy, or quite simply as belonging to philosophy.[21]

(c) *Scholastic Theology and Positive Theology.* Gregory of Valencia, in his *Commentarii theologici* published in 1591, speaks of the division of theology into Scholastic and positive as a current division. About the same time, Louis Carbonia also says: "Christian theology is usually divided into Scholastic and positive."[22] A little before these dates, the Master General of the Friars Preachers; Sixtus Fabri, in an ordinance of 30 October 1583, prescribed that in the convent of Perugia "in addition to the reading of Scholastic theology let there also be some reading of positive theology. . . ." The expression then must be current, since it is used without explanation in an official document. Nevertheless, it is without doubt quite recent at that date because Jean Altenstaig, in his *Lexicon theologicum* of 1576, does not mention it. Nor does Cano, although he formally knows the reality that the term covers and speaks twice about *ponere principia*: "There are two parts to every discipline . . . one

---

21. *In Iam part. Sum. theol.*, I^a pars, disp. VII, c. V; cf. disp. XII, c. III. Cf. J. Diebolt, *La théologie morale catholique en Allemagne au temps du philosophisme et de la Restauration,* 1750–1850, Strasbourg, 1926. In this work we can follow the change to which the study of natural law, in the wake of Grotius, gave a strong impetus and which tended to laicize, so to speak, moral theology.

22. *Introductio in sacram theologiam,* Venice, 1589, 1. I, c. VIII.

in which the principles themselves are posited, established, and settled as foundations, the other in which, the principles having been posited, we proceed to those things which are their conclusions."[23] And, farther on: "For absolutely no discipline proves its principles by reasoning. It posits them. For this reason they are called *positiones* or *petitiones*."[24]

We find the division of positive and Scholastic theology in the Rules of Orthodoxy added by St. Ignatius of Loyola (d. 1556) at the end of his Exercises, Rule XI: "To praise positive and Scholastic theology, for as it is particularly proper for the positive Doctors, such as St. Jerome, St. Augustine, St. Gregory, and others to excite the affections and lead men to love and to serve God, our Saviour with all their strength, so the principal goal of the Scholastics, such as St. Thomas, St. Bonaventure, the Master of the *Sentences,* and those who have followed them, is to define and explain, according to the needs of modern times, the things necessary for eternal salvation, to attack and point out clearly all the errors and false reasonings of the Church's enemies." We see in this text of St. Ignatius that positive theology and Scholastic theology answer less to two functions than to two finalities or rather to two genera or two forms of theology.

We can reach back beyond St. Ignatius and—until further information is available—we will consider as the first use of the term that made by Juan Mair in his commentary on the *Sentences* first published at Paris in 1509. Juan Mair disapproves of those "who profusely and at length insert into theology useless questions from the arts and assail frivolous opinions with a prodigality of words . . . Wherefore I decided as far as possible to pursue theological matters almost totally in this fourth part, now *positively,* now *Scholastically*,"[25] This text is remarkable and it puts us on

---

23. De *locis,* 1. II, c. IV.

24. Ibid., XII, c. IV.

25. In *IV^{um} Sent.,* 1509, fol. 1–2 quoted in R.-G. Valloslada, *Un teólogo olvidado: Juan Mair, in Estudios eclesiásticos,* t. XV, 1936, p. 97 and 109.

the road to a meaning of the word "positive" which could very well be its original meaning. For Juan Mair the word means both a matter and a method. It indicates a brief exposé, a religious exposé devoid of useless questions as well as questions mainly philosophical, and exposé offering not problematic or controversial things, but firm data, finally an exposé bearing on Christian material, on truths of fact which are not deducible by reason.

Beginning here, then, it would seem that the same word covers two notions which, despite their common origin, are not less notably different. There is a literary conception, according to which positive theology represents a certain *manner* in working out theology. Then there is a methodological conception, according to which "positive" is a certain *function* of theology. The first conception, which can be applied to the text of St. Ignatius and even to that of Juan Mair, will for a long time be the generally accepted meaning. It seems that this is what the word "positive" means most spontaneously by itself. The second conception represents an internal development of the notion of theology which was readied by Cano and could then have rolled along without being covered by the name of "positive." However it was finally presented under this ensign.

In the wake of Cano, positive theology will mean that part or that function by which theology establishes its principles or works on its foundations or its datum. A part or function which primarily deals with the Scriptures and the Fathers and which aims not at elaborating the content of their assertions but at seizing it as it is in its positive tenor. Consequently, a part or function which follows not a method of dialectical argumentation but a method of exposition quite exegetical and explicative. By this slant, positive theology thus understood rejoins positive theology understood in the literary sense, for it is distinguished from Scholastic theology by the "manner" and finally by the style itself. Also, a fairly large number of authors will blend or juxtapose the two notions.

The conception of positive theology taken in the literary sense is that which underlies the text of St. Ignatius cited above. It was by far its commonest meaning in the seventeenth and beginning of the eighteenth centuries. Petau himself, although he is effectively the father of positive theology in the modern sense of the word, did not define positive theology in any other terms. So with or without its label we finally come to the modern version. To what problems and to what needs did this relatively new activity answer? To two needs: Humanism and heresies.

We mentioned above the new exigencies of texts and history. Certainly, the need for their expression is paramount. Cano declared in 1560 that the people with education considered as singularly incompetent these theologians whose works contained no history.[26] History, however, was no less a stranger to the programs of intellectual formation in the sixteenth century. The seventeenth century was more blessed. Not only did it see published some very remarkable works of positive theology, those, in particular, of Petau (d. 1647) and Thomassin (d. 1695), but it saw history introduced, in more than one place, in the pedagogic regime of the clergy. Many treatises of theological methodology at this time will give considerable space to historical and scriptural studies.

Positive theology was not born solely from Humanism, but from the necessity of replying to heresies. That involved the obligation of proving the conformity of a given ecclesiastical dogma with its first sources. So the very first researches of positive theology in the Church were the collecting of texts and testimonies to be opposed to the innovators. The modern heresies were found so much more to instigate an activity of this kind, since they were presented as a radical reform of the Church and called into question its fidelity to its origins. This was the issue first of all, in the polemic with Wyclif, as we see, for example, in the *Doctrinale antiquitatum fidei Ecclesiae catholicae* of Thomas Net-

---

26. *De locis*, 1. XI, c. II.

ter, called Waldensis (d. 1431), and in that with John Huss. Positive theology was the key in the enormous effort made by the Catholics to reply to Protestantism. The activities of modern Catholicism have been conditioned in great part by the doctrinal revolt of the Reformation. Until then theology had been in peaceful possession of its sources. It received its supplies, so to speak, in the Church. It was in full tranquility that the Scholastic theologians not only drew their datum from the actual life of the Church, without growing disturbed about historical criticism, but they referred to the living Church whatever new factor they could find at any given moment in its development. This is very clear, for example, in the institution of the sacraments, question which will become crucial for the new positive theology.

Now, the authority of the Church, reduced by the Reformers to an entirely human level, will no longer suffice to justify the least tradition; and to answer the innovators on their ground, it was necessary to refer back to the ancient Church, indeed sometimes to a single text of Scripture. Hence the creation by the Catholic theologians of positive theology, on one side, and of the treatise of tradition, on the other; a double creation by which the manner of referring to the sources will be changed for theology and for the theologian, at least for the theologian who will not believe it possible purely and simply to continue Medieval Scholasticism.

The necessities we have just pointed out gave rise in the seventeenth century to innumerable treatises all orientated toward demonstrating the "perpetuity of the Faith." Before the famous book of Nicole, *Perpétuité de la foi de l'Église touchant l'eucharistie* (1669–71), which was a model for many others, we will have numerous demonstrations in the same spirit and of the same type in the course of the sixteenth century.

So it is that the effort of positive theology in the beginning was directed toward proving the conformity of the actual teaching of the Church with the biblical or patristic testimonies of the ancient Apostolic faith. This is what certain authors call "positive in sources."

(d) *Apologetics*. We are now at the epoch of dissociations. The secular world tends to recapture its independence and to think of itself as a stranger to the faith. In fact, feeling self-sufficient, it sets itself over against the faith. In politics, there are now two powers which can, as equal to equal, pass a concordat. In the matter of knowledge, there are two lights, outside of each other and each governing a world apart. Apologetics, which represents a use of reason external to the faith, though relative to it, is born of this situation and of the need to refashion the lost unity. Indeed, the project is, by using natural light to start a return to the faith by proving that the teaching of the Catholic Church represents the Revelation of God. A few decades before the epoch of which we are talking, the problem of the Reformation had brought to life a new activity of defense which, under the name of "polemics" or "controversy," was quickly constituted as a special branch of theology and ecclesiastical teaching. We will only make a simple mention of this fact. Here we are interested in apologetics only in so far as it concerns the notion of theology, that is, in so far as it has become a specialty of theology and its creation and development can influence the very conception of theology.

Apologetics will hardly constitute a separate treatise of dogmatic theology before the middle of the seventeenth century. But in the Scholastic treatises on the faith it is getting ready to branch out in two directions: first, the question of credibility, and second, the subjective certitude of faith.

The care to establish the foundations of Catholic dogma determines a new activity of reason regarding the principles of theology, which are precisely the dogmas.. There is no longer the question of elaborating the objective content of the dogmas (Scholastic theology), nor even of proving the conformity of dogma with its prime sources (positive theology), but of establishing in the eyes of reason their credibility (object of "Christian demonstration"). Thus, on one side, apologetic treatises inflate themselves with theological matter which they do not have to prove, while, on the other, theology itself before its objects often takes an attitude of apologetic preoccupation. Thus the controversy affects everything. Sometimes theology in its argumentative parts will seem to have for its object the apologetic establishment of the general truth of religion and then the particular truths of religion. The frequent substitution of the word "religion" for the word "faith" here displays its nuance. This conception—with a strong *positive* accentuation and a timid mention of the deduction of conclusions—is basically the one affirmed in Chapters I and III of Ellis du Pin's, *Méthode pour étudier Id théologie* in 1716: "All study of theology consists in looking for the means whereby we can be assured which religion is truly founded on divine Revelation and which truths are certainly revealed."

As for the question of the subjective certitude of faith, this has been extensively developed by Post-Tridentine and even contemporary theologians under the title of *analysis fidei*.

Chapter Six
From the Seventeenth Century to the Present

After having seen the new problems set before theology in the modern era, and then the effect of dissociation and specialization caused by these problems, it remains to outline the changes in the notion of theology which occurred from the seventeenth century to our time.

Theology Born of Modern Tendencies: Dogmatic and Scholastico-Dogmatic

From the standpoint of the notion of theology, it is toward the last years of the seventeenth century that the modern forms of this science are fixed. These forms spring at once from the modern movement of the Renaissance and the defensive movement of the Council of Trent. The great schools of thought which were the conventual schools or the universities are losing their renown. An important fact from the viewpoint of theology is the death of universities as centers of original thought. They are absorbed by the quarrels of Gallicanism or Jansenism, or discredit themselves in the domestication of Josephism. Nevertheless the teaching of theology continues in them as it does in the seminaries and the schools of Religious Orders. Hurter[1] points out that about 1680 these schools began replacing commentaries on St. Thomas and on the *Sentences* by courses and systematized manuals of theology in which the positive, the Scholastic, and the polemic viewpoints are all adopted at once and harmonized. Three things, which follow one another chronologically, seem to us characteristic of theology between 1680 and the end of the eighteenth

---

1. *Nomenclator,* t. IV, 3rd ed., col. 317.

century: (1) the dogmatic method; (2) the tendency to set up a "system"; (3) the pedagogic organization of theology of "Encyclopedias."

A. *The Dogmatic Method*

This springs from the new "positive" emphasis and from the need to propose for teaching, over and beyond the controversies which divide the schools, a doctrine which is acceptable to all. The idea of "dogmatic" is linked to the desire for a doctrine not subject to disputes. These will come to life anyway, but in a margin left open to liberty. This is the period when the famous formula was coined, *In dubiis libertas,* and when, for example, the Servite G.-M. Capassi publishes a book entitled, *Intellectus triumphans, in dogmaticis captivus, in scholasticis liber,* Florence, 1683.

The word *dogmaticus* already existed in theology and it had been used in opposition to *moralis* or *ethicus,* or to signify something theoretical which involved solid ideological positions and affirmations. In Catholic theology, the word, no longer employed in opposition to *ethicus* or *historiens,* but to *Scholastieus,* around 1680 seems to take on a meaning which the following text will suffice to explain: "(We understand as) dogmatic and moral, theology in which, having set aside all Scholastic questions and omitted questions of positive theology . . . only those things are treated which were defined or handed out as dogmas in the Council of Trent, or explained in the Catechism of this same council . . ."[2] The word is still used in distinction with *moralis* but it derives a very clear meaning from the common doctrine in the Church; the kind which avoids the disputes between schools and is immediately founded on the documents of the *magisterium.*

This idea of a "dogmatic" theology is allied at this epoch to quite a movement of thought regarding the notion of

---

2. Noël Alexandre, *Theologia dogmatica et moralis,* 1693, t. I, praef.

dogma and the theological *loci.* There is frequently found in the authors of this time new and complicated precisions on dogma and its different varieties. The distinctions made in 1705 by Fr. Annat in his *Apparatus ad positivam theologiam methodicus* between *dogma imperatum, liberum,* and *toleratum* are accepted by the authors. These same writers devote much care to distinguishing different kinds and different degrees of theological conclusions. Moreover, they develop quite a complicated *De locis* and devote a great deal of space to defining the different theological notes.

It is this line of the *theologia dogmatica* which will end in the modern *Dogmatics.* This will be an exposition of Catholic doctrine. Not an extremely systematic and dialectical elaboration, like the *Summa' s* of the Middle Ages, but a kind of developed "Christian doctrine" or an explanation of the datum of faith taken from positive expressions of the sources.

The courses and manuals of the period which follows 1680 frequently contain the words "dogmatico-Scholastic" in their titles. This title indicates the intention of marrying the positive element and the rational element, the explanation of the faith and the interpretation of the Schools. This is very clear, for example, in the work of Martin Gerbert. This intention commands a method. The technique of the *quaestio* was abandoned and in its place a scheme of exposition was adopted. This had already appeared in the Scholasticism of the fourteenth century and was indeed Cano's method. It does not follow a dialectical order of invention and proof, blit a pedagogical order of explanation. It involves the following steps: thesis, *status quaestionis* (that is, an exposé of opinions), positive proofs from authority, proofs from theological reason, solution of the difficulties, corollaries, and in particular corollaries for life and piety. This schema has become that of practically all our manuals.

B. *The Tendency to Set Up a "System"*

Toward the middle of the eighteenth century, theology,
especially in Germany, underwent the influence of Wolf's
philosophy. This influence is felt in content and perhaps
still more in method. Wolf accents the tendencies of those
who inspired him: Spinoza, with his *more geometrico*, Leibniz, with his *Systema theologiae*, and develops what will be
called the *systema* or the *methodus scientifica* ("scientific
method"). This is a method of geometric type characterized by research of a deductive order connecting all the
elements to a unique principle. O. Ritschl has studied the
growth of the idea of "system" and of "systematic" process
in theology, principally in Protestant theology from the
beginning of the seventeenth century to the middle of the
eighteenth. It is very probable that the example of Protestant theology, which quite early juxtaposed to the Sacred
Scriptures a "system" more intricate than the ancient Scholastic *Summa's*, influenced Catholic theology.

In the second half of the eighteenth century Catholic
theology voluntarily tries to construct itself into a "system"
by following the *methodus scientifica* of Wolf's school of
thought.

C. *The Pedagogic Organization of Theology into "Encyclopedias"*

At the same time, theology of the eighteenth century is
partial to methodological treatises. The *Introductiones*,
the *Apparatus*, the *De locis* multiply without number. The
old notion of gathering all the ideas into one *corpus* where
they would be distributed and ordered reappears and animates the movement of encyclopedias. Toward the end
of the eighteenth century and the beginning of the nineteenth century, the idea of uniting and organizing the various branches of theology into some sort of whole becomes
a reality as attested by a great number of "Encyclopedias"

or "Methodologies." These two words correspond to the ancient *De sacra doctrina,* to the *De locis,* and to the new need to distribute systematically the different branches of theology which had sometimes been divided and subdivided to excess. By this notion of systematic distribution and order deduced from a single principle, the "encyclopedia" links up with "system," as can be seen even in the title of one of the most celebrated productions of this type from the Catholic standpoint: *Enyklopädie der theologischen Wissenschaften als System der gesammten Theologie* by F. A. Staudenmaier, published in 1834.

The Apathy of Theology During the time of Philosophism

Theology penetrated by the miasma of philosophism is characterized by the inability to associate Christianity with things of the human spirit. It fails to see that, beyond the possibilities and initiatives proper to man, Christianity introduces a new order of objects which are mysteries, inaccessible to any rational discovery and once these are revealed and received into the faith, they occasion a new contemplative activity of supernatural intellectuality. The *Vemunft-theologie,* during the Enlightenment and philosophism, recaptures the intention of apologetics which had developed since the seventeenth century against the "libertines." It wishes to refashion the unity of aspirations in Christianity in a world where faith on one side, science and culture on the other form two separate planets. It wants to open a bridge from reason to religion, from science to Christianity, through the resources of reason and science. G. Hermes (d. 1831) gives to this intention a scholarly form in which the apparatus in great part is borrowed from Kant and corrected by Fichte: *Einleitung in die christkatholische*

Theologie. He defines faith in purely intellectual terms as that state of mind which setting out from positive and absolute doubt arrives at a position where it can no longer doubt. Grace of course intervenes to make efficaciously salutary the "faith" thus obtained. But the entire intellectual content of this faith, whatever the mind receives from the object and by which it conducts its vital activities, was, according to Hermes, a thing of reason. He did not see that between reason, on the one hand, preparing the way to faith by the demonstration of *the praeambula fidei* and that of the general credibility of dogma and, on the other, reason undertaking an activity in faith and on the objects of faith by theology, there was inserted a supernatural act by which the spirit was elevated to a new order of objects.

Thus Hermes shows the danger of an apologetic conceived as a demonstration of dogma such that theology could pass from one to the other with no loss of continuity. In the different types of *analysis fidei,* whenever a search was made for the act of faith itself and not merely for its rational preparations, a conscious resolution based on evidence, the investigation seemed directed toward a philosophical faith or a *Vernunfttheologie.*

Philosophism affects theology quite differently in France than it does in Germany. In France, the philosophy was strictly secular; it excluded Christianity. In Germany, Fichte, Schelling, and Hegel assumed in their system a sort of ideological double of Christianity and it had very great religious attraction. We see theologians making theological explanations of great Christian dogmas according to Hegel or Schelling. In this theology, the entire ideological and speculative side, the internal necessity and the logical sequence of mysteries, seem to set off nothing but a philosophical system which boasts a knowledge of the "Absolute." The positive side of Christianity seems to offer only an element of fact which, as such, involves no original intelligibility.

The Renewal of Theology in the Nineteenth Century and the Contemporary Period

This last part of our historic exposé is divided as follows: (1) The renewal from romantic inspiration; (2) The renewal of Scholasticism; (3) The development of positive and critical studies; (4) The crisis of ecclesiastical studies and Modernism; (5) The syntheses; (6) The tendencies and needs of today.

A. *The Renewed from Romantic Inspiration*

The romantic current in theology is the first factor to bring about reconstruction in the course of the years from 1810 to 1840. Its action promotes unity and the reintegration of the elements dissociated in the preceding period. It regains first of all a sense of the past, of the Fathers and even of Scholasticism through its interest in the Middle Ages. In this way, it begins to recapture a sense of the contemplation of truths of the faith and of speculation about them. Each of these points is very clear in the history of the Catholic school at Tübingen and in particular in the writings of J. A. Möhler (d. 1838). In this very manner, Romanticism recaptures or discovers a sense of development and history.

It also conveys a sense of connections and a viewpoint of the living organism. Thanks to this vital and organic directive, the dissociations already accredited are denounced. It is extremely impressive to see the elimination of rationalism bring with it an immediate demand for the reunion of moral and dogma. At the same time the romantic current orders an end to the separation between theology and the world and its culture. The program drawn up by Drey embraces this order. He inspires the School of Tübingen, as Lamennais does France.

Finally, Romanticism brings to theology a sense of the vital and, so to speak, of the "lived." It repeats the request ceaselessly renewed in the course of time: that of a theology allied to life, indeed of a theology in which life gives expression to itself. Let theology be allied to the gift, made by God to man, of a new, supernatural life, let it pursue its work in an ambiance of faith and piety and, in its turn, let it inspire life! But, in the romantic school of Tübingen, insufficiently freed of German philosophical and theological idealism, ite theology appears as too concretely concerned with faith as lived in the Church. The sources and objective criteria of theology are not sufficiently disengaged or elevated from the ordinary. Certainly, theology had never been defined there, as in the liberal Protestantism sprung from Schleiermacher, as an analysis and a description of religious experience. The thought of the greatest among those at Tübingen is thoroughly orthodox. But their theology is conceived too much as an intellectual realization of what the Church (and the theologian in the Church) has received and by which it lives. It is not sufficiently the human construction of a faith rising up from a datum objectively established and from objective criteria. In a word, their theology is too much a science of faith and not enough a science of Revelation.

B. *The Renewal of Scholasticism*

The eighteenth century had, on the whole, discredited Medieval Scholasticism. So it is notable that the first interventions of ecclesiastic authority in favor of Scholasticism were to defend it against the accusation or suspicion of rationalism.[3]

It does not enter into the purpose of this work to trace the history of the restoration of Scholasticism during the

---

3. Cf. the condemnation of Bonnetty, 1855; the Encyclical *Tuas libenter* of Pius IX, 1863; the 13th proposition of the *Syllabus,* Denz.-Bannw. n. 1652, 1680 and 1713.

nineteenth century, beginning with the efforts of a tradition still preserved in Spain and especially Italy, up to the Encyclical *Aeterni Patris* of Leo XIII, 4 August 1879, and to documents which have followed since. On the contrary, we should point out here what this restoration of Scholasticism means from the standpoint of its influence on the notion of theology in the nineteenth century. The seventeenth and eighteenth centuries had not eliminated Scholasticism as a method, but little by little they had seen it atrophy as an object or content of thought, because they had abandoned that which properly animated it, viz., Christian philosophy. What is most striking in the period which stretches from 1760 to about 1840 is to see theology seek its philosophical ferment not in the Christian tradition of Augustine, Thomas Aquinas, and Bonaventure, but in the miscellaneous philosophies, which by turn had their day in the sun. For example, M. Emery in his *Pensées de Descartes sur la religion et la morale,* or Fr. Valla, author of *Philosophie de Lyon,* which was followed in numerous seminaries, and of a *Theologia* which was put on the Index in 1792 looked to current philosophy for inspiration. Then there were the influences of Leibniz and Wolf, as we saw above; Kant and Fichte, who influenced Hermes; then Schelling, who inspired M. Dobmaier's *Systema theologiae dogmaticae,* P. B. Ziemer's *Theologia dogmatica.* And there was Sailer. Also there were Hegel and Schleiermacher who, in a certain measure, influenced Möhler, as Malebranche did Gerdil. There were the sensualists, empiricists, and naturalists. Locke, Condillac, and Rousseau affected Abbé Flotter, author of *Leçons élémentaires de philosophie,* followed in numerous seminaries. Finally, there was Lamennais' effect on Abbé Gerbet's *Des doctrines philosophiques sur la certitude dans leur rapports avec la théologie* (1826), and on *Coup d'oeil sur la controverse chrétienne* (1828).

Now, it is precisely *Christian philosophy* which the popes try to restore first of all in teaching, then by their doctrinal statements on the relations between science and faith, finally, by the series of documents which surround or follow the encyclical *Aeterni Patris,* whose subtitle is quite significant: "The establishment of Christian philosophy in the tradition of St. Thomas Aquinas, the Angelic Doctor, in our Catholic schools, 4 August 1879." The documents on this topic are numerous.[4]

The philosophy which the popes wish to have restored is that of the Fathers and the great medieval Doctors. In addition to *Aeterni Patris,* there were the encyclicals *Communium rerum,* 21 April 1909, for the centenary of St. Anselm; *Jucunda sane,* 12 March 1904, on St. Gregory the Great; *Doctoris seraphici,* 11 April 1904, for the reediting of the works of St. Bonaventure, etc. Nevertheless, from the encyclical *Aeterni Patris,* St. Thomas is proposed as the safest Master and the one in whose works Christian philosophy found its most perfect, elevated, and universal expression. From then, this preference becomes more precise and more efficacious: "We wish and We order," says the encyclical *Pascendi,* "that Scholastic philosophy be put at the base of the sacred sciences . . . ; and, when We prescribe Scholastic philosophy, and this is capital, what We mean by that is the philosophy which has been left us by the Angelic Doctor."[5] If the doctrine of some other author has been especially recommended, Pius X again declares, it is evident that this is done only to the degree that that doctrine agrees with the principles of St. Thomas.[6]

This *motu proprio* was followed, a month later, 27 July, by the famous twenty-four theses which state precisely the

---

4. Cf. the tables of the *Enchiridion clericomm. Documenta Ecclesiae sacrorum alumnis instituendis,* published by the Congregation of Seminaries and Universities in 1938.

5. Actes *de S.S. Pie* X, Bonne Presse, t. III, p. 160; *Enchir. cleric.,* n. 805.

6. *Motu proprio Doctoris angelici,* 29 June 1914, in *Acta apost. Sedis,* 1914, p. 338.

essential principles of St. Thomas to he held "in every philosophy school."[7] This formal promotion of St. Thomas'
thought was continued by Pius XI, not without some wise
interpretations in his encyclical *Studiorum ducem,* 29 June
1923, and the letter *Officiorum omnium* on the Seminaries,
1 August 1922. The *Codex juris canonici* obliges professors
in teaching philosophy and theology to follow "the reasoning, doctrine, and principles of the Angelic Doctor." The
constitution *Deus scientiarum* of 24 May 1931 recalls this
obligation for the faculties of philosophy as well as those
of theology. So it is that contemporary theology is developed under the aegis of St. Thomas and Scholastic philosophy. It is from them that it derives the principles and the
developed synthesis between faith and reason that it has
found wise to follow. We can really speak of a renewal of
Scholasticism. For, just as Albert the Great and St. Thomas
had already brought to theology a truly scientific outlook,
that of Aristotle, so current theology has recaptured their
heritage and has truly reintroduced into its work Scholastic
reason which is Christian philosophy.*

C. *The Development of Positive and Critical Studies*

The nineteenth century sees the definitive advent of a new
form of rational study, viz. historical and critical study: that
is, biblical critique, history of dogmas, science of religions.
Certainly all this existed before to a certain degree. In the
Catholic Church, the seventeenth century had been a great
historical century. Biblical criticism begins with Richard
Simon, and the very term "biblical theology" first appears
at the beginning of the eighteenth century. The science of
religions begins with the eighteenth century and our mis-

---

7. *Acta apost. Sedis,* 1914, pp. 383–86.
*   *Translator's Note.* Nevertheless, the Second Council of the Vatican
    has expressed itself with discretion on the duty to follow St. Thomas
    as a master (Decret. *Optatam totius Ecclesiae renovationem,* n. 16,
    1965) or as a model (Decret. *Gravissimum educationis momentum,*
    n. 10, 1965).

sionaries are not strangers to this beginning. Nevertheless, these disciplines did not then constitute a real search into the principles of theology. On the contrary, this search really began in the nineteenth century, thanks mainly to two causes: the critique grounded on comparative history; and the new viewpoint of historical development.

Up until this date the Bible had been interpreted almost exclusively by itself. The discoveries in the field of Egyptology, of Babylonian civilization and Palestinian archaeology, etc., henceforth put the sacred text into relationship with a medium where ideas and institutions had lost their character of uniqueness and individuality. Many works are published on the history of dogma, especially in Germany. And critical questions on the subject of several dogmas are considered at length; of this type the most perfect example, perhaps, is the question of the origins of penance. From all this, the result is that the assertions of the Bible, on the one hand, dogmas, which furnish theology with its principles, on the other, are the object of new interpretations and discussions, and seem to lose their character of absolute verity that seemed to be essential.[8]

So by this very fact the idea of historical development demands serious consideration. An idea or an institution bears in its very fabric a date and it is not the same in the first, the thirteenth, or the nineteenth century. However, it may be noted that the idea of development was integrated by both the philosophers and theologians into their respective systems. This is true, for example, of Hegel and Möhler and the Catholic theologians of Tübingen, as well as Strauss and Renan. Independent of these influences and in a much purer atmosphere, we have the example of Newman. This viewpoint, which applied just as well to Revelation, as to the history of Israel, to Christianity, its dogmas and its

---

8. On the rise of critical and historical studies in the nineteenth century, see A. Briggs, *History of the Study of Theology*, London, 1916, t. II, p. 189 sq.

institutions, would have to be given a place in the theological sciences.

Under these influences, the task of ancient historical or positive theology faced new conditions. There could no longer be question of justifying by old texts the actual doctrines or institutions, after the manner of the old positive approach, as seen in the *Perpétuité de la foi*. Nothing points out better the difference in perspective between the old manner of research and the modern than the confrontation of these two texts which Mgr. Batiffol quotes in the *Bulletin de littérature ecclésiastique*. Bossuet: "Catholic truth, having sprung from God, has first of all his perfection"; Newman: "No doctrine is complete from its birth, for there is none which the researches of faith or the attacks of heresy cannot help to develop." In Newman's time, the ancient conception of things was represented by Perrone, then by Franzelin, for whom a knowledge of texts had no other purpose than to furnish matter for proof and sometimes even simply for citations to "back up" "theses" in speculative theology according to a scheme, worked out by Perrone, of a triple probation: *Probatur ex Scriptura, ex Traditione, ex ratione*. But now positive work was considered as pure historical research which aimed at knowing the past from extant documents which would help determine past facts. Such work is pure history. What would be its situation with regard to theology and what would happen if its results did not agree with the exigencies of the sacred science? The crisis had to begin sooner or later. The problem had to be debated at the time of the Modernist crisis, under the form of discussions on the true nature of positive theology, on its relations with speculative theology and on the liberty of historical research.[9]

---

9. Lee M. McGrath, *The Vatican Council on the Evolution of Dogma*, Rome, 1955; O. Chadwick, *From Bossuet to Newman: The Idea of Doctrinal Development*, Cambridge, 1957.

D. *The Crisis in the Teaching of Theological Sciences and Modernism*

In face of the new needs, the state of teaching and of Catholic works in the realm of religious sciences left much to be desired. The manuals of theology, skeletal résumés of works of the preceding epoch, were almost totally foreign to the new needs. Moreover the last years of the nineteenth century and the first of the twentieth were to see quite a literature produced on the programs of ecclesiastical studies and their readaptation. The claims in this field touched at times merely the form and the style rather than the heart of the matter but they also asked some questions of structure which benefited history, the positive sciences, and science as such. Sometimes, too, we have to admit there was displayed a certain ignorance of speculative values and Scholasticism.

We see the same state of things at the origin of the Modernist crisis. We mention this only because and insofar as it concerns the conception of theology in that day. The Modernist crisis was born of attempts made by diverse Catholic scholars or thinkers to solve the questions raised by the inadequacy it was thought there existed between the texts or facts and the corresponding ecclesiastical doctrines. Addressing themselves to these problems, the Modernists are going to study the bases of religious knowledge and then the principles of theology. They will do this by presenting in the name of history a critical reduction of whatever this knowledge contains that is objectively absolute. This will offer a new way of justifying the agreement between doctrinal affirmations and historically known facts. In every case this new manner will consist in replacing the relation of objective homogeneity of the dogmatic concepts and theological notions, on one side, and the primitive state of the datum, on the other, by a relation of symbol to reality. The Modernists always dissect the primitive fact, separating its divine and hence absolute value from its intellectual expression, considered as relative, variable, and subject to the vicissitudes of history. The result is that the Modernists are united in their common criticism of intellectualism and Scholasticism.

One of the misfortunes of the Modernists was that they did not know how to distinguish theology and dogma. Certainly at that time the distinction for all practical purposes was not as clear as it is today. This was one of the benefits of the Modernist crisis. With Tyrrell and M. LeRoy especially, the confusion is flagrant. They want—and rightly so—to avoid any tie between the absolute of faith or Revelation and the theology of St. Thomas or in general the theology of the thirteenth century, with its particular type of intellectualism, its conceptual and philosophical apparatus, etc. But, to reject this particular theology, they think they must disengage the revealed facts and dogma itself from all properly intellectual content and value.

Theology in this perspective can no longer be the scientific construction and human elaboration of revealed statements. It is an interpretation, a scientific construction, a human elaboration of Christian affirmations and it is no more than that. Between it, and what proceeds from God to man and is called Revelation, there is no longer that continuity of objective and speculative content on which theology must live and without which it cannot exist as theology. Revelation, in the opinion of M. Loisy, is nothing but human, religious intuitions springing up as part of man's effort in search for the true and the perfect. Dogma is only the authorized explanation of primitive assertions of the "faith," that is to say, of the religious consciousness. In Tyrrell's opinion, Revelation is a "prophetic" phenomenon, an internal ethic. The Church's guardianship of this deposit is merely a custody of the heritage of an inspiration. The dogmatic formulas which come to light in the course of centuries are only a useful expression of that which we are led to think conforms to the spirit of Christ. Between them and the primitive, revealed fact, the relation is not that of a formula to an objective and intellectually definite datum, but that of a formula born of the needs of a given time and adapted to them and to a spirit, that is the Christian spirit which dwells in each believer and animates the entire Church.

Modernism with considerable acuteness set before Catholic theology the twofold problem, first, of its homogeneity, when taken in its scientific and rational form, with Revelation, and second, of its relation to its positive sources, henceforth subject to historical and critical methods, viz., the Bible, ancient and progressively developing traditions and institutions.

E. *Syntheses in the Line of Tradition*

A new and fruitful effort in theological methodology was the product of Catholic reaction to the Enlightenment and semirationalism, and then to Modernism.

The pontificate of Pius IX was orientated against rationalism and naturalism. It affirmed (1) the supernatural order and, in the order of thought, matters of the faith; (2) relations of subordination and harmony between reason and faith, human intelligence and the divine magisterium. These affirmations promulgated at the first Council of the Vatican were to assure theology of a status in conformity with its true nature and what it had been in the Catholic tradition. It is in this perspective that we find Franzelin (d. 1885) direct collaborator with the Vatican Council; M. J. Scheeben (d. 1888); in France J.-B. Aubry (d. 1882) who follows Franzelin; J. Didiot (d. 1903); C. Labeyrie, who follows Scheeben and Didiot, etc. All these authors labor to recapture the grand theological tradition, to regain a synthesis enriched by modern needs and contributions but based on the patristic and medieval synthesis both in type and inspiration. This is a state of affairs, in which reason is not separated from faith but organically bound to it, in which the different parts of theology regroup themselves and articulate together in a living unity. With these authors as with the Vatican Council, the *understanding* of theology is to be sought from the side of faith, which is turned directly toward Revelation and the Word of God.

This is particularly true of M. J. Scheeben. It is in a very rich and lucid view of the supernaturalism of the faith that this author has drawn up his notion of theology. His notion of faith itself is integrated with his theology of the supernatural, of the new being which grace gives to the children of God. This is indeed the traditional line of *Fides quaerens intellectum.* Theology is a knowledge which proceeds from this gift of light, from this new look opening on the world of supernatural objects, which constitutes faith. Its very order is that of faith. As when he says it is "only the knowledge developed from faith."[10] Its first role is to bring the faith, by expressing and explaining it in the intelligence of man, to a firmer, more luminous, more intimate, and more personal state. The first activity of theology and the first stage of its development is the deepening of faith by the *understanding* which we take from it. All the later development of theology into a *science* of faith depends on this first *intellectus.* All the intelligibility of theological science comes to it from man's intelligence of the thing revealed. The science of faith is principally constituted by an effort to discover and organize into a doctrinal corpus the connections which the revealed mysteries have with themselves and the truths of the natural world. Scheeben insists much on this point by which theology seems to him to merit the name of science.

This search for connections and this penetration into the internal logic of the mysteries is a work of reason seeking *cur res sit vel esse debeat* ("why a thing is or should be"). In other words, the internal and external possibility of the mystery, the "why" of its realization. In this work, reason assumes and puts to work the natural knowledges and analogies borrowed from our world. If Scheeben does not exclude all possibility of theological conclusions in the modern sense

---

10. *Dogmatik*, n. 957.

of the term, he does not make the deduction of conclusions the principal and proper object of theological work. Rather he sees this object as the interpretation of revealed truths and their construction into an organized whole.

Finally, to establish itself in this way as a science of faith, theology must have a certain activity aimed at setting up the propositions of faith. By this function theology seeks to establish: (1) that the dogmatic teachings proposed by the Church are truly contained in the divine sources of Revelation; (2) that the proposal which the Church makes of these teachings is really based on a divine mission. This is the positive or apologetic-dogmatic function of theology. Positive theology then is that activity by which theology establishes the agreement of ecclesiastical teaching (which is its immediate datum) with the sources in which Revelation is presented and transmitted to us.

On the matter of theological methodology, it is also a synthesis and of an inspiration similar to that of Scheeben, which Fr. A. Gardeil brought out in his *Le donné révélé et la théologie,* 1910. It is much more than a polemic or an apologetic tied to the difficulties of the moment, for Fr. Gardeil rose to the very principles of religious knowledge, both dogmatic and theological. On truly structural points the *Donné révélé* reestablished theology in its proper status: the homogeneity of theological work relative to revealed truths; a unity which integrates the two great disciplines, positive and speculative theology; the definition of "positive" as a theological function and work on its principles conducted under the guidance of faith; the distinction between science and theological systems; the full rational value and full religious value of theological work. Several contemporary works, quite notable in their theological methodology, spring from Fr. Gardeil's volume. This is particularly true of Fr. Marin-Sola's *La evolución homogénea del dogma católico* (1923), which develops and systematizes, with regard to the problem of the growth of dogma and theological conclusions, Fr. Gardeil's main idea on the homogeneity of theology with dogma and of dogma with primitive Revelation.

F. *The Problems, the Tendencies, and the Tasks of Today*

For the past forty years or so, theology, more than ever, is inquiring about itself, its object, methods, possibilities, and place among the other disciplines. It would seem that this effort can be characterized as follows. After having had its very existence called into question and made a groping return, theology seeks a unity over and above the dissociations introduced by Nominalism, the Reformation, theology of the seventeenth century, Rationalism, and Modernism. It wants a unity similar to that which it enjoyed in its golden days of the Middle Ages, yet at the same time enriched by the addition of data, questions, new methods, and by the compilation and assimilation of the auxiliary disciplines which have sprung up since the Middle Ages. At the same time, theology better realizes its dependence with regard to the ecclesiastical community and its magisterium.

The turning point when theology starts reflecting on itself has had two principal points of application: the question of the scientific value of theology and the status of positive theology.

It was tragic that since the fifteenth century the scientific value of theology had been persistently denounced. Nevertheless the turning point came about only when Christians—and not merely unbelievers—raised the question whether a discipline feudalized to one faith and one orthodoxy could still be counted among the sciences and, as such, be taught in the universities. It is in Germany and in Protestant circles that the question was broached by C. A. Bernouilli's famous book, *Die wissenschaftliche und die kirchliche Methode in der Theologie* (1897), to which Overbeck, Lagarde, Duhm, and Well-hausen gave their vote of approval. It was Bernouilli's plan to distinguish two theologies: one liberated from all ecclesiastical control, free in its research and worthy of the name of science; the other adapted to the practical finality of clerical education and under the guidance of the Churches. The problem thus posed did not fail to arouse the Catholic theologians. So in recent years they were very careful to justify the scientific quality of their discipline, to defend the uniqueness and value of religious knowledge, to find a proper place for theology in the ensemble of scientific disciplines. On this last point one of the most original and certainly most successful efforts is that of G. Rabeau. Using Stuart Mill's "collocation" theory he was able to justify the existence and define the status, object, and method of theology as a science in an order of facts, complete with its own ontological and epistemological specifications.

However, the problem of theological status these past years has been especially concerned with positive theology. The necessity of giving greater consideration to the original datum, plus the manifold results acquired during the nineteenth century in the positive domain caused a lengthy discussion on the nature of positive theology. Some of the topics debated were: the place of positive research in theology; the consequent necessary reform of this latter; the place—if any—to be reserved for Scholastic theology. For many authors the problem henceforth was to set theology under the sign of "positive," as up to then it had been under that of "Scholastic." Several of the studies devoted to the debate on the "positive" are rather defenses of Scholasticism which was disowned and rejected by others as the embarrassing heritage of a dead age. Some authors devoted themselves to the question of the status and method of positive inquiry over against theological work. Those who had been formed in historical disciplines were tempted to call positive theology a simple historical inquiry into doctrines and Christian institutions. It is thus that Mgr. Battiffol thought it sufficient to reply to Fr. Laberthonnière's objections: "Our studies which are historical by their method, are theological by their object."[11] In this way positive theology was given a *lumen sub quo* and hence a method of a purely historical and natural order. And so the new discipline was called "historical theology" or "patristic theology" or "history of dogmas," with hardly any discrimination of the different kinds of knowledge contained under these diverse headings.

It is the intervention of Fathers Lemonnyer and Gardeil which at this time contributed the most to pointing out the need for a formally theological viewpoint in the definition of the object and method of positive theology insofar as it is distinct from a *history* of dogmas. At the same time Fr. Gardeil proposed the idea of a "regressive method" as characteristic of positive theology.

This reflective effort both on the status of theology as a science and on the proper requirements of a positive *theology* went with equal courage into contemporary theology. There was also an emphasis on the essential connection which exists between theology and the magisterium of the Church. This seems to have been one of the benefits of recent discussions on how best to understand the implications of the ecclesiastical magisterium in the work of positive theology. It is in this sense that already in Franzelin's *De divina Traditione et Scriptura*, 1870, and then in the work of more recent years, positive theology has become more and more conscious of the *ecclesiastical* character of its method. This accentuation of the relationship between the *sacra doctrina* in its positive function and the magisterium of the Church was consecrated by the encyclical *Humani generis*, 1950. For several years prior to that encyclical this relationship had been reenforced by studies on tradition which went far to restore its ancient ecclesiastical meaning—so well understood by Möhler. The datum of theology is tradition. This means whatever the Apostolic preaching

---

11. *Questions d'enseignement supérieur*, p. 149.

delivers to each generation, and the treasure constituted by that preaching in its development through space and time.

But the most notable feature of the present idea of theology comes from the effort made to surmount the dissociations which arose after the fifteenth century and to integrate the acquisitions of positive technics into the theological structure. The two great dissociations are, on the one hand, that which Nominalism and the Reformation favored, between human cognition and faith, and, on the other, that which theology of the seventeenth century started between theology and moral, theology and mysticism or the spiritual life. They both proceed from an insufficient comprehension of the true nature of faith. It is only when the contemplative character of faith has been grasped that it can be seen as the principle of a new system of knowledge inside which theology is constructed. Only then can we assign to theology the direction of human life and the study of spiritual life in the entire extent of its development. Finally, only then can we comprehend the union of the positive and speculative functions of theology and establish, in the conditions of *our* faith, the social and ecclesiastical status of the "positive."

With some authors the tendency to restore the connection of theology with the values of faith and life in the Church veers toward a theology immediately and intrinsically allied with life as its source of inspiration. In Germany, the tendency has always been very strong to unite and almost to fuse together life and theology, knowledge and experience. Recently this movement has taken on new vigor in the current supplied by *Lebenstheologie.* Another source of supply comes from the liturgical movement which advocates a return to the Fathers and to a form of theology which would be living contemplation as much as intellectual speculation. All this links up with the growing tendency to consider the deposit of faith as immanent to the life of the Christian community and theological work as akin *to Christ* and allied to "life in Christ."

Finally, one of the tasks of contemporary theology is properly to absorb, without detracting from its unity or the laws of its work, the data of auxiliary sciences and, in particular, of documentary and positive techniques, viz., exegesis, archaeology, epigraphy, history of dogmas and institutions, science of religions, philosophy of religion, psychology, etc. In these areas there is still much to do. During the Modernistic period many points were formulated on these topics which have not yet received a satisfactory answer.

The Speculative Notion of Theology

A. *Data and Indications of the Magisterium*

The magisterium of the Church gives us a definite teaching on theology, its bases, rule, law, or method. We will confine ourselves, as do the *Enchiridion symbolorum* of Denzinger and the *Enchiridion clericorum,* to the acts of the great Councils and especially to those of the Apostolic See. Their interventions have reference to three great crises in religious thought: (i) the introduction of Aristotelian philosophy at the beginning of the thirteenth century[12]; (2) the semirationalism of the nineteenth century, condemnation of Hermes, Günther, and Froschammer[13]; (3) and finally, the Modernist crisis and the problems or renewal of problems which it involved.[14] After this crisis an attempt was made to reform and improve ecclesiastical teaching. In this connection there are a certain number of recent documents to be found in the *Enchiridion clericorum. Documenta Ecclesiae sacrorum ahimnis instituendis,* Rome, 1938; in particular see the constitution *Deus scientiarum Dominus,* which in 1931 determined the status of the teaching of sacred sciences in ecclesiastical universities.

---

12. Ab *Aegyptüs* of Gregory IX in 1228, *Denz.* 442 sq.
13. Letter of Pius IX to the Archbishop of Munich, Council of the Vatican, *Denz.* 1618 sq., 1634 sq., 1655 sq., 1666 sq., 1679 sq.
14. Encyclicals *Pascendi* and *Communium rerum, Denz.* 208–687 and 2120.

Since then the papal magisterium has intervened in the context of what has abusively been called "the new theology," in the form of various allocutions of Pius XII and of *Humani generis*.[15] The Pope warned against an infatuation for the ancient status of questions and formulas, against a certain historical or philosophical relativism, against the idle talk of putting everything into question, against a misguided irenicism. He recalled the fact that theologians should submit even to the ordinary magisterium; next, he emphasized the value of dogmatic formulas, even when recognized as perfectible, and the value of the traditional theological language.[16] Finally, he expressed the desire that serious research be encouraged.

John XXIII from his first encyclical recalled the legitimacy of diverging opinions and the liberty of discussion, while still preserving the communion of faith.[17] Then, in his opening discourse at the Vatican Council II, he stressed the necessity of study and of presenting the doctrine "according to the methods of research and presentation used by modern thought. On one side is the substance of the ancient doctrine contained in the deposit of faith, on the other is its formulation which is guided in its forms and proportions by the needs of a magisterium essentially pastoral."[18] Vatican Council II has followed this program. It has well absorbed the presentations of recent theology. It has not fashioned a new charter for theology, but it urges an opening for research and questions of the world as it is today.

Briefly, here are some of the arrangements relative to theology contained in these documents. The basis or the source of theology is not rational evidence but supernatural

---

15. AAS, t. XLII, p. 561 sq.; *Denz.* 3875–99.
16. "What in the first case (Gregory IX), by reason of its novelty, gave rise to disquiet in the Church, is precisely, in the second case (Pius XII), what the magisterium is trying to favor." Schillebeeckx, *Révélation et théologie*, 1965, p. 125.
17. *Ad Petri cathedram*, 1959, AAS, t. LI, 1959, p. 513.
18. AAS, t. LIV, 1962.

faith in the mysteries revealed by God[19]; its soul, says Leo XIII, is Sacred Scripture.[20] The encyclical *Pascendi* insists on the error which would try to subordinate theology to a religious philosophy and its positive aspect to pure historical criticism. The rule of theological thought is the teaching of the Church and the tradition of the Fathers.[21] Theologians must be on guard against the dangers of innovation, not only in thought, but even in expression.[22] Finally, medieval Scholastic theology is formally defended and shown not to be out of date nor inclined to rationalism.[23] Moreover, while affirming the necessity of a positive method, its limits are marked, and the necessity of an adjoining speculative method is affirmed with greater force.[24] At last, after having the dangers pointed out and the errors condemned, we are given a positive formula of what could be called the status of the charter of theology:

> Reason, enlightened by faith, when it dedicates itself to research with zeal, piety, and moderation, can, with the help of God, arrive at a very fruitful understanding of mysteries, by using the analogy of realities already known to our spirit, as well as by considering the links which the mysteries have between themselves and with human destiny. Nevertheless, our reason will never come to know these things in the way it knows the truths which constitute its proper object. . .[25]

In the *Adnotationes* of various theologians to the text of the preparatory schema (for Vatican Council I), which corresponds to the above definitive text, we read some

---

19. *Denz.* 1619, 1642, 1656, 1669 sq.
20. *Enchir.* cler. 515; also *Spiritus Paraclitus* of Benedict XV, and the constitution *Dei Verbum* of Vatican II.
21. *Denz.* 1657, 1666 sq., 1679.
22. *Denz.* 320, 442 sq., 1657–58, 1680, 1800 (where it is shown that tradition does not exclude progress).
23. *Denz.* 1652, 1713; *Enchir.* cler. 414 sq., 423, 602, 1132, 1156.
24. *Enchir.* cler. 86, 1107, 1133 sq., 1156.
25. Vatican II, sess. III, c. IV, *Denz.* 1796.

precisions which, though they do not emanate from the dogmatic authority of the hierarchy, are nonetheless specially authorized:

> Any purely philosophical knowledge or science of the mysteries is excluded. . . . But there is another science which proceeds from principles revealed and believed by faith, and which is based on these principles. Far be it from us to exclude such a knowledge (*intelligentia*), which constitutes a great part of sacred theology. In this latter, faith being supposed, one function is to find out how the truths are proposed in Revelation and this is positive theology (as they say). Next, still assuming certain truths and rational principles, we arrive (*deducitur*) at a certain *analogical* intelligence of the things known by Revelation and of what they are in themselves. This is *Fides quaerens intellectum* and is our speculative theology. In this discipline, it is the meaning of dogmas, as found in Revelation and declared by the Church, which is the norm of this work of purification and thinning down (*expoliendae*), which the philosophical notions must undergo before being applied to our understanding (*intelligentia*) of the mysteries. The Fathers and Catholic theologians have always practiced this form of moderation. Inversely, it is not in the purely natural notions of philosophy that we should try to find a meaning of the dogmas different from what we find in Revelation as the Church comprehends and proposes it. This is the reason for the dictum "In religious things, human reason and philosophy must not reign, but serve."[26]

In these recent documents the necessity of a careful philosophical preparation for theology is underlined, as well as the role which philosophical disciplines are expected to play in the very constitution of that theology.

---

26. Mansi-Petit, *Council*, t. I, col. 84–85; Th. Granderath, *Constitutiones digmat. S. oec. concilii Vaticam . . .*, Freiburg-im-B., 1892, p. 90.

Idea and Definition of Theology

A. Birth and Necessity of Theology: Philosophy, Faith, and Theology

We must begin by situating theology in the general economy of our knowledge of God. This comprehends divine knowledge, human knowledge, and theandric knowledge. God is knowable in two ways: according to His manner of knowledge and according to our manner of knowledge, each nature having its own mode of knowledge, determined by its connatural object.[27]

God, Who is Being itself and the perfect Infinite, has Himself as a proper and connatural object. The mode of His knowledge is to know Himself intuitively and all other things flowing from Him and in Him as participations of Himself. Divine knowledge follows in this manner: it is the created, the order *in se* of things, and their intelligibility.

Our connatural objects, which is at the level of our own ontology, is the quiddity of sensible things, the nature of physical objects. Our knowledge goes from the exterior to the interior, from things less primary and less intelligible in themselves to realities more primary and more intelligible. It is thus that we come to know God, as the efficient, exemplary, and final cause of sensible things, in an analogous type of knowledge, which is based on our connatural object, viz. the quiddity of sensible things. It seems that since the fifteenth century the name of "natural-theology" has been given to that knowledge of God which we have from reason, starting with our knowledge of created things.

The knowledge which God has of Himself is communicated to men by grace. It is perfect in so far as that is pos-

---

27. Cf. St. Thomas, In *I^{um} Sent.*, prol., a. 1 sol. and ad 1um; a. 3, sol. 1; In II^{um}, prol.; *In Boet. de Trin.* prol., q. II, a. 2; q. V, a. 4; *Cont. Gent.* 1. I, c. III and VIII; 1. II, c. IV; 1. IV, c. I; *Sum. Theol.*, I^{a}, q. XII, a. 12.

sible for creatures—and after a manner which permits of degrees—in the beatific vision. It is imperfect in our knowledge through supernatural faith. Faith is "a reality of things for which one hopes, a firm assurance of things which one does not see," *Hebr.* 11, 1. It is a perceptive power of objects or rather of the Object connatural to God Himself. But, if it is a "firm assurance," if it is the germ of the "vision," and if as of now it has *in se* the potentiality to attain the mystery of God Himself as an Object, it must be remembered that the knowledge of faith is conditioned in us by an exterior communication of objects, which operate according to Revelation. God unveils Himself to us and speaks to us of Himself. He does this in a manner proportionate to our human condition, that is, on one side, according to a collective or social manner, on the other, in a language of men, in images, concepts, and judgments like our own. In the world of our natural knowledge, God chooses things, concepts, and words, which He knows and guarantees for us by that very fact to be the truthful signs of His own mystery. So it is that across the images, concepts, and judgments of the same type and extraction as ours, our faith survives and adheres in God Himself, Who is our total destiny. It is only in the images, concepts, and formulas of Revelation and dogma that faith can perceive its object. But across the precariousness and insufficiency of verbal veils which reveal God only imperfectly, faith tends to a less imperfect perception of God.

This reaching up to a more complete perception of divine Truth operates in the heart of a believing man who is sensitive to God's approaches. In this way the believer achieves God's work by vitally joining his activity to the gift he has received. Thus we see born a third knowledge of God which is not purely divine or purely human, but divino-human or theandric. This is no longer the purely philosophical knowledge of God, obtained solely by our personal efforts and limited to what we creatures say about Him. Nor is it the properly divine knowledge communicated in the intuitive vision and, here below, in an inchoative and imperfect manner in the act of faith. It is a knowledge, which starting from faith and completely exploiting this gift, tends, by an effort in which man gives God's grace an active response, to perceive better the divine Object already made present by grace and the propositions of faith.

But this effort of perceiving the revealed Object can be done in two different ways, which are also the two ways of dogmatic progress. It can be done on the way of supernatural contemplation, based on an affective union with God. Or it can be done by way of theological contemplation, based on an activity of knowledge of the rational and discursive type. These two ways are characterized by two different manners of possessing the principle, which is God in His supernatural mystery. In the first case, the soul possesses the principle and is united to it by way of experience. The soul penetrates the object of faith to a greater extent by charity. It is not so much that the soul works on the mystery of God, as it is this mystery which works on the soul interiorly rendering it vitally agreeable, conformed, and sympathetic. In the theology of St. Thomas this activity of perception in a vital manner is attributed to the gifts of the Holy Spirit, especially to the gifts of intelligence and wisdom.

In the second way, man possesses God in His mystery, no longer in the order of vital connaturality, but in that of cognition, which is an order of *intentional* conformity with the object. The penetration of this object is done in a work which is properly rational and in which we are active and no longer passive and in which each can profit from the work of others and communicate his own acquisitions. Love, certainly, enters into this work but only as it is in every activity, namely, as a motive. Formally, the penetration of the object is made by rational activity, according to the laws and methods of intelligence or more precisely, of reason. It is in this latter order which theology belongs, for here is properly intellectual contemplation and a rational mode of presenting the faith. It is quite certain that if we must distinguish theology and mysticism on their rational formalities, it remains forever true that the theologian will find, and this for his own theological work, an incomparable profit in being both a rational and a mystic. God alone speaks well of God. It helps to study the things of God and to speak about them, to live the things of God. In theological contemplation faith is developed and radiates in the man according to his mode, which we presume to be rational and discursive. It develops and radiates in his reason, there taking the form and obeying the needs of human wisdom. As to these needs, there are two which will give a proper shape to theology: (1) a need of order; (2) a need of unity in the objects of knowledge.

1. NEED OF ORDER AND HIERARCHY. On the one hand, God has made all things with order and measure. This order proceeds from the creative science of God. From the science of God this order passes not only into His works, but into His Word which communicates to us something of this science. Thus, while we decipher something from the order of creation and the science of God in the "book of nature," we receive another knowledge in Revelation to which we adhere by faith. Now this faith is that of a man whose reason brings him objects which have legitimate claims to intelligibility and order. Faith does not have the competence of pure reason but, however he receives it, once man opens his heart to it, it demands of him complete submission and occupies his whole being including his reason. The mind then cannot refuse to accept it, and since it can no longer renounce the claims of light and order which it has received from God as its constitutive law, it is obliged then to bring into the consideration of new objects of knowledge, which faith has brought into our ken, its own native needs of intelligibility and order. And these are needs which God's work,

God's Word, Revelation, and faith have the wherewithal to satisfy. What is quite simply given to man for his salvation, his reason, now believing, will consider in its own manner, will explicitate, translate into concepts and definitions conformed to its needs. Above all it will construct it into an ordered body of truths and statements in which what is first in intelligibility will be given as foundation to that which is second. In this way the hierarchy of the intelligible reconstructs itself in an order which, by seeking all indications both in reality and Revelation, forces it to reproduce the order of the creative science of God. We will see shortly in what this program is engaged.

2. NEED OF UNITY. The second need is still common to faith and reason. It is that of unity in the objects of knowledge. On the one hand, reason cannot admit the theory of the double truth. What is certain and demonstrated by human reason in the order of speculative truth cannot be denied or contradicted by faith. Therefore the mind will always seek to set up a certain unity with the knowledge it holds from its evidences or demonstrations and the new contribution of objects and statements for which faith is the source. If it is revealed that God made Himself man, it will strive to think through this mystery with whatever it knows of man. And similarly it will apply to the Sacraments, to evangelical morality, to the theory of justification, etc., the different notions which seem connected to the realities which are held by faith.

Now, on the other hand, faith itself is no less exacting of unity in knowledge. In fact, in the believer, it is not a separate realm or like a new specialty which comes as an addition to others but remaining separate from them. True, it is a novelty, but it is also total and, modifying man in his entirety, it tends to subordinate and annex to itself whatever there is of sound and certain knowledge as, for example, the basic principles of moral activity. And, again, God cannot

reveal Himself through faith as having become man without the authentic certitudes of the human mind concerning
human nature being subordinated to that Revelation and
without demanding to enter with the revealed mystery into
an order of knowledge which is *one*.

Of course, the confrontation between revealed and rational truths necessarily involves at least apparent difficulties.
Now the believer has to set his reason in good relations
with his faith, and, with regard to Christian teaching, to get
it started on an activity of defense which is a new form or
way of applying reason to matters of faith. Under these different headings revealed teaching develops and branches
out in human reason as such and tends to take a properly
rational, discursive, and scientific form which is theology.

The Light of Theology and the Different Forms of the Activity of Reason in Faith

Having seen its genesis and thereby its necessity, we can
define the light proper to theology, its *lumen sub quo*. It
is supernatural Revelation received in faith insofar as it
expresses and develops itself in a human intellectual life of
a rational and scientific form. From the time of Bañez, St.
Thomas' commentators call it *Revelatio virtualis* ("virtual
Revelation"). Properly speaking, then, it is neither the light
of reason, for theology lives only from faith; nor is it the
light of faith, for theology is built up by a rational activity
being applied to the datum of faith. But it is a light which
is formed by the vital and organic union of the two. In
short the light of faith insofar as it joins with that of reason, informs and directs it and uses it to construct its object
into a body of doctrines of rational and scientific form. This
use of reason in the faith, which is the work of theology, is
performed in different manners, which we will set down
briefly.

A. *Establishment of the "Praeambula Fidei"*

A first manner is to furnish rigorous rational demonstrations of the preambles of faith: the existence of God, unity of God, creation *ex nihilo,* immortality of the soul, etc.[28]

B. *Defense of Christian Truths*

A second manner concerns the defense of Christian truths and it admits of two different activities. One activity is applied to demonstrating the rational credibility of Catholic dogma and the magisterium taken in their ensemble. A second activity is applied to defending each one of these dogmas in particular.

The first activity makes a special part of theology its object, apologetics or fundamental theology. The second is divided over the entire length of theology. It amounts to this, in effect: after having rationally contemplated and constructed them, it now defends each of the dogmas in particular against the objections of reason or the human sciences. In this activity of particular defense, theology cannot bring forth rigorous, positive, and direct proofs of the truth of the mysteries. It can only suggest the rational suitability of these mysteries, and show, by solving the proposed objections, that it is not absurd to hold the truth of these things by faith. We have the same activity in another direction when the magisterium intervened to condemn Rosmini for trying to demonstrate indirectly the possibility of the Trinity.[29]

C. *Construction of the Revealed Truths*

But by far the most important manner in which rational activity applies to Christian doctrine has to do with the intellectual construction of the mysteries into a body of

---

28. St. Thomas, In *Boet. de Trin.,* q. II, a. *3, In IIIum Sent.,* dist. XXIV, a. 1, sol. l.
29. *Denz.* 1915.

doctrine. For the mysteries are coherent relative to each other and coherent also with the natural realities and the certain statements of reason. It is as a result of this connection of the mysteries among themselves and of this kind of proportion which they have with the things we know, that theology exists. Under the name of "analogy of faith" these relations inspire the charter given by the Council of the Vatican to theological labor.[30]

1. ROLE OF ANALOGY. "(Reason) has some understanding of the mysteries from the analogy of those things which it knows naturally." There is no question here of demonstrating the mysteries. But since these are known by faith, there is hope of procuring some understanding by having recourse to the things, laws, and relations which are rationally known to us and with which the mysteries have a certain similitude or proportion. Justification for this rests entirely on the validity of analogical knowledge and, hence, partly, on the relative or proportional unity of the natural and supernatural world, and, partly, on the transcendent range of human cognition.

This second point is a question of philosophy. In part, the first is also, since it is tied to our notion of being, to the claims and justification of that idea. But it is also a theological truth, flowing from Revelation. First, from the very fact of a Revelation formulated in notions and terms borrowed from our world of knowledge. Secondly, from certain significative affirmations in Sacred Scripture according to which the God Who is Revealer and Savior, the God of faith and the new life is also and identically He Who created the world of our natural knowledge and lives.[31] Even though the supernatural world is constituted by an entirely new participation in the intimate life of God, the two creations do not cease to be both of them *being*; both too are participations in God and hence not only

30. *Providentissimus, Denz.* 1943; "Oath against Modernism," *Denz.* 2146.
31. Cf. Hebr., I, 1 sq., and John I, 1 sq.

cannot completely contradict each other, but are bound together by a certain order.

This is why man's reason can truly unite with supernatural faith and become a new and original power of knowledge, which is no longer simple faith, for it reasons, nor is it simple reason, for it applies its activity to an object held because of supernatural faith, but which is theological reason.

2. CONNECTION OF THE MYSTERIES. For the understanding which the believing reason can obtain from mysteries with the aid of God, the Church attaches great importance to the contemplation of the relations which these mysteries have among themselves and with the final goal of man.

As a matter of fact when we look for what gives fullness and scope to the dogmatic and moral writings of the Fathers, we find that it is principally their sense of the connection and living harmony of the dogmas. They have had this sense, because they lived and thought in the Church, because they wrote in answer to the needs of its life, and because in this way they reflected in their works the consciousness which the Church has of its faith. When the Fathers expound a point of Sacred Scripture or of Catholic doctrine, we have the feeling that all the rest, which they are not setting forth, is present in the particular point they are treating.

The more scientific form which theology received from the great Scholastics is necessarily more analytic than were the writings of the Fathers. Less allied to the immediate life of the Church, this form is more purely scientific or didactic. Partly because it is a more erudite elaboration of doctrines and partly because it is a more fragmented distribution of these same doctrines, theology in its scientific form renders the contemplation of mysteries more difficult. In some manuals issued by a generally debased Scholasticism, the doctrines have often been divided into "theses" and presented in a packaged, inorganic state. Theologians of the value of Scheeben attach great importance to the organic presentation of doctrines. This need was satisfied by the great Scholastics. It found satisfaction in their concern for a complete approach and in their determination of the unity of matter or "subject" of theology.

It would take too long to show how the admirable plan of St. Thomas' *Summa* meets these needs. But it is certain that the plan of the *Sentences*, first of all, based on the Augustinian categories of *res et signa* ("things and signs") and *frui et uti* ("enjoy and use"), and then the other systematic treatises, *Compendia* or *Summae,* have been and remain the elements of the *intellectus fidei* ("understanding of faith"), by the harmony which they disclose and express between the revealed mysteries. The mystery of the Incarnation, for example, can be understood as the achievement and the means of our return to the arms of the Father and it can thus be seen in relation to the mysteries of the Trinity, of the "Divine missions," of grace, of the man-image of God and of all His equipment of theological or moral virtues and of gifts or charismata, finally of the sacraments, predestination, adoptive filiation, and judgment. Obviously, this shows in a general way what the believer can find in this mystery and how he can see it as related to all the others. This establishment of a relationship between the mysteries gives theology a most fruitful process for developing and elaborating its doctrines.

Finally, we recall that Vatican I made a special mention of the relation of mysteries to man's final goal. This relation immediately concerns the place of this particular doctrine in the economy of Revelation. There are some things, says St. Thomas, which are material for Revelation, and hence *objectum quod* of faith as well as principles of theology, "primarily, essentially, naturally, directly," by very reason of their content. And there are others which are material only *in ordine ad alia,* that is, by the relation of application or illustration which they have to the preceding group.

Now, the things which fall under divine Revelation and concern faith directly, are summed up, according to St.

Thomas, as "that through which man is made holy," namely, the double mystery or the double "economy." That is, (1) the necessary mystery of the end, "the vision of which we shall enjoy in eternal life," and (2) the free mystery of the means, "through which we are led to eternal life."[32] This is a profound doctrine, which makes our beatitude and the truth of our total destiny the direct object of Revelation and, hence, of faith, dogma, and theology. And, we might add, puts it under the care of the ecclesiastical ministry. All this is a technical translation, but nonetheless faithful, of the Pauline definition of faith as *substantia rerum sperandarum* ("the substance of things to be hoped for").

Here we already have a presentiment of how little theology consists in a pure application of philosophy to a new datum. It is truly a "religious science," having an object which, technically and in its very epistemological condition, refers to our destiny. Hence this special title of intelligibility, as evidenced by Vatican I, which accrues to this science from a consideration of each doctrine in its relation to man's final goal.

In this intellectual penetration and construction of the mysteries, counting whatever the world of our natural knowledge can furnish us in analogies, as well as the evaluation of the relations these mysteries have with themselves and man's last goal, the interventions of reason can take different forms which may be reduced to three: (a) the simple explanation of the revealed truth; (b) the reason of suitability; (c) the deduction of new conclusions.

(a) *The Simple Explanation of the Revealed Truth.* This is a very frequent function of reason in theology. The explanation can be sought intrinsically or extririsically to the revealed truth itself.

---

32. *Sum. Theol.*, II^a-II^{ae}, q. I, a. 6, ad 1um; a. 8, copr.; q. II, a. 5, copr.; a. 7, corp.

(1) INTRINSIC EXPLANATION. This mainly consists in giving the revealed realities a more precise notion, sometimes even a definition answering to the exactions of a rigorous logic. Examples: dogma announces that Christ is seated to the right of the Father. It is theology's task to explain by reasoning out the case what this "sitting at the right" means. In cases of this kind the work involved is rather close to that of biblical theology and the catechesis. Nevertheless it is well within its role of *sacra doctrina* and a number of questions in St. Thomas' *Summa* respond to this function. Another example, in which the scientific elaboration is clearer. The theology of pontifical primacy and infallibility as explanation of the biblical texts which announce them: Math. XVI, 15-20; Luke, XXII, 31-32; John, XXI, 15-17; or the formulas of the magisterium. In the more important cases the explanation will go so far as to give the revealed reality a technically rigorous definition.

(2) EXTRINSIC EXPLANATIONS. It also falls to theology—in this, keeping itself quite dose to catechesis—to furnish, by analogies taken from our world, explanations which are less an elaborated formula of the revealed fact than a *manuductio*, i.e., pedagogic assistance suggesting to the faithful an understanding of the dogma. This pedagogic use of natural analogies is to be distinguished from the preceding use and from uses described later. In the first or preceding method analogies are used for their intrinsic content of truth, even if that truth is not entirely adequate. In the second or pedagogic method analogies are aids from the outside and their role is relatively independent of their intrinsic value. This is why in theology we continue, on the one hand, to use old *manuductiones* like those which are borrowed from ancient cosmology, for example, the idea of light as a physical medium, while, on the other, we can borrow entirely new theories from science but if they have not yet given sufficient proof of their truth, we would not know how to introduce them as elements of explanation into theological science itself.

(b) *Arguments of Fitness or Suitability.* These form considerably the most important part of the arguments in
theology and the appropriated realm of that science. They
consist quite simply in exploiting the general agreement,
which a supernatural, Christian fact, known by Revelation,
has with the everyday course, laws, and structure of our
workaday world. This agreement is susceptible of very different degrees, since the element naturally accessible to us
sometimes represents only a distant echo of the revealed
reality or fact. However, it can also represent a datum so
homogeneous to Christian things that it practically gives
us, in the law or essence naturally known, a true explanation of the revealed datum. In any case, the reason or analogy offered is not a direct proof of the supernatural fact. It
only gives motives to think that this fact is true and, under
this title, the reason or analogy should be listed in the category of "probable." They offer, as St. Thomas says, "true
similarities," "natural likenesses," which permit us—the
supernatural fact having been given us—to understand it
in some way. On this subject it can be noted that the vocabulary of the Fathers and the great Scholastics must not
deceive us and that often what they talk about as "necessary" or "obvious" only involves *fittingness.* When, in order
to give a theological reckoning of the Redemptive Incarnation, St. Thomas appeals to the metaphysics of *bonum est
diffusivum sui* ("the good is self-diffusive"),[33] he does not
intend to prove the fact of the Incarnation and knows very
well that the application of this principle in the supernatural world is subject to God's free initiative. But, to the extent
that so elevated a principle applies to the very life of God,
we can legitimately ask it to show us any intelligibility the
mystery may conceal. Analysis does not supply the reason
for a supernatural fact, but guaranteed by the wisdom of
God which reconciles all things in a world made by Him on

---

33. *Sum. Theol.*, III, q. I, a. 1.

two levels, it tends to help the human mind see whatever is intelligible in the supernatural fact.

This procedure will produce excellent results in the case where the agreement between the Christian fact and the naturally known law will come into reality from an essential structural community and, hence, from a real unity of law. Such a case is realized when by natural reason we come to know a form and its essential laws which will remain the same under the different modes in which that form can be realized. This is the case with our knowledge of human nature, so that it is necessary to find how our knowledge of human nature applies to the different questions which this nature presents in anthropology, morality, Christology, even mystical experience.

(c) *Deductive Theological Reasoning.* The explanation of a revealed truth often takes the form of reasoning whereby the mind disengages the more or less involved content of Christian teaching. It becomes then an explication. So it happens that we explicate truths which were really, though not manifestly, revealed. Again it happens—and this is most frequently the case—that by a rational detour we encounter a truth which was revealed elsewhere but without that revelation making known its logical connections or its metaphysical reason. Thus in the following syllogism:

> What is spiritual is not in a place;
> But, God is spiritual;
> Therefore, God is not in a place.

It also happens, especially when we introduce a premise of natural reason into our argument, that we obtain a new truth which we cannot pretend is revealed. This is an example, inspired by St. Thomas:[34]

> Being is attributed to the person;
> But, in Christ there is unity of person;
> Therefore, in Christ there is unity of being.

---

34. *Sum. Theol.* III, q. XVII, a. 2.

The conclusion is a new acquisition, which is so little a part of the datum of faith that theologians do not agree on this subject. The conclusion is obtained thanks not only to formal reasoning but also to the intervention of a rational quantity into the very constitution of the object finally known. This, in addition, involves a definite philosophy of *esse* and "person" which is adopted for its content and truth value. This deductive function of theology with the assumption of natural truths entering into the constitution of a "knowable object" poses some special questions. We will ideal with these later.

"Objectum Quod" and Subject of Theology

The subject of a science is the reality which is treated in that discipline. Still more exactly, according to Aristotle,[35] it is the reality whose properties are demonstrated. If we consider the subject of a science formally, i.e., under the aspect according to which the reality is treated in that science, the unity of the subject is as essential to the unity of the science as is the unity of light or the formal object *quo*. So Aristotle and St. Thomas say that the two things correspond to each other and that the unity of a science requires the unity of its *genus subjectum* ("generic object") as well as of its *genus scibile* ("knowable object"). Hence the great care of St. Thomas to show the unity of the subject of "Sacred Doctrine," that is, the unity of the reality which it treats.[36]

In theology this reality is God Himself. It is of Him and ultimately of Him alone that we treat in this science which is a "discourse on God." It is a discourse on God not considered under the formality of causality, which we know only in a very relative manner, "not as the subject of a science, but as the principle of the subject."[37] But on God consid-

---

35. II *Anal.* 1. I, c. VII, 75b 1 and c. X, 76b 15.
36. *Sum. Theol.*, I, q. I, a. 3, ad 1ᵘᵐ and a. 7.
37. *In Boet. de* Trin., q. V, a. 4; Cont. Gent., 1. II, c. IV.

ered in Himself, in His absoluteness, as He appears in His own regard and as He cannot be known to others save by supernatural Revelation. Theology has for its subject the same Reality which is the Principle of our beatitude, the One which the word of God reveals to us and to Whom our faith adheres, the One "whose vision we shall enjoy in eternal life."

Our knowledge of this God is measured by a Revelation which itself was ordered for our salvation, *salutis causa.*[38] The God Whom this word causes us to know is He Who wishes to form an alliance with us,[39] Who has conceived and Who pursues this design in the history of mankind. He is the Living God. To Moses who asked Him His name He replied, "I am Who I am."[40] He is known by what He does and what He wishes for us, supremely by the Incarnation, the death and resurrection of Jesus Christ. The subject of theology, then, is not "the Supreme Being," nor "the Eternal Axiom," nor even "the Great Architect." It is the Living God such as He has made Himself known in the history of His people.

However, it will be objected, theology also treats of the Angels, the Blessed Virgin, men and their moral life, the Church, the Sacraments, etc. It is true and in theological teaching these different realities are the object of just as many particular "treatises." But, as St. Thomas remarks, theology treats of these realities only "under the formality of God, because they have an orderly relation to God as to a Principle and a Goal."[41] Theology is by no means made up of anthropology, angelology or a study of sacramentary realities pursued for themselves. It is and it is uniquely a study of God insofar as He is God, i.e., *sub ratione Dei.* But, since the entire world has an orderly relation to God, an

---

38. Vatican II, Const. *Dei verbum*, n. 11.
39. *Ibid.* nn. 1 and 2.
40. Exod. III, 14.
41. *Sum. Theol.*, I, q. 1, a. 7.

order of procession to its efficient and exemplary Cause, order of return as to its final Cause, so theology considers all things insofar as they verify to some degree the *ratio Dei,* or God is implicated and as it were invested in them.

This is the program worked out by St. Thomas, letting this very simple idea organize his synthesis into the plan of the Summa which the prologue of the I^a *pars,* q. II, announces in very sober terms. Just as by charity we love in reasonable creatures the divine good which they possess or of which they are capable, so by Revelation and in the faith first of all, then by a rational manner in theology, we know God in Himself and all other things insofar as they have any relation to the mystery of God and, for the beatitude of the elect, insofar as they are associated with this mystery. So, while treating of angels and sacraments, etc., theology preserves its objectively theological character. But the Living God, the God of Revelation and salvation, is a God *for men.* Theology, after Revelation itself, has something to say about man and the universe. It cannot separate them from God, if He is the Living God of the Bible. There will be a "theology of terrestrial realities."

It is to this theological constitution of theology, the science of the objects of faith, that the very profound view of St. Thomas is attached. It deals with the unity and order of dogmas or *articuli fidei.* Theological tradition paid great attention to the text of the Epistle to the Hebrews on the necessity of believing "that God exists and is a rewarder to them that seek him."[42] St. Thomas gives to this definition of St. Paul the equivalent already noted: "that vision which we shall enjoy in eternal life and through which we are led to eternal life." For him, all the Revelation, all the faith, and hence all theology have reference to this double object: (1) God beatifying, or the divine economy of the means of beatitude—this is again the double mystery of God; (2) the necessary mystery of His Triune life and the free mys-

---

42. *Hebr.*, XI, 6.

tery of our salvation by the redeeming Incarnation. All the other dogmas return to these two essential *credenda*. For St. Thomas, the other articles of faith are only applications or explanations of these two essential articles.[43] So, there is in Revelation and hence in theology, a hierarchy, an order in which the unity of the subject is manifested.[44]

At the beginning of the nineteenth century, several theologians, inheriting the tendency to construct the dogmatic datum into a "system," but enlivening it by a romantic inspiration of the vital or the organic and by the philosophical viewpoint of an "idea" which is dynamically developed, have used as an organizing principle for dogmatic theology, not the mystery of God, but the notion of the Kingdom of God. Thus J. S. Drey, J. Hirscher, B. Galura, Cardinal Katschthalter, etc. The idea has been resumed in our days by L. Bopp in his *Theologie als Lebens-und Volksdienst*. These ideas proceed rather from a descriptive viewpoint and an empirical organization of the elements of dogma, than from a truly formal viewpoint: "Giving attention to what is treated in this science and not to the formal reason for considering them."[45]

Fr. Mersch while treating this question of the *subjectum* of theology, recently outlined a position very close to that which once assigned *Christus totus* as the object of theology. Fr. Mersch agrees that God in His Divinity is the subject of theology and *in se* the principle of intelligibility of all Revelation. But he then poses the question, Which mystery for us is the means of approach and the principle of understanding all the others? What doctrine unites all dogma and represents the "first intelligible" so that all the rest is accessible and systematizable? He answers that this is the doctrine of the mystical Christ, *Christus totus*. He has no trouble in showing that all the other mysteries are related

---

43. De verif., q. XIV, a. 11.
44. Cf. the Decree, *Unitatis redintegratio* of Vatican II on ecumenism, n. 11.
45. *Sum. Theol.*, I, q. 1, a. 7.

to that of the mystical Christ, Who is indeed the central mystery.

It is true that from the standpoint of an effective union and a vital assimilation to these mysteries, the Trinity and grace are accessible to us only by Christ and in Christ. It is true also that Christ is the perfect *Revealer* of God, of grace and our own condition. These things are finally known to us through Him, but these are the mysteries *of God.* The subject which theology treats is truly God, and the rest *sub ratione Dei.* God creating, choosing and making a covenant; God incarnating Himself, God author of the sacraments and operating through them, God divinizing us; for Revelation is an unveiling of our supernatural goal and this goal is a veritable divinization, for which the incarnate Christ is a means and a way. The Indices of Denzinger-Schönmetzer's most recent edition show all this very well. God is known only in what He does for us. In the scientific function of the *sacra doctrina,* says St. Thomas, we use in place of a definition of the subject (a definition which we do not have . . .), the effects which He produces, either in the order of creation or in the order of grace (I, q. 1, a. VII, ad 1). We reach Him as *He Who* has done all that fulfills the economy of Revelation, and supremely *He Who* is manifested in Jesus Christ. So it can be said with Fr. E. Schillebeeckx "that speculative theology is essentially Christological *quoad methodum* ('as to the method') and Theocentric *quoad subjectum* ('as to subject') . . ."[46] The investigation is about God. Unfortunately many confuse the theses or conclusions which theology formulates and which represent its *material object,* with the *subject* it treats, Who is the Living God.

Theological Science

Theology is the rational and scientific form of Christian teaching. Depending entirely on supernatural faith for the

---

46. *Révélation et théologie,* Bruxelles, 1965, p. 109.

possession of its object, the question arises does theology verify the quality of science and how? The answer to this question depends on what notion we have of science. So first we will look at the notion of science borrowed from Aristotle, which was that of St. Thomas, then at a notion of science which may be considered as quite commonly admitted today.

A. *Theology as Science from the Scholastic Standpoint*

There is science, according to Aristotle and the Scholastics, when we know one reality in another which is its reason, and then when we know the cause of a thing which makes it what it is and in such a way that it cannot be otherwise.[47] Science is knowledge in the cause, in the principle, *in principio*. With man, that knowledge is not intuitive but discursive. We do not see the consequences in their principle, the properties in their essential subject, but we have to deduce them or grasp them by proper reasoning which is of the demonstrative type. Science for us is not only knowledge *in principiis* ("in principles") but *ex principiis* ("from principles").[48] The ideal step of science constructing itself by demonstrative reasoning is to begin with the definition of the subject, which is the reality being treated, and to use that definition to demonstrate that such or such a property belongs to the subject. So the light of the initial definition communicates itself to the conclusions and, accordingly as the definitions, postulates or initial principles are known in this light which itself is determined or characterized by a given degree of abstraction, we obtain conclusions of a certain scientific quality. Thus the ancient idea of science is to reconstruct by the mind in its reasoning process, the ontological sequences upon which what is derived or subsequent in things is grounded on and to find its explicative reason in that which is first and principal.

47. *II Anal.*, 1. I, lect. 4.
48. *Sum. Theol.* I, q. LXXXV, a. 5.

When St. Thomas asks if Christian doctrine, *sacra doctrina,* verifies the quality of science and replies affirmatively, it is to be presumed that he understands science after the manner of Aristotle, in so far as that manner can be applied to theology. For St. Thomas, there is no question of purely and simply identifying theology with a science, that is, with a science corresponding on all points to the Aristotelian schema. And, it may be added, perhaps his commentators have too exclusively affirmed that identification. The manner in which St. Thomas introduces this question can be found in his *In Boetii de Trinitate*[49] and it takes this form: In its eminence, can Christian doctrine verify the function and quality of science? Now, theology, founded on Revelation, answers to two requirements of science. First, Christian doctrine presents us with truths which are effectively the foundation of other truths. Certainly faith, which has for a unique and direct formal motive the testimony of God as proposed by the Church, adheres as immediately to one set of truths as to the other. But when we try to find the real intelligible values and relations between the truths of Christian doctrine, then these truths are construed according to an order of intelligibility in which those which express secondary and derived realities are attached to those which express prime and principal realities, as conclusions to their principle, effects to their cause, or properties to their essence. It is thus, for example, that Christian doctrine gives me both the idea of the divine omnipresence and that of divine omnicausality. They tell me so little indeed that certain theologians, like Suárez, ground God's omnipresence in His immensity which is also taught by the faith. We see how the very elements of Christian doctrine on the mystery of God can become the object of a scientific study in which we are forced "to find in some aspect of God's Essence reason for the existence of other aspects which are posterior

---

49. Q. II, a. 2. See also *Sum. Theol.,* I, q. 1, a. 2.

from the standpoint of our understanding and also find reason for the existence of everything He causes."[50]

According to St. Thomas, there is science when *ex aliquibus notis alia ignotiora cognoscuntur* ("from a few known things other unknown things become known") and Christian doctrine takes on a form of science when "from those truths we take from faith while adhering to the First Truth, we come to know others by means of our method, namely, by moving from principles to conclusions."[51] Our science is discursive and proceeds by reasoning. But on the basis of what God has communicated to us of His science of Himself—to which we adhere by faith—we strive to connect the *ignotiora* ("less known") to the *notis* ("known"), and finally all things in hierarchical fashion to the unique Mystery and to the first and only Light of God. Theology is science and *humano modo* it even tries to imitate the science of God— St. Thomas goes so far as to say *impressio divinae scientiae* ("the imprint of divine knowledge").[52] That is not an eloquent formula, but a technically precise expression of what theology is for St. Thomas. So theology appears to us as an effort on the part of a rational believing creature to rethink reality as God thinks it, no longer on the level of a simple adherence of faith, but on the level of our discursive, rational knowledge, using all its means and resources. It is a "double" of the faith, but of a rational and scientific mode.

B. *The Science of Theology from the Modern Standpoint*

Modern theologians are no longer interested in the Aristotelian notion of science, save perhaps from tradition in the School, since the question of whether or not theology is a science is for them no longer urgent. But even if we remain strangers to the ancient concept of science, it is neverthe-

50. R. Gagnebet, in *Revue Thomiste*, 1938, p. 219.
51. *In Boet. de Trin.*, q. II, a. 2.
52. *Sum. Theol.*, I, q. I, a. 3 ad 2[um]; *In Boet. de Trin.*, q. III, a. 1, ad 4[um].

less interesting to ask the modern theologian whether his theology can justify the quality of science. But, the moderns do not have a notion of science of the same type and scope as that of Aristotle. The modern notion, insofar as one exists, that is, the ensemble of conditions which any learned man would say is a science, is much more external and more relative. A science is any discipline which can justify a proper object and a proper method and arrive at certitudes of a certain type which may be communicable to other minds. In these terms, history and sociology, for example, would be considered sciences.

This notion of science can be applied to theology by way of comparison and the result will be favorable if theology can present a similar front to the other disciplines which no one hesitates to qualify as sciences. Modern minds then will judge theology according to its object of knowledge and the method employed. This methodological viewpoint will generally lead them to consider the different particular methods which are used in theology to justify the existence of so many special sciences: biblical theology, historical theology, etc., which may be likened to the secular, historical, and social sciences. In this perspective where does theology proper, that is, speculative theology stand? Considered as a system of thought and representations, theology will be certainly and at least, matter for historical *science*; but considered as a philosophical treatment of certain convictions derived from faith, it seems indeed to possess a proper object, in accordance with a proper method of investigation. Hence it can find a place in the modern world of sciences.

In his *Introduction à l'étude de la théologie*, G. Rabeau tried to justify, even to the eyes of non-Christian philosophers, the existence of theology as a science and to determine its place in a classfication of sciences which answer the demands of modern logic. He claims that theology has the right to be listed with the sciences, because: (1) it has a scientifically founded object, since there is a speculative problem of religion posed by modern science and a practical problem of religion posed by daily life; (2) it has a method which can be analyzed and should be placed among the other scientific methods; (3) finally, to work upon its object it uses all the modern sciences which can help achieve its goal. It deserves, then, to be classed among the sciences. How can this classification operate and be justified? To answer this, the author proposes to apply the theory of "collocations" formulated by Stuart Mill. There are complex sciences whose status is not defined by the existence of their elements but by the fact of their coexistence. For example, it is the conjuncture of fossils and terranes which permits the stratigraphic and the paleontologic data to be synthesized in geology. Similarly, theology is not defined by its elements, history or Scholasticism, texts or deductions, but by the fact of their coexistence, by a fact of synthesis, in short, a collocation. Now, what puts history and facts in relation with dogma or religious thought is faith; just as stratigraphy and paleontology are united by the fact that these fossils lie in these terranes, so history and theological speculation find their unity in the faith of the believers, the unity of individuals and especially that of the total Church. This is human collocation which defines theology as an original science, and over and above that we can find in the very science of God a supreme collocation which sovereignly justifies the former.

The Problems of Structure and Method

Under this heading we have to examine: 1. The problem of the datum and positive theology; 2. The problem of rational support and theological reasoning; 3. The problem of the theological conclusion and of the homogeneity of theological science with dogma.

A. *The Problem of the Datum and Positive Theology*

It is generally agreed that the task of positive theology is to establish some new truth as a part of Christian doctrine. We have seen above that its proof, conceived first of all as an appeal to the texts of Sacred Scripture and to the monuments of tradition, has been considered for the past several generations as guided by the actual teaching of the Church and as capable of being produced only in its light.

1. NOTION OF POSITIVE THEOLOGY AND REASON FOR ITS EXISTENCE. Positive theology is the means by which theology takes possession of its datum. All rational science puts the natural light of intelligence to work; but it must receive from without, and finally through the senses, its particular matter. Theology is the science of the faith. Its light exists then in every believing man who, by his faith, has a principle of knowledge of the supernatural mysteries and, in his reason, the possibility of an elaboration and scientific construction of these mysteries. But still it is necessary that faith, a mere possibility of cognition, encounter the determination of its objects. And since these objects are supernatural, their determination can be made only by divine Revelation. Certainly this Revelation could be interior to each believer, as it was for the Prophets and the Apostles. But this has not been God's plan. God takes men as they are, engaged as parts in a whole in a specific unity and in social communities. He treats humanity as one kind, as one people, as a single Church, and He addresses to them a unique Revelation, social and collective. So the determination of the objects of faith, *determinatio credendorum,* is received not as an independent and personal experience but through a supernatural Revelation and the medium of a magisterium. (*In Boet. de Trin.,* q. III, a. 1, ad 4[um].) It is because the supernatural light given to each one in the faith is too weak to procure for him a knowledge and discern-

ment of the objects of faith, that there is, in the supernatural order, a magisterium and that the Church possesses a real power of teaching.

Hence, the entire development of faith is linked to Revelation, which is transmitted, proposed, conserved, and explained by the living Apostolic preaching in the Church. Thus we have this simple formula: "Faith is principally from infusion and as such we receive it with baptism; but as to its determination we receive that from preaching: hence man is instructed in his faith by catechism."[53]

But is the catechism, which is sufficient to explain the faith to a simple believer, satisfactory to construct rationally the faith of the theologian? It is quite clear that in hearing the simple preaching of the Church, the theologian receives the basis of his principles. And this is why it is often said that for him positive inquiry is only a question of *bene esse* and that, if he could not have theology without speculation, he can have one without special inquiry on the datum. This remark—which is a good, honest observation—has sometimes moved certain theologians to conceive positive theology as a sort of ornament pinned to theology's coat, but not forming a part of its essential activity and representing rather a concession to the taste of the day, or a purely apologetic operation, or lastly a sort of alibi for those who, having lost their sense of theological contemplation, took refuge in "erudition."

In reality and quite simply, positive theology is the very core of theology. It is essentially an act or function of theology and proceeds—by twofold right—from the same necessity as speculative theology. (1) It is necessary to speculative theology, which borrows its subject matter from a positive datum. It is exact to say that this datum can be acquired in its main lines by the simple *auditus fidei* which corresponds faithfully to the Christian catechesis. But a

---

53. Cf. Fr. Marin-Sola, *Évolution homogène du dogme cathol.*, t. I, p. 202, sq.

speculative theology which stops there would never achieve its plenitude in the order of speculation. It would become a sort of philosophy of Christian truths unless it limited itself to rudimentary questions and then it would not be nourished by its own sap and would be incapable of fully setting itself up in the category of a science. (2) Not only is the positive position necessary to speculative theology, but, in its own way, it corresponds to the need which faith has to constitute itself in a rational and scientific state by assuming the resources proper to reason and science. To this twofold activity of faith there corresponds in the believing and, hence, theological reason a double function. One as well as the other needs to establish itself in a truly rational and scientific condition by assuming the needs and the instruments of reason; together, positive and speculative, they constitute the total development of faith in reason; theology's full development as a science.

Faith of its very nature involves contemplation of its object; when this is promoted to a rational and scientific level, we have speculative theology. On the other hand, faith also involves submission to God's Revelation as transmitted by the Church; when this, in its turn, receives rational and scientific development, we have positive theology. The first is the scientific state of the *intellectus fidei;* the second is the scientific state of the *auditus fidei.* St. Augustine commented on the famous formula, *Nisi credideritis, non intelligetis,* by saying that the two elements were divided between authority and reason: "What we understand we owe to reason, what we believe we owe to authority."[54] But it is clear that faith is at the root of the *intellectus* and that reason finds, in its very submission to *auctoritas,* the means to give a scientific status to the theologian's notes, sources, and authorities. So, on the one hand, the mere union of theology with its sources is not purely scientific or rational. It is really a labor of theology, as we are soon going to show by

---

54. *De util, cred.,* c. XI, n. 25, P.L., t. XLII, col. 83.

distinguishing positive theology and the history of Christian doctrine; and, on the other hand, this union is not a labor of pure faith, or a stranger to all rationality. But, just as reason applies itself to the interior of faith, there to find an *intellectus,* so with equal interest it must apply itself to the interior of faith with all its resources, this time to find an *auditus* as rich, as precise, and as critical as possible.

It remains to set forth precisely this notion of positive theology by successively determining its formal object *quod,* its formal object *quo,* and its method.

2. FORMAL OBJECT "QUOD" OF POSITIVE THEOLOGY. While the formal object of speculative theology is the rational and scientific intelligibility of the revealed truth or of Christian doctrine received in faith, positive theology is concerned with the very reception of this revealed truth or this Christian doctrine. As positive, it studies the revealed truth in order to receive it and know it in its state of transmitted reality, offered to the adhesion and contemplation of the believing reason. To achieve this goal it uses all the resources which reason presents to grasp a datum, or more precisely, to discover this particular datum which is the faith and teaching of the Church. The object of positive theology then is the knowledge of what the Church teaches and delivers to our faith; which is practically the same as saying that its object is *tradition,* in the sense which recent studies have restored to this term.

When the treatise *De divina traditione* was constituted as a special study in the sixteenth century, it was orientated, as a function of the Protestant polemic, in the sense of a distinction in the objects of faith or the dogmas between the dogmas contained in Scripture and those contained in "tradition" and in the sense of a justification of the tradition thus understood. Thus we were led to conceive "tradition": (1) as designating a certain order of objects, (2) as distinct from Sacred Scripture, and (3) as constituted by ancient texts and documents. In short, it is this idea of post-Tridentine theology which in our manuals of theology still inspires the famous schema of *Probatur ex Scriptura, ex traditione* . . . ("proving a thesis from Scripture, from tradition . . .").

But recent writings have shown that the ancient and authentic conception of tradition was somewhat different. The first meaning of the term "tradition" is that of teaching or doctrinal preaching, either in the objective sense, as that which is taught or transmitted, or in the active sense of the action of transmitting or teaching. But the oldest meaning, going back to and including St. Irenaeus, is the objective meaning: tradition is the teaching, the object transmitted by Christ and the Apostles, then, from age to age, by the Church. This teaching comprises at once Sacred Scripture with its content and the truths not contained in Scripture, which can be called "traditions" in the strict sense of the term. In a secondary sense, we can designate as tradition the memorials or testimonies which the Church constructs and leaves of its doctrine in the course of the ages and which are preserved for us in certain documents: writings of the popes, Fathers, theologians, texts of the Councils, liturgy, inscriptions, etc.

Revelation is a deposit. The Church is able to gain a progressive consciousness of this deposit and realize a progressive development from it. And it will add nothing to it which is objectively foreign. If there are in the Church and through the course of its history some "revelations," these add objectively nothing to the knowledge of God's mystery. They are either a special light given to the hierarchy or the Fathers or to the Church as a whole, for a new and more profound understanding of the revealed doctrine, or perhaps some "private revelations" concerning the life of the Church, the orientation of piety, the basic inclinations relative to the conduct of souls.

This is why in the continuity of the "tradition," understood in the sense of revealed doctrine transmitted by the

Church, there is placed for a distinction between the *traditio constitutiva*, which is the doctrine-revelation of the Prophets, of Christ and the Apostles, the *traditio continuativa*, which is the primitive deposit as the basis for doctrinal development, and the *traditio explicativa*, which is the proposal, the conservation, the explanation and the development by the Church of the primitive deposit. The *traditio constitutiva*, formed by the revelatory contributions from the Prophets, Christ and the Apostles, without detriment from the *sine scripto traditiones* ("unwritten traditions"), is principally derived from the Sacred Scripture where the ancient Fathers found the doctrinal substance of the ecclesiastical *Paradosis*. As for the *traditio continuativa* and *explicativa*, they consist in the faithful proposition and the progressive explanation of the deposit as they have been produced in the Church animated and directed by the Spirit of Christ since the day of Pentecost to our day. It is this social testimony, in all its concrete reality and its successive development, which is the object and the matter of positive theology.

The object of positive theology, then, is tradition. That is, the doctrine transmitted by the Church from the time of Christ and the Apostles to our day. This has developed little by little both in its expressions and in the understanding which believing humanity has had of its tenets. It lives in the teaching of the present Church: "what has been given and what is given us." Positive theology is *sacra doctrina* insofar as it is conscious of its acquired content. It finds its object in the expressions, first, of the present Church, then, of the total Church in the living continuity of its development (*traditio continuativa et explicativa*), lastly, in the sources which, being the expression of our *traditio constitutiva*, are the interior rule of the ecclesiastical *Paradosis*. So the object *quod* of positive theology is the total testimony on the mystery of God as told by the Prophets, Christ and the Apostles; it exists, is preserved, interpreted, developed, and proposed in and by the Church of Christ and the Apostles, in and by the Church which is One and Apostolic.

3. THE FORMAL OBJECT "QUO" OR THE LIGHT of POSITIVE THEOLOGY. Positive theology is knowledge of a revealed doctrine. It is also scientific knowledge of this doctrine, not in the pure *auditus fidei*, but, since it is an intellectual inquiry, in the research and interpretation of documents of the ecclesiastical tradition. However, the intellect which is here associated with the faith is not the speculative intellect. Rather it is the intellect which studies biblical and historical documents in which ecclesiastical tradition finds its expression. The light of positive theology is then theological, i.e., it is the light of Revelation as, beyond the simple act of faith, it illuminates the human reason, inspires it to set up a human, rational, and properly scientific state to utilize the *auditus fidei*. This notion, quite simple in itself, can best be explained in these three propositions.

(a) *Positive Theology Is a Theology, Not a History.* The history of biblical doctrines and Christian doctrines materially have the same object as positive theology, but they view and attain that object under a different light and according to different criteria. Of the Christian datum we can have a formally natural and historical knowledge: history of the people of Israel, history of biblical doctrines, history of Christian doctrines, etc. But it is not such a knowledge of the datum, formally rational and historical, which furnishes theology with its principles. For in this case, between the revealed truth and theology which should simply be its rational interpretation, there would be a rupture of continuity. Both from the noetic and the epistemological standpoint, there would be a complete change of direction. To remain a science of revealed truth, theology must directly encounter its datum and recognize its principles in a formally theological light, using only theological criteria. This is why positive theology is formally different from the history of Christian doctrines.

(b) *Positive Theology, Being Theology, Develops in Depen-*
dence on the Church's Magisterium. The task of positive
theology is to find and interpret documents and to know
the past as far as documents and past testimony attest to the
revealed mystery of God. Hence it is only the magisterium
which can say what are the documents, who are the men
that bear witness to revealed truth, and the respective value
of their testimony. For Sacred Scripture, it is quite clear.
The Church has determined its canon, so that Scripture
exists for us as Scripture, that is as an inspired document
and an expression of the Word of God, only in the Church
and thanks to the Church's declaration. And again it is the
Church which possesses the meaning of Scripture; the total
Church, that of today as well as that of the past. Hence the
Church rightfully requires that we interpret Sacred Scripture according to the consensus Patrum, which is the tradition of the Church.

(c) *If There Is Question of Fathers and Theologians*, it is
from the approbation of the Church (an approbation which
can take many forms) that, as theologians, they hold their
position as witnesses of the Christian datum. "The doctrine of Catholic doctors has its authority from the Church.
Hence the authority of the Church is to be trusted more
than the authority of an Augustine or a Jerome or any
Doctor."[55] This will be immediately noted in the work of a
positive theologian giving him an aim, an orientation and
criteria different from those of the pure historian. The reason why, in studying Sacred Scripture, he will not search for
his datum in the *IV*[th] *Book of Esdras* or in the *Gospel of Peter*,
is because of the strictly theological decisions received from
the magisterium of the Church. The same is true relative to
patristic thought. One of the results of the Modernist crisis
was to bring this point more clearly to light.

It is from this difference of criterion and real source of
knowledge and appreciation that there are different results
which come from positive theology and pure history. It is

---

55. *Sum. Theol.*, II^a-II^{ae}, q. X, a. 12.

a difference which at times is hard to reconcile. Sometimes from the historian's viewpoint there is a certain disproportion between the affirmations which the theologian holds as data and the positive proofs or the documentary supports invoked in favor of these affirmations. Certainly, as regards method, positive theology is never dispensed from loyalty and rigor, but it is guided in its reading of documents by a certain sense and a certain knowledge of what it is looking for, and thus naturally finds more in them than does the historian.

4. THE METHOD OF POSITIVE THEOLOGY. What we have just said about the light of positive theology indicates the method it should follow. In a simple phrase, it uses the resources of historical reason exactly the way speculative theology uses the resources of philosophical reason. This involves two affirmations, in whose delicate conjunction resides the secret of positive theology. These two affirmations respectively concern the two notions of the resources of historical reason and their utilization.

(a) *The Resources of Historical Reason.* What speculative theology demands of philosophical reason is that it be loyal to itself, so that it can bring to theology an authentic service of truth. In the same way, positive theology demands the service of a loyal historical reason, master *au maximum* of the different historical technics. Quite simply, then, we want to bring to the service of revealed theological knowledge the maximum of authentic resources by which the believing reason can make contact with the ecclesiastical *Paradosis,* thanks to biblical and historical documents. Of course, it is evident that we cannot expect one and the same man to possess all these competences. Theological work is a social work and requires instruments of communication and collaboration, such as, collections, libraries, congresses, but especially technical publications, which have become the most efficacious instruments of scientific exchange and collaboration.

If some progress is still to be made in Catholic theology as far as the volume and exactitude of its positive support–especially in biblical matters–is concerned, it should be noted that considerable progress has already been made in this century. In a matter of this kind it is clear that each epoch has different needs and will make different demands. Positive theology has had to follow the evolutions of exegetical and historical reasoning. This in its modern sense is fully true only after the Nominalist criticism and the Humanist Renaissance and later in the nineteenth century, culminating in the crisis we have discussed earlier. But, before that, reason had its own manner of studying documentary evidence and what was considered satisfactory at that time will no longer satisfy a more informed historic reason.

(b) *Their Utilization.* In the same manner that philosophical reason is not master in speculative theology but a servant, that is, accomplishing its work under the direction and control of faith, so historic reason is an aid to positive theology, which always remains truly theological. From its work on sources, positive theology tries to enrich the knowledge of the ecclesiastical *Paradosis,* which is the "datum" of theology, and to do this, it must employ as faithfully and integrally as possible, the resources of historical reason. But it looks at the past for testimony on the revealed mystery of God. It is interested in St. Augustine or in the Syrian liturgy, only insofar as they represent an expression of the ecclesiastical *Paradosis* and that the revealed truth finds it is developed and witnessed to by them. Hence positive theology does not try to build up history for itself, rather it studies it according to the direction and indications of current ecclesiastical preaching, thereby taking its start from the current intellectual interests of the Church.

The method of positive theology, because it is theology, will then be "regressive" according to the term proposed by Fr. A. Gardeil. Positive theology takes its departure from the present, from the actual teaching in the Church, but it tries to enrich that teaching with a knowledge obtained by putting to work all the resources of historical reason as well as the *total* teaching of the Church, its integral social testimony on Revelation, which comprises together with Scripture—its *principalior pars*—*all* the development and all the expressions which Revelation has received in the Church through time and space.

This is why positive theology sometimes finds in a document, which for the historian would not have a similar meaning, some sign or expression of the actual faith of the Church. So that where the historian would be unable to draw a conclusion, the positive theologian interpreting the sign recaptures the continuity of development. This is because he proceeds from the certitude of the homogeneity of this development, the sense of that homogeneity and knowledge of the final result at least in substance.

When, for example, pontifical infallibility is officially expressed in the common faith of the Church, the positive theologian finds it expressed or suggested in texts, in facts or institutions where the historian legitimately does not see it. For the historian can give as meaning to a text only that which springs from the text taken in itself. For him the implicit does not exist, the signs of ulterior homogeneous developments are admitted only with difficulty and the existence of a doctrine is recognized only if its explicit documentary expression is discovered.

For the positive theologian, the meaning of a text is clarified from within. The fullness of its sense is given by way of an interior reading which through help from doctrinal continuity lights up the implicit by the explicit and gives the direction which will open up further development. For the theologian a text is only the means of a fuller communion with a living thought whose core meaning is actually given him. For him there is question of finding in the past the elements of its unique life, and thought. In theology any reference to a documentary datum is not an extrinsic proof of the proposed assertions. It is an element of the Apostolic word or theological science itself. From this standpoint history is rather a justification or enrichment of present thought and life than a restitution of the past according to documents.

Hence, while the history of biblical or Christian doctrines may have irreplaceable technical value, it will always be only a partial view and will never have the worth of a total explanation. Biblical theology, however, will have that worth, because it is a positive theology and, in its order, is a wisdom. Of course, it runs the temptation of every wisdom, but especially of theological wisdom which is to devote one's time exclusively to transcendent explanations and neglect the use of proper causes. This sort of mentality will give to positive theology a false supernaturalism which, under the titles of the Transcendent, will in reality cover over an ignorance of the real. Positive theology, if it is a use of historical technics by a higher wisdom sprung from faith, lives only by a loyal exercise of the authentic and integral resources of historical reason.

5. REPLY TO SOME DIFFICULTIES. It remains for us to state precisely the method of positive theology by examining some very real difficulties in its use. These concern either the value of the objective and historic truth of positive theology or its dogmatic and regulating value for speculative theology.

First Difficulty. The viewpoint of a justification of an actual datum by documents of the past and the use of a regressive method risk leading the positive theologian not to look for the truth of what was held by St. Leo, for example, or St. Athanasius or St. Paul; but simply for texts which support what one may wish to say himself or which can serve as a *confirmatur* to a thesis held by others. In history, it can be dangerous to read the meaning of an epoch or a text in the light of what has followed. Did not critics have to correct Burckhardt's interpretation of the Renaissance which he had viewed in the light of the modern world and classical art?

Reply. Properly speaking, in positive theology it is not a question of learning what St. Athanasius or St. Leo thought. That is the viewpoint of the history of Christian doctrines and the field of interest of the historical method. Rather, in seeking to know what the Church believes and, hence, what God has revealed, the task of positive theology is to examine St. Athanasius and St. Leo as witnesses of the Church's belief at a given moment and under given circumstances. It looks for nothing from them but the Church's belief. Nevertheless, this research can enrich our knowledge of the ever actual testimony of the Church only if it brings to light a more precise version of this testimony—precisely that version which St. Athanasius and St. Leo grasped in their individual set of circumstances. This knowledge can be obtained only if the thought of Athanasius or of Leo on the point in question is known in its historical circumstances by a loyal use of the resources of history. The contribution of positive theology to theological work presupposes and utilizes the method and results of the history of Christian doctrines.

The order then is as follows, (1) A historical reconstruction of the Christian past, as reliable as possible, thanks to all the resources of history: this is the history of Christian doctrines. (2) An act of faith and the *auditus fidei* as dependent on the Paradosis or ecclesiastical preaching which continues homogeneously through the ages. (3) Scientific research of this *auditus fidei* and the enrichment of our knowledge of the Christian datum contained and presented in Church preaching through the understanding of different conditions, forms, and expressions of the belief and doctrine of the Church in their first constitution and in the course of their development: this is the work of positive theology pursued under the direction of faith, by the build-up and use of the results of doctrinal history. (4) Scientific research of the *intellectus fidei* using the light and resources of reason to set up Christian doctrine as known in its most precise and richest form as datum.

Second Difficulty. This renews a point from the preceding difficulty. Positive theology "uses" the work of history wrongly, since its viewpoint is not purely historical. Searching for an enrichment of its knowledge of the faith of the actual Church, it is led to see a formal continuity and homogeneity in material which is similar only in expressions. For example, if a Father speaks of the *dona Spiritus Sancti,* positive theology will unduly understand this formula in the sense we use today when speaking of the seven gifts of the Holy Spirit as distinct from virtues. Again in the texts of the Councils, we seek justification of theological positions of certain Schools, which nevertheless the Councils expressly did not want to take up and which, in some cases, were printed long after the Councils took place.

Reply. These original notions arise from the honesty and rigor both in the documentation and interpretative methods set up by positive theology. Documentation and interpretation must be worked out to a truly scientific and critical degree. If these are lacking, there will be no positive theology, despite citations and a window display of references. To be faithful to its position it must set up a twofold critique of interpretations. It is first of all historical; it is secondly theological, springing from that methodological and critical treatise on the sources and the rules of theological thought which is encompassed in considering the theological *loci.*

Third Difficulty. Science is made by the scholar. The intellect has a role not only in the interpretation of facts, but in the construction of the fact as such and in the reception of experience. No matter what claim it may make in its advance, positive theology remains a theologian's work. It involves an irreducible portion of personal interpretation, even of choice in documentation. Often the texts do not stand out so clearly that they exclude the personal factor of choice or interpretation which with each one will play a role in his personal or collective options. The Scotist will find texts from the Greek Fathers which to him will evidently seem to support his thesis on the primacy of Christ. Similarly, the Molinist will also find texts in the Greek Fathers which will seem to him to support his theory on predestination *post praevisa merita* and the physical non-predetermination of free acts, etc.

Reply. Fr. Simonin considered this difficulty in a "Note sur l'argument de tradition et la théologie."[56] First of all, as a criterion of interpretation he eliminates any option inspired by religious experience, or, if you will, the personal "spirituality" of the theologian. Next, he discards as another criterion the harmony of an interpretation with the internal coherence of an intellectual interpretation or even with a speculative system, because this would be to use as a criterion precisely that which is in question. In short, he retains as our interpretative principle, docility to the ecclesiastical magisterium: for there is no question of finding support for a personal theory, but simply of enriching, by the knowledge of all its expressions, the *auditus* of an Apostolic testimony which is deposited, explained, and perpetuated in the Church. It is the Church's thought which the positive theologian seeks. He asks of those who, having lived and thought in her, had learned to express and sometimes to explain the faith of the *Catholica,* a testimony on what they held from her, what she had expressed in them and can teach us through them. The theologian at the same time can have recourse to the directions of the magisterium and to that control and enrichment which each one receives from communion and commerce with all the others. This collaboration, this mutual criticism of the norms of probability and their reenforcement are some of the elements of life and of scientific progress. The theologian is a scholar and his method benefits from this collaboration and mutual control of which scientific interchange is the source. He is

---

56. *Angelicum,* 1938, pp. 409–18.

also a believer and he finds the same benefits in the order of faith and religious thought in the heart of the Catholic community as long as he is living in this communion.

From this, then, we see that there would be some narrow-mindedness in limiting a theologian's investigations to data which has already been clearly interpreted by the magisterium. First of all, the ordinary magisterium of the Church in reality has very varied forms, and it goes so far as to teach in a tacit manner by letting people in some unimportant matters think, say, and act on a contrary interpretation. Secondly, in the silence of the hierarchical magisterium, there is a conservation and an education in the faith which is felt in the whole body of the Church. Finally, the historical inquiry by itself can furnish data firm enough to give theology certain principles, even in the absence of any "definition" by the magisterium. As, for example, in the case for the notion of the instrumental causality of Christ's humanity.

The Problem of Rational Support and Theological Reasoning

A. *The Problem*

can be stated thus. Even admitting that between the universe of our natural knowledge and the universe of faith there is a certain proportion, *analogia entis,* the revealed world is proposed to our faith precisely as something other than our natural world, something new, which we can represent by way of reason only in the smallest possible way. Revelation is given us precisely to help us know things inaccessible to our knowledge but nevertheless necessary for the achievement of our destiny. And even when it speaks of things which we know, at least from one side, it speaks of them not to help us know their nature, their ontological or physical properties, but to teach us how to use them in conformity with our orientation toward God. Is this not basically the problem which certain texts of Scripture set before us? "We preach a wisdom which is not of this world . . . of things which the eye has not seen, nor the ear heard . . . Now we have received not the spirit of this world, but the Spirit that is of God; that we may know the things that are given us from God. Which things also we speak, not in the learned words of human wisdom; but in the doctrine of the Spirit, comparing spiritual things with spiritual."[57] How can there be a Christian theology which employs the philosophical knowledge of this world in its formulation?

Technically, the difficulty may be presented this way. If we make use of philosophical notions to set up theology, either we will have four terms in our syllogisms, or what we conclude will mean nothing and contribute nothing, or Sacred Scripture will be reduced to the worn-out terms of philosophical categories. As a matter of fact, let us examine a reasoning process of this type, where there is no reason to ask if it terminates in a new theological conclusion, contained in Revelation or not.

> Christ is King (revealed in John, XVIII, 37);
> But, every king possesses the power to judge and condemn his subjects (philosophical principle, in *Sum. Theol.*, III, q. XLIX, a. 4, ad 1um);
> Therefore, Christ possesses the power etc.

The royal quality of Christ is revealed in many passages of Sacred Scripture, but it is revealed with a particular relationship. His royalty is expressly presented as being "of another world" and obeying laws quite different from those followed by terrestrial kings. Now in the minor (or major, if the argument is put in proper form), "royalty" is taken in its human philosophical notion. And we try to progress in the knowledge of Christ's royalty and its "properties," thanks to the knowledge contained in the philosophical minor—

---

57. I Cor. II, 6, 9 12–13.

above—of one property of all royalty and hence, conclusively, of Christ's royalty.

The difficulty is evident. Either there is no philosophical support and therefore this reasoning process means nothing; or there is support, but then we are reasoning about two notions of royalty, one revealed and special, the other philosophical and general. Hence, we are syllogizing in four terms. Or, finally, we reduce Christ's supernatural and revealed royalty to the generic notion of royalty, such as men understand it and rational sociology defines it. If we put our syllogism into form, then the philosophical principle plays the major role. It subordinates revealed truth and Christ's royalty is treated only as a case of human royalty in general. This means that it loses its supernatural uniqueness and God becomes *one* king *among others,* while all Revelation tries to tell us that He is the *sole King.* Some will say that this is precisely the mistake that all "Scholastic" theology makes, because it is constructed on philosophical assumptions. From this viewpoint a rational reconstruction of morality would have lost sight of biblical anthropology, where man is essentially flesh and spirit, and change it to a philosophical anthropology, where man is matter and form. The Church is a society of types like the others, different simply in their goal and in the powers they have at their disposal, for example, the sacraments.

Scheeben gives us a very happy comparison which may better help us realize the difficulty of the problem. Think of a traveler telling of his experiences in a distant country, of its climate and the flora and fauna totally different from our own. The simple believer is like a man who would be content to listen, to admit what was reported and to follow it through to its consequences, if any. But, the theologian is the man who, having heard and admitted the narration, will try further to comprehend it by traveling around and studying the flora and fauna *of his own country.*

B. *Reply*

Faced with the problem just outlined, we must say there is another hypothesis: the rational notions introduced into speculative theology are neither vain nor parallel or foreign to the truths of faith, nor domineering and assimilative, for they may be assimilated by these truths and used to convey their meaning. In reality this hypothesis is the true one, as we will now try to show.

In my mind, there is only one way to proceed intellectually in the investigation of mysteries and that is to analyze the content of the concepts in which they have been revealed by God, to deduce the properties from the essences, to link up effects to causes, in short, to analyze, explain, and organize in a rational manner. That is theology. For this reason it deals with concepts chosen by God from our world to fit corresponding concepts which we can attain by the different sciences which concern them. It is thus, that if God unveils Himself as a Person, and reveals to us that in Him there is Father, Son, and Holy Spirit, the manner of an intellectual perception of these truths for us will be to apply to this revealed datum, formulated in notions of our world, elaborations which these same notions can receive in the human disciplines which concern them.

But it is necessary to study the new condition of these notions borrowed by theology from the sciences. Certainly, the elaborate ideas from which theology profits today have been obtained from a study of created and sensible things which constitute our objects of knowledge. But their validity and effectiveness with regard to the representation of mysteries are the object of a guarantee, whose initiative and responsibility come from God Himself. Their application to the mysteries to represent them authentically is authorized by God Himself, Who in revealing Himself as a Person, as Father and as Son, Himself determines what are the created concepts and realities which have a value of "a likeness of His own wisdom." These concepts, then, are no longer philosophical analogies applied by man under his sole responsibility in virtue of a transcendent principle of causality. They are revealed analogies, received in faith and whose representational value man knows by faith.

We begin then to get a glimpse of the solution to our difficulties. The notions of reason employed in theology to express the teaching of faith according to a rational and scientific mode are no longer pure notions of philosophical reason. They are, as a matter of fact, submitted to the analogies of faith, judged, corrected, measured, and approved by them and thereby led to the dignity of a *theological anology,* object of theological reason, of that *ratio fide illustrata* about which the Vatican Council talks.[58] Theological reasoning is in no sense an application of philosophical notions to a datum which was received without being demonstrated. Certain manners of procedure, which rely more on the rational arrangement than on the revealed truth can fall under this reproach. This is the case when the Salamancans, for example, taking up the reasoning process *de potentia absoluta,* dear to theological criticism of the fourteenth and fifteenth centuries, contend that even if God were not the Father or the Trinity, our adoption by Him in the quality of son would still be possible. Looking back at *In III^am,* q. XXIII, a. 2, we can say that such a manner of reasoning, according to mere natural concepts and outside effective affirmations or the real economy of Revelation is very bad theology. For theology is not philosophy which reasons about faith.

From the standpoint of objective content, it is faith which dominates theology from one end to the other. It is uniquely to develop in a human intelligence according to the mode connatural to that intelligence, that it annexes and subordinates itself to philosophical notions. From them it receives no proper objective contribution, but only

---

58. Sess. III, c. IV, *Denz.* 1799.

a more complete explanation by assuming the resources and the ways of reason. So in this assumption the philosophical notions are verified, thinned down, and purified by faith in such a way as to fulfill a designated task. This type of work is evident in Scholastic theology. Just think of the refinement of notions such as person, relation, substantial conversion, subsistence, or mental word. These last two which are authentic philosophical notions have been precised in philosophy only under the pressure of theological work and for its needs. As for the first notion above, the rectifications and precisions it owes to its theological destination are quite well known. Such refinements would be a scandal for the philosopher who would be only a philosopher. They are in theology a consequence of the sovereignty of faith. To mention it in passing, it is to this role of faith vis-à-vis philosophy that we owe in great part "Christian Philosophy," in the sense in which this expression means a certain number of problems, attitudes, concepts, and certitudes which have been acquired by philosophy. The texts of the Catholic magisterium have often insisted on this benefit of certitude and this plus-value of precision that our human reason receives from this service of the faith.

We can now reply to the difficulties which represent the classical form of our problem.

There is no subalternation of theology to philosophy, for in theology of rational form what is given by faith judges and measures what is borrowed from philosophy and, far from being subordinated to it, it rather subordinates philosophy to itself.[59] On the other hand, theology-remains one science characterized by one *medium demonstrations* ("means of demonstration"). The premises of theological reasoning, in effect, are coordinated with one another to infer the conclusion. The analogical notion of reason has in effect been taken, worked on, measured, and finally

---

59. *Sum. Theol.* I^a, q. 1, a. 5, ad 2um; a. 6, ad 1um and 2um; *In Boet. de Ttin.*, q. II, a. 3.

approved and adopted by the analogical notion of faith. In
the theological argument we do not have a term of faith,
one of reason and a theological product, but a term of faith
vitally assuming and assimilating the rational truth to bear
the revealed analogy to a rational and scientific state and
constitute together with it a unique analogy of faith. Hence,
(1) there are not four terms in the theological argument; (2)
the two premises of this argument form a unique *medium*
("means") of demonstration in which the entire determination comes from faith and which is then, as Cajetan says,
divino lumine fulgens ("braced by divine light"). The conclusion of theological reasoning is expressed in the unique
causality of the organized and coordinated premises from
which the inference is drawn. All the light comes to it from
the premise of faith. Theology is truly the scientific development of faith, the science of faith.

C. *Consequences*

These consequences all go effectively to assure the primacy
of the datum of faith and the instrumental role of rational
support. We note the four following points.

1. The theologian will have to have a very lively consciousness of the fact that there is really only one world
of thought as a single world of reality and that the faith
assumes to itself all rational knowledge, just as the supernatural being does for natural realities. Faith and reason,
supenature and nature are distinct, but nevertheless not as
two quantities of the same genus and external one to the
other. The world of faith is the "whole" of the world of reason. It encircles it and overflows it. This is why it is necessary not to take the truths of faith as simple cases or simple
applications of the general laws of the natural world or to
consider that they will find their explanation in these laws.

2. Beyond every construction, however satisfactory it
may be, the theologian will have to preserve a very sharp
sense of transcendence and mystery. He must guard his

awareness of the insufficiency of the concepts he uses. Our human ideas can very well help us better to understand what it means to speak of Christ as King, for example. But the proper and positive manner in which He is King escapes us in its indivisible unity and remains a mystery. So, as a human science of the faith, theology can take an increasingly precise view of the revealed and mysterious reality which it studies. But what constitutes the core of the mystery itself cannot be elucidated by the use of human analogies. We define with precision the source of the mystery, but that does not help clear it up. Here again for the theologian St. Augustine represents a worthy example for meditation. When speaking about three *Persons* in God, he warns that he is writing "less to say something than not to say anything"[60]; he who had also written that what was already discovered and understood about God was simply an invitation to new and perpetual research.[61]

3. In theology, the datum is totally regulatory. Beginning with his concepts the theologian does not construct a world in which the mind encounters nothing foreign to its own ideas or its necessary ideological determinations; rather he refers constantly to a datum of realities received from without. These are the realities which he is forced to grasp. For that, his concepts are merely means of expression, and his reasonings are means of distinction or verification. The datum and the realities exercise an absolute critical function with regard to all conceptualization and all reasoning. This dependence exacts from the theologian an attitude of total submission and radical "poverty of spirit." It implies that in each one of its forward steps, the ideological system which the theologian constructs must be critical and yet supple with reference to all the elements of the datum, each one appreciated according to its respective value. Especially in certain questions, as on sacramental material, which com-

---

60. *De Trin.*, 1. V, c. IX.
61. *Ibid.*, 1. XV, c. II.

prises as many "institutions" as dogmas, the factual references must be constant. For the least fact must be respected
and if a theory proves to be too narrow or too rigid to take
it into account, then the theory must be remolded.

4. Finally, it will still be a matter of humility and submission on the part of theological science to accept a datum
whose elements are far from being on a level with the needs
of conceptual precision. Revelation is made in a style of
imagery to which M. Penido has given the epistemological
status of "metaphorical analogy" or "analogy of improper
proportionality."[62] Thus Christ is revealed to us as the
"Lamb of God," or "Head of the Church," while the Church
itself is the "Spouse of Christ" or the "Vineyard of the Lord,"
etc. The perfection common to the two metaphorically analogical terms is not formally in all the analogues. The metaphorical analogy expresses an equivalence of effects not
directly in the form of *being* or the essential definition but
in the proportion between two manners of *acting*. So since
God in His Revelation wishes to tell us what He is for us
and what He does for us rather than what He is in Himself,
(quite independently of the general principle of addressing
men by images since they are sensible beings), we can very
readily understand that Revelation must be filled with metaphors. Similarly when the theologian is trying to translate
these metaphorical notions into analogies of proportionality more rigorously defined, because they are revealed data
and analogies of faith, he will remember to submit his more
satisfying philosophical concepts to the approval of these
metaphors. So, on the one hand, he will translate into more
precise concepts the meaning affirmed by the similitudes of
the "Head" and the "Vineyard," but, on the other, the theologian will have to submit the conceptual material, borrowed
from philosophical sciences, to the judgment and measure
of these more majestic but imprecise images of "Head,"
"Vineyard," etc. For these metaphors are of Revelation and

---

62. *Le rôle de l'analogie en théologie dogmatique*, p. 42 sq., 99 sq.

their content must pass into the constitution of theology. It would be a serious error of method to construct, for example, an ecclesiology merely with humanly dear and rigorous notions, close to philosophy, society, power, law, etc., and neglect the great biblical images.

Problem of the Theological Conclusion and the Homogeneity of Theological Science to Dogma

If theological reasoning verifies the conditions of necessary reasoning and if reason on this level is assumed and regulated by faith, may we not recognize in the theological conclusion a certain homogeneity with Revelation itself, the object of our faith? In the case where a conclusion would follow in a necessary and evident manner, either from two premises of faith, or from one premise of faith and another of evident reason, can the conclusion be made the object of an affirmation of faith and its negation the object of a sin of heresy, before any definition of that truth by the Church? Can such a conclusion be defined by the Church as a truth of faith, and, if so, is that definition justified? Finally, after its definition does such a truth derive from theological faith or from a special adherence distinct from both theological faith and from human faith? Such are the questions raised by the theological conclusion.

A. *Adherence to a Theological Conclusion Before Its Definition*

The great theologians of the thirteenth century willingly admit an increase of dogmatic formulas by the canonization of propositions *consequentia ad articulos* ("consequent on the articles of faith"). But for them these propositions as to their content are secondary revealed truths and not theological conclusions. The modern problem of the epistemological quality of the theological conclusion in its proper sense is announced in the fourteenth and fifteenth centuries but not truly studied until after the Council of Trent. The most notable position in this early epoch is that of Vásquez and Suárez. In effect these authors introduced a distinction to this problem which has been handed down since their day and passed into a great number of works. With regard to a necessary theological conclusion they distinguish two assents. One which is given to the conclusion insofar as its inference by reasoning is evident, and that assent is theo-logical. It is given to the truth precisely as the conclusion presents it. Disengaged by reasoning for the benefit of the human mind, it appears as objectively and really contained in the revealed proposition. The second assent, which is given to a truth contained in another truth that is revealed, springs from faith. However, to distinguish this from the first assent given to revealed truths explicitly proposed by the Church as dogmas, Suárez speaks, in this latter case, of Catholic faith and, in the former, of simple divine faith or "theological faith." This is a distinction which since Suárez's day has been widely accepted in the Church.

Hence, the great principle of discrimination is that every adherence depends on its motivation. If my adherence rests on God's testimony as proposed in Apostolic preaching, it will be theological *faith*. But if it rests on what I see by the industry of my intellect in God's testimony, it will remain human or rather humano-divine, which is simply *theological*.

However, it is not always possible to apply this principle conveniently. The simplest *auditus fidei* always implies a certain amount of intellectual activity merely to compre-hend the meaning of the words. The very purpose of faith cannot be satisfied with a purely passive reception of the word of God. As far as possible it tries to penetrate God's meaning. And to that end, even while it is docile to the Church's teaching and to the declarations of its magis-terium, it runs the risk of actively interpreting. It tries to comprehend all that the sacred message is meant to convey. Isn't it possible for a Christian to adhere with theological faith to the meaning which he sees in a given passage of the Scriptures, even though the Church has not given it an explicit official interpretation? And again can he not adhere with theological faith to what he sees with evidence belongs to a dogma but to which the Church has not yet given an explicit definition?

It seems we can say this much with certainty. When the human mind confines itself to the limits of an understanding of revealed statements *as such*, an assent of faith is possible with regard to what is seen evidently to belong to the revealed truth or to be the sense of these statements. At most, it seems that the same adherence of faith can be given to what is evidently seen to be linked to these statements of faith in such a manner that if it is denied, the officially declared meaning of the statements would be necessarily perverted. Such at least is St. Thomas' position apropos of the divine "notions."[63] St. Thomas says we can sin against the faith, if we deny the doctrine of divine notions. Not because this doctrine is explicitly of the faith, but because it concerns the faith indirectly (*indirecte ad fidem pertinet*). The sin of heresy can be committed not merely by directly denying a truth of faith, but by maintaining a position in such a way that the orthodox meaning of faith cannot be preserved. Perhaps St. Thomas here is looking at the "indirect" of faith—not from the standpoint of an inventory of what can be found in the objective limits of Revelation, but from a concrete and existential approach with relation to the attitude of the person adhering to the message of salvation.

On the other hand, it is important from the foregoing position to distinguish carefully the theological conclusion, which recently has been called the "virtual illation." In

---

63. *In I*um *Sent.* dist. XXXIII, q. I, a. 5; *Sum. Theol.*, I, q. XXXII, a. 4; cf. II^a-II^ae, q. XI, a. 2.

this case, we no longer have the intellect trying its utmost to comprehend totally and translate simply into technical values a given statement of the faith, but rather, by the introduction of an element foreign to a formally revealed truth, trying to detach an object of thought which proceeds only mediately from the statements of faith. We are in the order of *mediate* Revelation. Intellectual activity intervenes not merely to enable the Christian to comprehend what is expressly revealed, but to constitute an object of thought which is only mediately related to a revealed truth. There can be no question of giving to this object an adherence of faith, since the motive is *nihil aliud quam veritas prima* ("nothing other than the Prime Truth").[64]

In this matter it is helpful to use John of Saint-Thomas' distinction between two modes of reasoning. (1)There is the case, where there is question merely of disposing and accustoming the believer's mind to comprehend as totally as possible what is truely revealed. Next, we have the case of producing, *by the use of a new middle term,* certain notions which can be attributed to a revealed truth only in a mediate manner. It seems that Suárez's and Vásquez's distinction cannot apply in this second case and that, in strict theological reasoning once the conclusion is obtained, we cannot set aside the means of inference which produced it and simply contemplate truth as such, as objectively contained in the revealed premise. What is true of the effort by which the theologian becomes aware of the content of a formally revealed truth, is not true of the effort by which he disengages the "virtually revealed" truth, which always implies the intervention of reason. Moreover, what is believed at a given moment as merely virtually revealed, perhaps one day will be defined by the Church. It is clear that in the beginning there was simply formal Revelation. But no science. This is why the theologian must conduct his work in a spirit of perfect docility toward the Church's magisterium.

---

64. *Sum. Theol.,* II^a-II^{ae}, q. I, a. 1.

B. *After the Church's Definition*

The question of knowing which assent should be given to a theological conclusion after its definition by the Church is nicely settled by Schultes' thesis.[65] He strongly criticizes the "ecclesiastical faith," which is neither theological nor a human faith inspired by divine faith and submitting itself to the Church's authority. Father Marin-Sola has more profoundly criticized the "ecclesiastical faith." He clearly shows that by the Church's definition a new motive of adherence, which springs from theological faith, is substituted for theological science.[66]

C. *Dogma and Theology*

At the close of this study of structural problems raised by theology and this last question of its homogeneity with its initial datum, it can be useful to set down clearly the distinction between theology and dogma and then to explain and determine the role of a plurality of intellectual constructions in the very interior of theology.

Theology is distinguished from dogma where we find the object of faith defined in such a manner that it implies the work of a human intelligence and hence is precisely a purely human labor. Faith, on the other hand, is a pure adherence to the Word of God motivated solely by the sovereign authority of the revealing God. Even though man plays a role in the expression of this divine Revelation, his statements are not guaranteed as the pure Word of God by the charism of inspiration. Man's part is more notable in the properly dogmatic formulation of the object of faith. For dogma, the more elaborated expression of Revelation, is the work of the Church, which is not directly inspired in this labor, but only assisted *ne erret* ("so that it might not err"). In this respect, dogma is human workmanship.

---

65. *Introductio in historian dogmatum*, pp. 130–31.
66. *Evolution homogène*, 1.1, n. 225–97.

Hence its formulas are not without relationship to the intellectual conditions of the times which give them birth. For
dogma is nothing but the official formulation of truths contained in Revelation and already proposed by the Church
which transmits it to us with the authority of Scripture and
Tradition. Dogma merely explains and explicates the real
content of the revealed Word without adding anything to
it. Hence, human labor can be notable in the explanation of
the primitive datum and elaboration of its dogmatic formulas. However, in no sense of the term does the product of
this "human labor" enter into the intrinsic constitution of
the object of our religious adherence. This object remains,
under a more elaborated and precise form, exactly what it
was as object in the prophetic, evangelical, and Apostolic
Revelation. Not only do we add nothing to its content but
we change nothing of its essence as our object of assent.

To explain Revelation intellectually and construe it
scientifically, theology consciously tries to remain within
the content of *revealed* assertions. Thus, as to the assertion of the real presence of Christ living in the Eucharist it
refuses to add any further assertion. It only confines itself
to penetrate intellectually and to scientifically construct the
affirmed reality. But what theology perceives and affirms in
the revealed object is perceived and seen by it thanks to
a human effort and by the use of epistemological human
means, which are aided neither by the assistance the
Church receives nor the inspiration given to a prophet. In
the theologian's vision, the human mind on its own power
intervenes as a principle of cognition. The object, as object,
that is, as the terminal of knowledge, is constituted by the
mixture of two lights very unequal in quality and certitude,
one of revealed truth, the other, the human reason of the
believer. These two lights fuse together to determine a new
kind of adherence, viz., theological knowledge.

The distinction between dogma and theology under one
form or another has always been recognized and practiced

in the Church. This was true even before theology was clearly defined as a rational and scientific activity of the believer, when it was not possible to distinguish between what is unanimously held by the Church and imposed on the faith of all and what is the viewpoint of the individual proposing a given doctrine on his personal responsibility; or again when it was not possible to distinguish between the simple affirmation of Christian facts, the object of ecclesiastical preaching and the explanation of *how* and *why* to which the preaching of the Doctors was dedicated. Origen had already remarked this at the beginning of his *De Principiis.*

However, the distinction between dogma and theology has not always been sufficiently present to the mind of some theologians and of non-theologians who have touched on the domain of theology. Several difficulties raised by the Modernists against dogma spring from the failure to distinguish between the Church's dogma and theological systems or even the science of theology. The clear distinction, then, between dogma and theology, the theological science and the particular systems of the theology was one of the benefits of the Modernist crisis.

It is in the perspective of what has just been said about dogma and theology that we must comprehend the difference between the theological science and theological systems and the inevitable diversity of these systems in the Church. There is the Catholic faith which is imposed on all believers, because it is not particularized in the thought of a single man but is the treasure of the Church as such. Then, there is the human elaboration of that faith, which is theology. By the very fact that this elaboration is the work of particular believers and that it is brought about by the organic addition to dogma of elements borrowed from rational knowledge, its product, theology, is necessarily inadequate to the *fides catholica* ("Catholic faith"). And somewhat similar to the way in which the inadequation of particular goods to the universally willed good founds liberty of choice, so this inadequation justifies and, in some measure, involves a certain diversity of theologies. This diversity proceeds from three principal sources.

1. Neither theology nor, for that matter, philosophy is an absolutely impersonal work, a sort of purely logical construction which would render the concrete reality of the thinking man, his temperament, his history, his exterior and interior experiences amorphous and unimportant. In philosophy, for example, these factors, on the contrary, turn the thinker toward certain attitudes which themselves command the inspirational options of the system. Now theology has for its rule a datum proposed by the ecclesiastical magisterium, just as philosophy has for rule the datum of natural knowledge. And it is well established that the first step of the theologian is an act of submission to this datum and the magisterium. But the datum is so rich that it authorizes different manners of approach and, according to the intellectual orientation of each one, different manners of posing the problems themselves. What the Catholic faith tells us of the knowledge and will of God as to our free acts certainly authorizes different constructions not only of responses but of the problems themselves. These constructions depend on a certain angle of vision, which itself is commanded by an initial orientation whose reason is to be sought in a certain intimate experience, a tradition, a personal comprehension of the very first data. So it is, for example, that the most recent historians of Nominalism have pointed out in this movement a consequence and, as it were, an expression of a very strong initial intuition of the sovereign and free, divine Omnipotence. Similar remarks could be made about Molinism, Franciscan Augustinianism, about Augustine's theology of grace or that of Pelagius, about the ecclesiology of St. Cyprian, etc.

2. If theology is the elaboration of faith by a human reason using its own resources, it is clear that the content and

inspiration of a "milieu," the content and inspiration of a tradition of religious life and of philosophical thought will determine in large measure the theological work and the rational construction of faith. The intellectual climate of Alexandria was not that of Carthage and the importance of this diversity has been justly underlined with regard to the diversity of theologies which flourished in those two places. In a more general manner, the theological traditions of the East and the West in the matter of the Trinity have each a relative internal homogeneity and nevertheless are diverse in their manner of approaching the mystery and of intellectually constructing it. Similar differences on other points exist between the East and the West. They proceed from a different manner of approaching the same mysteries, the difference being due to a diverse orientation of outlook and speculative effort; the orientation itself is conditioned by a culture, by a tradition of philosophical and religious thought.

3. Beyond the initial religious intuition, beyond the general sphere of thought, the diversity of theologies can be born of a deliberate choice of conceptual instruments and diverse philosophies. The Church indeed imposes on all the same datum of faith, but, by very reason of its transcendence, this datum supports, in its rational organization as theology, the service of diverse philosophical apparatus. If the project formed by some in the sixteenth century and continued into the middle of the eighteenth century of using Plato's logic and dialectics instead of Aristotle's had borne fruit, we would have had in the Catholic Church perhaps quite a different type of theology from that which has prevailed. The attempt to apply to the Eucharist Descartes' theory of extension has been condemned by the Church but a similar attempt inspired by the philosophy of Leibniz has not been condemned. The Thomist philosophy on matter and form differs radically from that of St. Bonaventure; Suárez' philosophy on composition differs profoundly

from that of St. Thomas, and all these differences have their immediate repercussions in the theological structure. Examples could be multiplied.

Having thus shown and justified the possibility of several theological systems, it is right to affirm no less strongly that this does not authorize a pure and simple relativism in this matter. Indeed, on the one hand, there are zones in which the rational interpretation is so tightly linked to common philosophical certitudes that a scientific and necessary knowledge is reached of a kind that leaves no room for a more particular systematization. This would be the case, for example, of the doctrine which teaches that he who deliberately denies an article of faith loses the total *habitus* of faith; of the theology of the blessed knowledge of Christ; of a certain number of conclusions relative to the Blessed Virgin, to man's last goal, to certain points of social or international morality . . . The ensemble of these theses would delineate the area of what, in opposition to the *systems,* can be called theological *science.*

On the other hand, all of the systems are far from giving plenary expression to the revealed datum with all its virtualities, just as they even fall short of the assumed rational elements. A system which, like that of St. Thomas, shows itself capable of assuming and ordaining a multitude of particular aspects—which are also put to work elsewhere, but in a dispersed and fragmentary fashion—evidently from its superior viewpoint possesses an overall value not possessed by a particular system fashioned to describe some antinomy of detail.

The Habitus of Theology in the Theologian

After having defined and studied theology from the standpoint of its object and method, we must define its status in the subject, in the theologian, by studying first of all the *habitus* of theology, then the conditions of theological work and progress.

A. *The Habitus of Theology*

Three affirmations characterize the *habitus* of theology. Theology is a science. It is at once speculative and practical, but principally speculative. It is a wisdom. The first point has been treated above. It remains to talk of the other two and to ask whether the *habitus* of theology is natural or supernatural.

1. THEOLOGY IS A SPECULATIVE AND PRACTICAL KNOWLEDGE, BUT PRINCIPALLY SPECULATIVE. We have already seen, apropos of the notion of science, how St. Thomas complied with the idea that knowledge must correspond to the object and to its internal conditions. Now, there are objects which are made to be known and the mere knowledge of which exhausts the relation we can have with them and there are objects which are made to be realized by us. That knowledge is speculative, which considers its object as a pure object to be known; as a spectator. That knowledge is practical, which considers its object as a thing to be realized and constructed; as an actor and cause. As St. Thomas says,[67] speculative knowledge aims at the *cognitio generis subjecti* ("knowledge of the generic subject"), and practical knowledge at the *constructio ipsius subjecti* ("contents of the subject itself").

Up above we have summarized the positions taken in the Middle Ages on the speculative or practical character of theology. They are all inspired by the sentiment that theology is an original, superior knowledge irreducible to the categories of merely human disciplines. This inspiration is also that of St. Thomas, but it leads him to a position somewhat different from the others. Theology is not constituted or specified like the human sciences. It is an extension of faith which is a certain communication and a

---

67. *In II Anal.*, 1. I, lect. 41, n. 7.

certain sharing of God's knowledge. Now, God's knowledge
exceeds the division into speculative and practical. This is
why faith, then the intellectual gifts of science, intelligence,
and wisdom, then the *doctrina sacra* and theology, which
is its scientific form, are at once speculative and practical,
and have from the superior viewpoint of God's knowledge
a unity which would not exist if it were just a question of
human knowledge. Nevertheless, theology is more speculative than practical. For (1) it principally considers the mysteries of God before which the believing intelligence is a
spectator and not active; (2) even the practical matter of
human action is considered as ordained to beatitude, which
consists in a perfect knowledge of God.

Hence, there is only one theology, the science of the
revealed mystery of God. This theology is principally speculative but it is also undeniably practical. For, the God of
Revelation is not only an Object, but we know Him also as
our goal. This is why the study of God involves a morality,
centering on the activity whereby man returns to God as
to his final goal, according to the concrete economy of this
world of the Fall and Redemption by Christ. Theology then
has for its object, first of all, the knowledge of its generic
subject, next a certain *constructio ipsius subjecti,* namely,
the construction of God in us, or rather the construction
of Christ in us. Certainly, as much for pedagogic reasons as
for reasons drawn from the nature of their objects, moral
and dogma are distinguished from one another. But we
would gravely deceive ourselves if we separated dogma
and moral as representing two independent systems of
knowledge. This would be the case if we said that, on the
one hand, there is dogmatic theology, which studies the
mysteries, such as original sin, grace, and the indwelling
of God in the souls of the just, and, on the other, there is
moral theology, or an ensemble of practical rules for solving concrete "cases" in real life. This moral, cut off from the
study of God's grace and beatitude, in which the consider-

ation of the theological virtues would be extremely thinned out and that of the gifts of the Holy Spirit omitted, would hardly represent anything more than a casuistry. This faulty moral would treat, as an extrinsic addition, some "ascetical" considerations, valuable for the majority of the faithful, and some "mystical" considerations, concerning particular and "extraordinary" cases.

This approach would be contrary to the true nature of theology and to that of its two functions or quasi-parts. It would be contrary to its speculative activity with regard to the mystery of God revealed, which is that of God beatifying, of God communicating Himself to men and constituted as their final goal. It would be contrary to His practical function with regard to Christian activity and the consummation of God's image in us. For action, image, and consummation can be conceived as such only in dependence on the mystery of God and as constituting a part of this mystery itself.

In the first place, all of theology, because of the connection its practical elements have with the speculative, appears normative and has, as is said, "life value." Secondly, asceticism and mysticism find their place in theology, not as special parts added to a moral itself separated from dogma, but as elements organically integrated in the scientific study of the revealed mystery of God beatifying. This is theology. It belongs then to this science to develop, in their own corresponding places, the elements of doctrine which render account of the different realities which have been made the object of asceticism, mysticism, and pastoral theology. And without doubt there is still room to complete the work of the ancient theologians on these doctrinal points.

It is quite certain that the science of moral theology is not sufficient to regulate concrete action directly. Between the knowledge of the principles of action and action itself, there is room for a practical knowledge which is directly regulatory. This knowledge is one no longer of a science, but of a virtue at once intellectual and moral; the virtue of prudence.

But between the science of moral theology and the virtue of prudence is there not room to place an intermediary type of knowledge which would be more practical—and differently so—than the moral science? Jacques Maritain thought so and proposed to insert between a speculative science of action and prudential management, a practically practical science. This would not distinguish several sciences by different objects, but only by a difference of formal viewpoint and method in the consideration of the same object. There would be, first of all, a speculative consideration of the moral reality which would propose only to know this reality and in it the nature of the moral agent. The nature of the moral action and its conditions, that of its end and general rules would be studied following the analytic method, going from concrete to abstract, which is the method of the speculative sciences. There would be, in the immediate direction of action, the virtue of prudence. Finally, there would be, between the speculative science of the practical or the speculatively practical science and the virtue of prudence, a practically practical knowledge. This is knowledge of the moral reality to be achieved practically; borrowing its lights from the speculative science of action, to which it would be subordinated, in view of its proposing more proximate rules of action. In this practically practical knowledge, personal or imparted experience would play a prominent role. This would be the science of the prudent man as such, of the practitioner, and the spiritual director.

Some theologians have approved this approach to the problem. They have thought that the distinction proposed would help give status to a "spiritual theology," distinct from the moral theology as the *Summa* of St. Thomas proposes it, where it appears to be only a speculative study of Christian action. It seems indeed that this category of "spiritual theology" refers to something. First, to a literary genre, that of "spiritual writers"; then, to a utility, even to a pedagogic necessity, since the ways of Christian perfection can be taught only by making a special study of them; finally, to a certain psychological reality, to that particular state which theological knowledge assumes in the theologian truly animated by a taste and zeal for the spiritual growth of people.

In all of this, however, there is nothing which justifies our ascribing to spiritual theology the quality of a special theology, distinct as a science from theology in its practical function. To the critical eye, this intermediary knowledge seems to distribute itself quite well over the two moral disciplines, that of the theological science and that of prudence, on condition that we restore to this latter everything which belongs to it of science and to the former the plenitude of its practical character and the necessary information it receives from experience, both our own and that of others. In this way, "spiritual theology" would be only one of the practical functions of theology, which, for reasons pointed out above and from a pragmatic standpoint, still could be considered as a specialty of some sort. This seems to be the opinion of a majority.

2. THEOLOGY IS WISDOM. In the first question of the *Summa* as St. Thomas in article *two* had asked himself whether Christian doctrine verifies the quality of science, so now in article *six* he asks if it verifies that of wisdom. As he always does in articles of this type, St. Thomas recalls what the conditions of wisdom are and then outlines their application to the *sacra doctrina*.

In each order of things, he writes, the wise man is he who retains the principle of order, which gives to all the rest its meaning and its justification. This is why the science which has for its object the first and universal cause, the sovereign principle of all things, will be the supreme wisdom, wisdom pure and simple. This is the case of the *sacra doctrina* or Christian doctrine, of which theology is its scientific form. Theology is truly an ultimate and universal criterion. It is queen and ruler of all knowledge. In the words of St. Paul: *Spiritualis judicat omnia* ("What is spiritual judges everything").

This leads to the following consequences:

(a) Theology, being wisdom, that is, supreme science, has nothing above it. In the scale of sciences, each discipline proves its own conclusions, but leaves to a higher discipline the task of defending its principles. The supreme science itself insures the defense of its own principles and the principles common to all the other sciences. It is thus that metaphysics develops itself into a "critic" to defend the value of the first principles of reason and the validity of knowledge itself. Likewise theology must defend its principles which are the revealed truths proposed by the Church. It does this by developing in itself a critical section which is called apologetics or fundamental theology, without prejudice to the particular defense of such or such a point which theology presents in its different treatises. This idea of apologetics conceived as the critique of theology appears to us most satisfactory.

(b) Theology is apt to use for its own end all the other sciences. It equally tends, under conditions to be seen later, to exercise with regard to all other sciences a certain function of regulation and control, which contributes a certain measure of security and truth.

(c) On one side, because of the fact that it utilizes the service of numerous auxiliary sciences, on the other, by reason of the amplitude and richness of its object, theology has a diversity of functions and parts, unequaled by any purely rational science.

(d) From its quality of supreme wisdom and as moderator of other sciences, theology holds a role of fulfillment, unification, and organization with regard to man's spiritual experiences. It is thanks to this wisdom and either to its service or under its direction that the different acquisitions of human intelligence can be orientated toward God and turned to His service, not only from the standpoint of exercise and *usus,* but according to their intrinsic content and richness themselves. This is why theology, as wisdom, appears as the necessary principle, if not for such and such an individual, at least for the community as such, of a Christian humanism and a Christian state of culture. A secularized century would necessarily want to suppress the faculties of theology or deny them any reason for existing.

The danger of theology would be precisely in its superior point of view, which could become a simplistic theological mentality. If it is an error to admit only immediate causes and so to remain in the limits of a strictly technical viewpoint, it is also wrong to become attached only to transcendent explanations by the efficient cause and the ultimately final cause while neglecting all immediate causes. This mentality would terminate in rather disastrous results: in politics, in a theocratic regime which would easily degenerate into clericalism; into mysticism, in a false supernaturalism, in apologetics, in an easy concordat, sometimes dishonest, in which truth, instead of being sought out and served, would be used and falsified.

3. Is the Habitus of Theology Supernatural? The position of Contenson is well known.[68] Grounding his thought on the fact, quite generally admitted, that theology is supernatural in its source or root, which is the faith, he wants it to be supernatural also entitatively as an activity. For (1) its Object and its Light are supernatural, surpassing all humanly possible assent; (2) the motive of the assent given to the conclusions is not the human discourse, but the truth of faith which the discourse only adapts; (3) theology has qualities such that it can only belong to a supernatural habitus. For example, it is subalternate to a properly supernatural knowledge; it is more certain than any natural knowledge.

---

68. See his *Theologia mentis et cordis,* t. I, p. 11 sq.

Contenson's intention is to underline heavily the objective homogeneity of theology with the order of faith. But Contenson admits that theology is an acquired *habitus,* whose role is to dispose the faculties, not to give them power itself. He is then far removed from the opinion connected with that of Henry of Ghent (and curiously upheld in recent days by J. Didiot[69] of an infused *habitus theologicus.* However we cannot agree with him on his intrinsically supernatural habitus. For, the object of theology is not *purely and simply* supernatural, neither is its light, nor its certitude. Theology's object, light or motive of assent, and certitude are indeed of supernatural origin and participate in the supernatural quality of their root, which is faith. But object, light, and certitude are intrinsically modified by the fact that theology considers them in the alteration they receive from the rational activity of a believing man, which indeed can be directed, fortified, and raised aloft by faith, but not formally possessed and qualified by it. The object which finalizes, terminates, and qualifies theological work is not purely and simply supernatural, but is rather that which is seen *by the believing reason* in the supernatural object of faith.

Conditions of Theological Work and Progress

A. *Theology and Spiritual Life*

First of all we will show how the religious life and theological speculation unite and what they receive from one another.

1. What Theology Contributes to the Religious Life. It is, for the spiritual life, a safeguard and an aid. Theology prevents the spiritual life from going astray; it preserves it from subjectivism in all its forms and from a poorly enlightened particularism. It permits the spiritual to radiate more completely in a man because it spreads the

---

69. *Logique surnaturelle subjective,* theor. XXII.

luminous reign of the faith over a greater number of convictions, consequences, and aspects. Finally, theology is an eminent work of faith and charity, a very elevated cult rendered to God, for it consecrates to Him our reason as such, thereby achieving the consecration that faith had made to Him of our understanding as such.

2. WHAT THE SPIRITUAL LIFE CAN AND MUST CONTRIBUTE TO THEOLOGY. First of all, the grace of faith is constitutionally necessary for theology. A theologian who lost his faith would also lose the habitus of theology. In its place he would have only a "habit" of opinions which would no longer have any relation with that science of God and the Blessed on which theology relies and into which it tends to resolve. Still, it is proper to note that theology is not linked with charity from the standpoint of its noetic structure. As we have seen above the mode of its union with its object is intentional and intellectual, not real and affective.

However, it behooves us to see clearly all that would be lacking in the theology of a theologian who had lost the state of grace. He would lose first the religious motivation for his research and the conditions without which he would no longer have any taste for theology. Nor will he have any desire to draw from its principles the practical conclusions which interest life, nor to contemplate any longer the mysteries which are joined to the most delicate attitudes of the soul: truths concerning the spiritual life, the angels, the Blessed Virgin, sin and penance, etc., in short, all the details which accompany what is called the spirit of faith.

But charity, taste, and a certain personal experience of the things of God are necessary in order that the theologian may treat the mysteries and speak of them in a befitting manner. Although the object of theology is of an intellectual and scientific order, it is supernatural by its roots and essentially religious by its content: "Those things by whose vision we are in beatitude for eternity and by which we are led to eternal life." The knowledge of faith, which gives to theology its principles, does not end in statements and formulas but in realities which are the mysteries of the life of God and our salvation. We have seen above how faith tends to the supernatural perception of divine realities. It is fitting then that the theologian lead a pure, holy, mortified prayerful life. His work can be done only with the aid of actual graces and on the basis of a certain religious potential. And if—as St. Thomas holds—the gifts of intelligence and wisdom are necessary for the believer correctly to perceive the meaning of the statements of faith, we can certainly think that the theologian cannot bypass their assistance.

B. *The Life of the Theologian in the Church*

1. THE THEOLOGIAN MUST LIVE IN THE CHURCH. This is necessary for several reasons. (a) From the fact that theology is a science, it supposes collaboration. Now, there is question at once of the collaboration of the other believers, anxious to bring their faith to a rational and scientific state. Hence we see that the theologian cannot isolate himself from the community of believers which is the Church. (b) In its development, theology is dependent on the development of faith. But, according to Saint Paul,[70] the development of faith into knowledge, *gnosis,* is linked to our growth in the mystical body, as members of this body. (c) The condition of an orthodox knowledge of the objects of faith is communion in the Church, for the correct view of these objects is given by the Holy Spirit, Who unveils the truth only to those who live in the communion of love. (d) The last and finally only efficacious criterion of this orthodox knowledge is the teaching Church. For the Church cannot live as a body and ecclesiastically in the unity of truth, except thanks to an ecclesiastical criterion of unity and belief. This is why, as much apropos of the *auditus fidei* and positive theology as apropos of the *intellectus fidei* and speculative theology, we have pointed out the necessity for the theolo-

---

70. *Eph.,* IV, 13; *Phil.,* I, 9.

gian to refer constantly to the teaching of the Church, to have within himself the sense of the Church and the sense of the magisterium.

Theology without doubt is a science, but it is a fact that the Fathers and the greatest theologians orientated their work toward the satisfaction of the needs of the Church at a given moment. These could be the defense of the faith, spiritual needs of souls, requirements or bettering of the formation of the clergy, replies to new forms of thought or to new acquisitions of knowledge. If we subtracted from theology the works which answer these different appeals and only kept those whose sole inspiration had been a thirst for knowledge, we would cross out the majority of the great masterpieces. However, it would be a danger to accentuate or develop the themes which give expression to a given moment or a given setting, at the expense of an authentic equilibrium of doctrine and even perhaps at the expense of truth itself. The theologian must not refuse to work for the service of the Church. But, to avoid this danger, which scientifically could be quite amateurish, he must also surround his work with conditions which are imperative for any scientific work: critical tools, a certain withdrawal in relation to the immediate actuality, an atmosphere of disinterestedness and contemplation, a share of leisure, divestment, and solitude.

2. The Church Draws Great Profit from the Work of Its Theologians. St. Augustine's statement that theology is the science by which the faith is nourished, comforted, and defended, also has its truth in the plan of the historic life of the Church as such. A developed state of the intelligibility of faith is practically necessary in order that the message can be communicated to minds which pose various questions in keeping with the current state of ideas and culture. Also the Church collectively has need of a situation of security which supposes that, in its midst, some men can reply to the critical requests of each generation. As to that, the hierarchy itself has need of theologians who

exercise a function of information and even, subordinated to the judgment of the magisterium, a critical function with regard to teaching in the Church. Finally, if the Church is the educative center of and truly nourishes the faith of the faithful, it owes this to the presence in its midst of an intense life of thought, expressed in doctrine and in works. This is why St. Augustine counted the Doctors among the agents by which Christ guards His Church from error and makes it grow in truth.[71]

3. The Church Must Permit or Procure for the Theologian the Conditions of Liberty which Are Necessary for His Work. Not that anyone would want in any way to demand the liberty of error or the right to error. But there is simply question of drawing a necessary consequence from the distinction, explained above, between dogma and theology. The teaching Church proposes and interprets the faith with the sovereign authority of the Apostolic magisterium. But, in the interior of this unity of faith of which it is the guardian and judge, there is place for research of a scientific type, which the theologian will conduct under his own responsibility and in accord with the axiom: *In necessariis unitas, in dubiis libertas*[72] ("In necessity unity; otherwise liberty").

So this distinction between dogma and theological science corresponds to a very important differentiation, in the heart of the Church, in the functions relative to the *sacra doctrina* or sacred truth. There are two essential ways in which this truth must be served. The properly dogmatic question is one function of conservation and continuity. It must transmit to each generation what has been handed down from the beginning. It is not its property to advance, in any sense of the word, our intellectual knowledge but to guard the deposit and to declare its meaning in an authentic manner. This is the role of the hierarchical magiste-

71. *Epist.* CXVIII, 32, *P.L.*, t. XXXIII, col. 418.
72. Recalled by John XXIII, enc. *Ad Petri Cathedram*, 1959, AAS, LI, p. 513.

rium. The scientific and properly theological function, on the contrary, is a function of initiative and progress; not, properly, a function of conservation, but one of research, indeed, of discovery. For, if theology works on an immutable datum to which nothing can be added, it is itself an activity of explanation thanks to the active intervention of rational resources. So at its own risk it has the opportunity to surpass the affirmations of dogma at a given moment; attempting syntheses where dogma only furnishes elements; approaching problems for which dogma only gives a more or less distant point of departure, in short, exercising the function of initiative and research which is that of science.

So theological work, as does any scientific work, demands a certain liberty in the field of its research—if not in that of its tradition. It is in effect utterly impossible for theology to fulfill its proper function if it is denied the possibility of trials, hypotheses, questions, and solutions which are put in circulation not to impose them as things defined and definitive, but to make them undergo the test of criticism and enjoy, to their profit and the profit of everyone, the cooperation of the thinking and working world. To refuse to run the least risk in this domain, or to decide that the theologian should do nothing but repeat what has been said before and proclaim only those things which are certainly irreproachable and inaccessible to criticism, would be to ignore the proper status of theology and therby prepare the way for its downfall. As Benedict XV declared to Fr. Ledochowski, "In matters which are not Revelation, we must allow liberty of discussion."

C. *The Progress of Theology*

That theology progresses is quite evident since dogmatic knowledge itself progresses and, for the most part, as a result of theological work. It seems we can analyze the conditions of theology's progress under these different aspects.

First, theology involves progress in that it is a science. It is developed in a regime of collaboration and by the dialogue of specialists, thanks to the normal means of such a dialogue: universities, institutes of research, congresses, collections, reviews with their sections on bibliographical critique. On one hand, the progress of theology is, at least in part, allied with progress in other sciences: historical, philological, liturgical, sociological, etc. Here, also, theology will follow in some measure the law of all progress made by specialization. The theologian truly concerned about the vitality and progress of his discipline must keep abreast of all those sciences which he can make auxiliary to his work.

Then, theology involves progress in its role as the science of a specific datum. If all progress involves holding to a principle, the progress of theology will consist in an understanding of its datum as found in Apostolic preaching rather than in the refinement of systematization. The Encyclical *Humani Generis* recognized that "The sacred disciplines always grow younger from the study of their sacred fonts, while, on the contrary, speculation, which neglects further inquiry into the sacred datum, as we know from experience, turns out sterile."[73]

Hence the law, which is that of all progress, is valid for theology in a more rigorous fashion since there is veritable progress and productive renewal only in tradition. The newness and progress in theology do not consist in change affecting the principles or the datum but primarily in a richer or more precise awareness of this datum itself. Several questions of theology can be taken up again, sometimes reviewed or orientated in a better fashion by a more critical study of the datum which concerns them. For example, this is the case with the notion of tradition, see above; this could be the case, without doubt, for more than one notion of ecclesiology or of sacramental theology.

But theology is a *reflection* on the datum. Hence it profits greatly, from everything that stimulates reflection, namely,

73. AAS, t. XLII, 1950, pp. 568–69; *Denz.* 3886.

human inquiry and philosophy which encourages inquiry. The dogmas can be seen in a new light, their content can be viewed more profoundly, either by a new elaboration of the concepts which they involve, or by starting from a new viewpoint set up by philosophy. So today even the dogmas of the Trinity, Christology, the Sacraments, the Eucharistic Presence, the act of Faith, profit from contemporary philosophical reflection on man and the existential experience of man. The questions posed in the current ecumenical dialogue are also sources of renewal and profit for theology.

Divisions or Parts of Theology

The progressive creation of different specialties in theology does not represent a process of disaggregation or decadence but rather a normal process of development. Progress generally engages a certain specialization and, hence, a certain division. In the historical section of this work we witnessed the growth of successive specializations in Sacred Science: division of teaching in *lectio* and *quaestio,* in commentary on Sacred Scripture and dialectical disputes, growth of a positive theology and a biblical theology, specialization of a moral theology, of an ascetic or mystic theology separated from the dogmatic, creation of an apologetic, separated development of a polemic theology. And we saw how in the tendencies of religious restoration and renovation at the beginning of the nineteenth century a "pastoral theology" was formulated.

We have also seen how toward the end of the eighteenth century quite a movement developed in the way of a reintegration of the different parts, thus divided, into an organic whole, that is, a "system" whose different parts would be like the development of a single idea. It is then, expecially in Germany, that *Encyclopedias* were written whose object was a logical distribution of the sacred sciences according to their natural articulations. But the modern authors *of Introductions* to theology again present a distribution of theology according to its different parts or auxiliary sciences. A rapid critical reflection on any one of these "Introductions" shows that in the different disciplines there are not different theologies but the distribution of a single theology made from a pedagogic point of view. It is in reality generally a division and distribution of the complex matter of ecclesiastical teaching in the universities and seminaries. The same is true of the enumeration presented by a certain number of official documents concerning the studies of the clergy. These documents usually give quite clear and extremely valuable indications on the object, method, importance, and spirit of theology. But it is quite clear from the purpose and character of these documents that the enumeration they make of principal, auxiliary, and special matter (the usual division) does not imply any speculative doctrine.

There is then no reason in these documents to look for a scientific division of theology into its necessary parts, for they are simply an organization and distribution of the teaching of ecclesiastical sciences. When the letter *Ordinamento,* the letter *Vixdum haec,* and the constitution *Deus scientiarum Dominus* speak of ascetico-mystical theology as a complement of moral, they intend in no way to pronounce that these disciplines have a separate epistemological status but simply give direction for a complete doctrine on morality. Similarly, when the *Codex* and Pius XI in *Officiorum omnium* speak of pastoral theology, they have in mind to promote a pedagogic reality and not to define an epistemological specialty. And so with the rest. The way then is open, according to the idea a theologian has of theology, for him to plan its unity and the distinction of its parts.

Theology in itself is one. It has a unique formal object *quod* and *quo,* namely the revealed mystery of God, insofar as it is attained by the activity of reason starting from faith. This definition, while it expresses the essential unity of theology, at the same time gives us a presentiment of the complexity of its elements and the contributions which go to integrate it: namely, an extremely complex positive datum, of which a really scientific knowledge would engage many disciplines, a rational contribution, considerable possibilities of developments and applications. Theology as a wisdom will normally subordinate to itself a plurality of methods and data, orientating them to its service but at the same time leaving them their autonomy. We will not pause here to define each one of the particular disciplines which come to theology's assistance or each part of the theological science. We prefer to set down rapidly, from a speculative standpoint, a classification of theology's parts.

We can distinguish a whole from the standpoint of its integrating parts or from the standpoint of its potential parts.

The integrating parts are those which together make up the integrity of the whole, as arms and legs insure the integrity of the body. In this sense, the parts of theology are: (1) from the viewpoint of its method or its formal object *quo,* the two acts which integrate its work, namely, the *auditus fidei* brought to a rational and scientific state in its positive function, and the *intellectus fidei* brought to a rational and scientific state in its speculative function; (2) from the viewpoint of its matter or its formal object *quod,* the different treatises by which it considers its object according to all its aspects: *De Deo uno, de Deo trino, de Deo creante,* etc. There are also different disciplines by which theology covers its entire field and which are only a development of certain elements studied in the different treatises: asceticism, pastoral, etc.

The potential parts are those in which the whole is present according to its entire essence, but does not realize its entire power. Part and whole are here taken in the order of a *virtus* or power which distributes itself unequally in different functions: thus the different powers of the soul, intellect, and will, or, in the theology of St. Thomas, the virtues which consider a secondary aspect in the object of another virtue, like religion or piety with relation to justice. We can then consider as potential parts of theology the different and unequal uses which are made there of theological reason, that is, of reason assumed, lighted, and positively directed by faith. This is why Fr. Gardeil made apologetics a potential part of theology. He saw apologetics as concerned with the natural credibility of religious truths and so directed to a secondary aspect of theology's formal object and using nothing but the resources of critical reason from which this natural credibility springs. But, if we were to consider apologetics as a special treatise studying the revealing God, like a tract on Revelation, in this respect we would rank it among the integrating parts. Likewise perhaps we could consider as potential parts those auxiliary instrumental disciplines which have been called "preparatory sciences": exegesis, history of dogmas and institutions, sacred philology, etc. Not that these sciences or parts of sciences, considered in themselves, would properly be theology: the history of dogmas is formally history and sacred philology is philology. But, if we consider these disciplines in the use that theology makes of them and as far as they subordinate themselves to it and obey its direction to serve its end, then they become appendages of theology. They can then be considered as belonging to a situation similar to that of apologetics, a discipline in which theological reason exercises only part of its power, using only purely rational resources—but under the direction of faith—and attaining only a secondary aspect of theology's object. For it is indeed the sacred object but only as it is found, say, in some historical documents which these disciplines are considering and that combines them with theology by a special title. On this account, the preparatory auxiliary sciences such as exegesis, the history of doctrines and schools, etc., can be considered as potential parts of theology. But they can also be considered as independent sciences whose services theology uses, as it also does that of philosophy.

On the eve of the last world war the idea was launched of a "kerygmatic theology" distinct, even by its object, from the scientific theology taught in the schools. The theology and even the catechesis, which derived from it, were presented under an atomized form, abstract, and of a dialectical systematization which had very little biblical support. So, alongside this it was proposed to create a theology adapted to preaching and to men's spiritual needs. It would be attached to the existential aspect of Revelation, not only as to its form and the more dynamic, warmer method of presenting the message, but as to the content itself. Its object would be Revelation less under the aspect of the true than the good and its value for human life. It would attach itself to a dynamic and historic exposé, centered on Christ and the history of salvation.

The desire was to remedy some real defects and there is no doubt that the kerygmatic propositions, supported by the biblical, liturgical, and patristic renovation, have helped to make us set aside a certain conception of Revelation, of faith and of theology itself as a sort of superior metaphysics, purely conceptual and impersonal. The program and the task of theology itself were in question. The possibilities of a true theology as an authentic reflection on faith were all too quickly despaired of. Certainly, in the plan of an activity and the modalities of work to be done, the moment of research or reflection is one thing, the moment of Apostolic communication to men: "We do not take on a chemist as a cook nor a mineralogist as a mason" (Newman) is quite another.

No doubt preaching presents problems. But this is only a practical application of the *sacra doctrina* of which theology is the scholarly elaboration. If theology were truly understood—its religious epistemological status, its unity, about Whom it speaks, from what sources it draws its notions—there would be ready agreement that it possesses the qualities needed for a living kerygma. To construct a particular "kerygmatic theology" would be to discharge theological science too quickly from the duty of being truly itself, and to run the risk of falling into a certain pastoral pragmatism, with the defects which a lack of true culture always entails: the narrowing of perspectives, a lack of recoil, the danger of remaining in the vague indefinite, and the greater danger of retaining from the mysteries only that which is human. However it must be added that theology owes it to itself to cater to the special circumstances which kerygmatism wanted to face, and to note that it has profited from the kerygmatists by their stress on the historic, Christological, salvific, and interpersonal characteristics of Revelation.

Theology and the other Sciences

Here we will simply propose quite briefly some conclusions regarding the relation of theology no longer with its own parts but with the secular sciences.

A. *Distinction of Theology and the Sciences Which, at Least Partially, Have Its Same Material Object*

Theology is distinct:

1. From Philosophy, even in that part where philosophy treats of God.[74]

2. From Religious Psychology, from an analysis or description of religious experience, for theology is an intellectual, scientific elaboration of the teachings of objective Revelation; a Revelation, which the interior grace of faith certainly meets in the faithful, but which is essentially constituted in its content by an objective datum whose conservation, formulation, and interpretation spring from the hierarchical magisterium prolonging that of the Apostles. Catholic theology is considerably different from descriptions of religious experiences in intellectual terms which Protestant liberalism put to work as dogmatic theology.

3. From the History of Dogmas, and for the very same reasons. If theology is nourished, by its positive function, from what has been thought in the Church, it does

---

74. *Denz.* 1795.

not identify itself with the history of that thought any more than philosophy identifies itself with the history of ideas. Theology is a rational contemplation of a datum, not the history of religious ideas.

4. FROM THE SCIENCE OF RELIGIONS AND THE PHILOSOPHY OF RELIGION. We distinguish quite generally the science of religions or history of religions, which is dedicated to describing in their genesis, their forms, their content and development the different religions with the help of resources from the historical method; religious psychology, which has for its object the different manifestations of the religious fact in individuals and in groups, and for its method that of psychology; and finally, the philosophy of religion, which studies the essence of religion, the bases of the religious fact in man's nature, the rational criteria of truth in matters of religion. The ensemble of these three disciplines form what in Germany is called *Religionswissenschaft*. Theology can be likened to these sciences neither by its object, which is the mystery of God such as it is known in the Judaeo-Christian Revelation proposed by the Church, nor by its method, which is in no way a historical or psychological inquiry and explanation, or even a philosophical demonstration, but which puts to work the resources of a historical and philosophical reason in the interior of a faith addressing itself to Revelation under the positive and constant direction of that faith.

If philosophy in general is a reflection on the totality of experience and of being, the philosophy of religion is a reflection on religious experience or religious being, that is on the relation between man and God. To the degree in which this relationship accords with Christianity, philosophy has this in common with theology, that it is an interpretation of faith. However, it differs from theology (1) by its formal object *quod*, which are not the objects of belief, vis., the mysteries, but religion as an act or activity, its conditions and the categories it employs, and (2) by its formal object *quo,* the angle and light under which it works. In the philosophy of religion, Revelation intervenes only as a negative norm and, of itself, is not a normative source of true propositions. However, the philosophy of religion is not purely descriptive, as is the science of religions or even religious psychology. It has always been an interpretation of religious facts and today it is on a better basis and operates by a better method than the documentary and inductive method of the science of religions. In short, it has adopted the phenomenological method. Abstracting—and without prejudice—from the existence or the objective value of the term "divine," phenomenology analyzes the content and intentionality of conscious facts in regard to their originality. It carefully seizes the essence of the seen object by reducing to the essential the diverse expressions which the consciousness may project from that object.

The philosophy of religion, whether it uses the inductive method or the phenomenological method, can go still further. It considers not only the content of consciousness, but also the entire religious activity, in order to separate the rational structures there involved, examine them critically and eventually even justify them critically. In this way the philosophy of religion can assume at least a small part in the program of apologetics. For example, by establishing the capacity, in fact, the need which man has to know and love God as the Absolute of his personal existence; by justifying the adventure of faith and very properly of the Christian and Catholic faith, with its structures of tradition and the Church, from the standpoint of a spiritual subject.

Necessarily, since it is *philosophical reflection,* the philosophy of religion studies the religious act, hence Christian faith, as an activity of consciousness. Its level of work and its method prevent it from forming a last judgment either on the existential conditions of faith or on its object. This judgment belongs to theology which, taking the affirmations of faith (even on itself) as the source of its own affirmations, draws from them its explanation of the genesis, structure, essence, and signification of this same faith, that is, of the reality in question. And this is taken for what it is, not only in its human phenomenality, but in its supernatural *reality*, which goes beyond the grasp of pure philosophy.

A critical proof and a rational justification of the faith, as content or as act, is totally an operation involving our rational resources.

B. *General Principles Concerning the Relations of Theology and the Secular Sciences*
We can formulate the thought of the Church on this matter in three statements: (1) Between faith and theology, on one side, and the sciences—which are truly such—on the other, there can be no real contradiction.[75] (2) The sciences have, vis-à-vis faith and theology, their own object and their own method and hence an epistemological autonomy.[76] (3) Theology, the science of faith, is nevertheless of itself superior to all the other sciences in light and certitude.[77]

C. *What Theology Does for the Sciences*
We have already pointed out above that theology, as supreme wisdom, was the crowning of all the sciences and ought to be the principle of a Christian order of culture and knowledge. As supreme wisdom, theology rules and judges the sciences. It uses their services for its own end, as we have already remarked, and it has, with regard to all of them, a certain role of critic, a role which can be expressed thus: theology does not prove the conclusions of other sciences, but, to the degree in which these conclusions touch it, theology approves or disapproves of them and thus intervenes in their work.

1. THEOLOGY DOES NOT PROVE THE CONCLUSIONS OF OTHER SCIENCES. It leaves them the autonomy of their

75. *Denz.* 1797 sq., 1878 sq.
76. *Denz.* 1670, 1674, 1799.
77. *Denz.* 1656, 2085.

own procedures. Its intervention in their regard is not intrinsic, concerning their internal work of research and proof. It makes no intrinsic or substantial change in their epistemological regime. And this is true not merely of physical or mathematical sciences, but of philosophical or historical sciences which theology directly employs in its service. Even then, in effect, the value, the certitude and evidence of the historical or philosophical data employed by it, remain intrinsically what they are in their respective science, according to the proper criteria of that science.

2. THEOLOGY INTERVENES EXTERNALLY IN THEIR WORK. Theology being—as compared to the sciences—of a higher and more certain truth, the relation of conformity or repugnance that the statements of the sciences will have with regard to those of theology will intervene from outside in the work of the sciences and thus will be able to rule them, change them, and, in a favorable hypothesis, even augment their certitude. Take for example the Cartesian theory of matter identified as extended substance. This theory clashes with the statements of faith and theology concerning the Eucharistic species (note that while theology speaks of "accidents," dogma avoids this philosophical term). The theory of extended substance will be judged and disapproved by theology and so will be condemned in the eyes of the believing philosopher. If up to that point he had held the doctrine for certain philosophical reasons, he will reconsider his reasons and his evidences. He will seek another way, by properly philosophical means. Theology, without intervening in the internal web of his thought, without intrinsically modifying the epistemological regime of his discipline, represents for the scholar an extrinsic criterion, a negative norm. Its intervention is, for the scholar as for his science, a benefit, for it keeps him from errors, from false ways; it guarantees him against illusion and frees him from falsehood.[78] In this matter the official documents

---

78. *Denz.* 1656, 1674, 1681, 1714, 1799, 2085.

are anxious to exclude the distinction which some make between philosopher and philosophy and to affirm the sovereignty of theology not only over the first but over the second as well.[79]

Now take for example a philosophical theory like that of subsistence, which theology uses in the very heart of its most important treatises, in the intellectual construction of the mysteries of the Trinity and the Incarnation. Using it in conditions which, we said above, were those of principles of reason in theological work, the sacred science obviously approves the theory of subsistence. It does not transform it intrinsically or epistemologically, and, in philosophy, the theory will remain what it was before, being worth what the reasons are worth which support it. But, in the eyes of the believing philosopher or of the theologian-philosopher, it will receive an extrinsic plus-value of certitude from the fact of its approbation by the science of faith which, so to speak, homologates and guarantees it. This is why in the numerous documents and in particular in the encyclical *Aeterni Patris*, the ecclesiastical magisterium has underlined, beyond a defense and protection against error, the positive benefit of certitude that philosophical reason receives from its subordination to faith through theology. Vatican II says of faith that "it instructs reason by multiple knowledge."[80]

It is the fact of this benefit received by philosophy from its contact with theology which led M. Gilson, then M. Maritain and those who followed them to speak of "Christian Philosophy." In Germany, about the same time but in a manner perhaps less "formal," there was talk of *Catholic* sciences and *Catholic* philosophy. In a slightly different sense, M. Blondel had, for some time, spoken of "Catholic philosophy." A certain number of theologians rebelled against this new category of Christian philosophy, wanting above all to maintain the distinction between theology and

---

79. *Denz.* 1674, 1682, 1710.
80. *Denz.* 1799.

philosophy taken from their formal object *quod* or *quo*, in terms of which all thought ruled by faith or dependent on faith would be theology, while all rational value, even if it owed its origin to Christianity, could receive no intrinsic qualification other than that of philosophy. This opposition underlines very well that from the standpoint of essential definitions and formal motives which are their principles, there is no *tertium quid* between philosophy and theology. But, all this granted, it seems legitimate to formulate a view from the standpoint of the genesis, the history, the conditions of exercise, and the concrete state of the historic forms of a given thought. In which case, there may be a thought inspired or aroused by faith but concerning values which epistemologically are purely philosophical and which reason develops and pursues by its own means and for its own end, which is pure and simple truth. Historically, this development of philosophical notions, thanks to the Christian faith, is often brought about by the activity of the *intellectus fidei,* that is, the intelligibility of faith, which is a properly theological effort.

Inversely, it happened to St. Augustine, for example, that the philosophical enrichment was obtained without any direct reference to the *intellectus fidei,* in a truly philosophical contemplation, pursued for itself and by ways proper to reason, but of which the datum of faith had been the occasion. In this way Christianity exercises one of its virtues which is to give back man to himself, and to reason its own value of reason. Opened by faith, the philosophical meditation is then developed according to its own requirements. So that by these two ways, that of the rational needs of theological contemplation, that of the possibilities opened up by faith for the benefit of philosophical contemplation itself, there has developed, during our long Christian history, a knowledge which, though purely philosophical from the viewpoint of its object, its procedures, its epistemological texture, has nonetheless the right to be qualified as Christian from the standpoint of everything which concretely made it possible: its point of departure, and the conditions and assistance necessary for reflection.

C. *What the Sciences Do for Theology*

The sciences are necessary auxiliaries for theology since they furnish it with that rational support without which it would not be able to be complete. What we have seen above about this support justifies the appellation of "servants of theology" which has traditionally been given to the sciences. However, to the measure in which the sciences do not bring to theology merely extrinsic illustrations or simple subjective preparations, but furnish it truly with an opening wedge in the elaboration of its object, they influence its construction, its orientation, and its progress. Not that theology in this way becomes subordinated or subalternate to the sciences, for it receives from them only what conforms to its principles and pertains to its goal. Theology regulates itself and develops itself by making use of sciences which have their own growth and development. And so the progress of the sacred science is in some way a function of the state of the sciences. It is clear that the development of psychology or sociology could in some measure modify that of theology in certain of its parts, as the development of metaphysics in the thirteenth century, of history in the seventeenth and biblical sciences in the nineteenth century have definitely influenced its growth in the past.

In this perspective some have advocated a renewal of theology, either in its method or in some one of its parts, like the treatise on the Eucharist, by its assumption of the techniques of new ideas, such as logistics of new scientific data, for example, in physics and chemistry. The idea is not false *a priori* and is in keeping with reasons of initiative. Structurally, methodologically, nothing denies that it can bear fruit. But it is a very serious question and a manner of procedure which cannot be entered into lightly or without a very serious testing of the new products which there would be question of assimilating. As to those cases which have concretely been proposed, it is not clear that we find ourselves in the presence of disciplines sufficiently mature or of a value, scope, or fecundity basically incontestable.

Bibliography

General Bibliography and Suggested Reading List

Adam, Karl: *The Spirit of Catholicism*. Image Books, Garden City, N.Y., 1954.

_____: *The Son of God*. Image Books, Garden City, N.Y., 1960.

Amiot, François: *History of the Mass*. Hawthorn Books, New York, 1958.

D'Arcy, M. J., S.J.: *Of God and Man*. University of Notre Dame Press, Notre Dame, Ind., 1957.

Attwater, Donald: A *Dictionary of Mary*. Kenedy, New York, 1956.

Augustine, St.: *The City of God*. Modern Library, New York, 1950.

Balthasar, Hans Urs von: *Church and the World*. Herder and Herder, New York, 1957.

Bars, Henri: *The Assent of Faith*. Helicon, Baltimore, 1960.

Bea, Augustin Cardinal: *The Unity of Christians*. Herder and Herder, New York, 1963.

_____: *Unity in Freedom*. Harper and Row, New York, 1964.

Boros, Ladislaus, S.J.: *The Mystery of Death*. Herder and Herder, New York, 1965.

Bouyer, Louis: *The Spirit and Form of Protestantism*. Newman Press, Westminster, Md., 1965.

_____: *Introduction to Spirituality*. Liturgical Press, Collegeville, Minn., 1961.

DeBovis, André: *The Church: Christ's Mystery and Sacrament*. Burns and Oates, London, 1961.

Boylan, Eugene, C.S.O.: *This Tremendous Lover*. Newman Press, Westminster, Md., 1947.

Brown, Raymond, S.S.: *New Testament Essays*. Bruce, Milwaukee, 1965.

Cerfaux, L.: *The Church in the Theology of St. Paul*. Herder and Herder, New York, 1963.

Congar, Yves, O.P.: *Lay People in the Church.* Newman Press, Westminster, Md., 1957.

_____: *The Mystery of the Church.* Helicon, Baltimore, 1960.

_____: *The Wide World, My Parish.* Helicon, Baltimore, 1961.

_____: *Power and Poverty in the Church.* Helicon, Baltimore, 1964.

_____: *Jesus Christ.* Herder and Herder, New York, 1967.

_____: *Ecumenism and the Future of the Church.* Priory Press, Chicago, 1967.

Connolly, James M.: *Human History and the Word of God.* Macmillan, New York, 1965.

Dalmais, Irenée-Henri, O.P.: *Eastern Liturgies.* Hawthorn, New York, 1960.

Daniélou, Jean, S.J.: *Origen.* Sheed and Ward, New York, 1955.

_____: *The Advent of Salvation.* Paulist Press, Glen Rock, N.J., 1962.

_____: *The Salvation of the Nations.* University of Notre Dame Press, Notre Dame, Ind., 1962.

Daniel-Rops, Henri: *Jesus and His Times.* 2 vols. Image Books, Garden City, N.Y., 1956.

_____: *What Is the Bible?* Image Books, Garden City, N.Y., 1968

_____: *Daily Life in the Time of Jesus.* Hawthorn, Garden City, N.Y., 1962.

Dohenry, William J., C.S.C., and Kelly, Joseph P.: *Papal Documents on Mary.* Bruce, Milwaukee, 1954.

Dulles, Avery, S.J.: *Apologetics and the Biblical Christ.* Newman Press, Westminster, Md., 1963.

Dyer, George: *Limbo: Unsettled Question.* Sheed and Ward, New York, 1964.

Fortman, Edmund, S.J.: *The Theology of Man and Grace: A Commentary,* Bruce, Milwaukee, 1966.

Freedman, David N. and Wright, Ernest G.: *The Biblical Archeologist Reader.* Doubleday, Garden City, N.Y., 1961.

Gelin, A. and others: *Son and Savior.* Chapman, London, 1960.

Gerken, John D., S.J.: *Toward a Theology of the Layman.* Herder and Herder, New York, 1963.

Gleason, Robert, S.J.: *Yahweh, God of the Old Testament.* Prentice-Hall, Englewood Cliffs, N.J., 1964.

_____: *The Search for God.* Sheed and Ward, New York, 1964.

LeGuillou, M. J.: *Christ and the Church.* Desclée, New York, 1967.

Häring, Bernard, C.SS.R.: *Christian Renewal in a Changing World.* Desclée, New York, 1967.

_____: *This Time of Salvation.* Herder and Herder, New York, 1967.

Hales, E. E. Y.: *Pope John and His Revolution.* Image Books, Garden City, N.Y., 1966.

Hardon, John, S.J.: *The Protestant Churches of America.* Newman Press, Westminster, Md., 1956.

_____: *Religions of the World.* Image Books, Garden City, N.Y., 1968.

Hulsboch, A., O.S.A.: *God in Creation and Evolution.* Sheed and Ward, New York, 1965.

Journet, Charles: *The Meaning of Grace.* Kenedy, New York, 1960.

_____: *The Meaning of Evil.* Kenedy, New York, 1963.

Jungmann, Josef, S.J.: *The Eucharistic Prayer.* Fides Publishers, Notre Dame, Ind., 1964.

Kilmartin, Edward, S.J.: *The Eucharist in the Primitive Church.* Prentice-Hall, Englewood Cliffs, N.J., 1965.

Knox, Ronald: *Enthusiasm.* Oxford, New York, 1950.

Küng, Hans: *Structures of the Church.* Nelson, Camden, N.J., 1964.

Latourelle, René, S.J.: *Theology of Revelation.* Alba House, New York, 1966.

Leeming, Bernard, S.J.: *The Churches and the Church.* Newman Press, Westminster, Md., 1960.

Lepp, Ignace: *Atheism in Our Time.* Macmillan, New York, 1963.

Love, Thomas T.: *John Courtney Murray: Contemporary Church-State Theory.* Doubleday, Garden City, N.Y., 1965.

De Lubac, Henri, S.J.: *Catholicism.* Sheed and Ward, New York, 1950.

_____: *The Splendour of the Church.* Sheed and Ward, New York, 1956.

_____: *The Discovery of God.* Kenedy, New York, 1960.

_____: *The Drama of Atheist Humanism.* Meridian, Cleveland, 1963.

McKenzie, John, S.J.: *The Two-Edged Sword.* Image Books, Garden City, N.Y., 1966.

_____: *The Power and the Wisdom.* Bruce, Milwaukee, 1965.

Mackey, J. P.: *The Modern Theology of Tradition.* Herder and Herder, New York, 1963.

Maly, Eugene: *Prophets of Salvation.* Herder and Herder, New York, 1967.

Marle, René, S.J.: *Introduction to Hermeneutics.* Herder and Herder, New York, 1967.

Miller, Samuel and Wright, Ernest: *Ecumenical Dialogue at Harvard.* Belknap Press, Cambridge, Mass., 1964.

Millot, René-Pierre: *Missions in the World Today.* Hawthorn, New York, 1961.

Monden, Louis, S.J.: *Sin, Liberty and Law.* Sheed and Ward, New York, 1965.

_____: *Signs and Wonders.* Desclée, New York, 1967.

Montague, George T.: *The Living Thought of St. Paul.* Bruce, Milwaukee, 1966.

Moriarity, Frederick, S.J.: *Introducing the Old Testament.* Bruce, Milwaukee, 1960.

Moran, Gabriel, F.S.C.: *Scripture and Tradition.* Herder and Herder, New York, 1963.

_____: *Theology of Revelation.* Herder and Herder, New York, 1966.

Mork, Dom Wulstan, O.S.B.: *The Biblical Meaning of Man.* Bruce, Milwaukee, 1967.

Mouroux, Jean: *The Meaning of Man.* Image Books, Garden City, N.Y., 1961.

_____: *The Mystery of Time.* Desclée, New York, 1964.

Murray, John Courtney, S.J.: *We Hold These Truths.* Image Books, Garden City, N.Y., 1964.

_____: *The Problem of God.* Yale University Press, New Haven, 1964.

_____: *The Problem of Religious Freedom.* Newman Press, Westminster, Md., 1965.

Neuner, Josef, S.J. and Roos, Heinrich, S.J.: *The Teaching of the Catholic Church as Contained in Her Documents.* Alba House, New York, 1967.

Newman, John H. Cardinal: *An Essay on the Development of Christian Doctrine.* Image Books, Garden City, N.Y., 1960.

Noonan, John: *Contraception.* Harvard University Press, Cambridge Mass., 1965.

Philips, Gerard: *The Role of the Laity in the Church.* Fides Publishers, Notre Dame, Ind., 1965.

Piault, Bernard: *What Is a Sacrament?* Hawthorn, New York, 1963.

Powers, Joseph, S.J.: *Eucharistic Theology.* Herder and Herder, New York, 1967.

Quesnell, Quentin, S.J.: *This Good News.* Bruce, Milwaukee, 1964.

Rahner, Karl, S.J.: *The Christian Commitment.* Sheed and Ward, New York, 1963.

_____: *Bishops: Their Status and Function.* Helicon, Baltimore, 1963.

_____: *Nature and Grace.* Sheed and Ward, New York, 1964.

_____: *The Dynamic Element in the Church.* Herder and Herder, New York, 1964.

_____: *Inquiries.* Herder and Herder, New York, 1964.

_____: *The Church After the Council.* Herder and Herder, New York, 1967.

_____: *The Christian of the Future.* Herder and Herder, New York, 1967.

Ricciotti, Giuseppe: *The Life of Christ.* Bruce, Milwaukee, 1947.

_____: *The Age of Martyrs.* Chapman, London, 1960.

Riga, Peter: *Catholic Thought in Crisis.* Bruce, Milwaukee, 1963.

Robert, A. and Feuillet, A.: *Introduction to the New Testament.* Desclée, New York, 1967.

DeRosa, Peter: *Christ and Original Sin.* Bruce, Milwaukee, 1967.

Schanz, John P.: *The Sacraments of Life and Worship.* Bruce, Milwaukee, 1966.

Scharp, Heinrich: *How the Catholic Church is Governed.* Paulist Press, Glen Rock, N.J., 1962.

Schillebeeckx, E., O.P.: *Christ, the Sacrament of the Encounter with God.* Sheed and Ward, New York, 1963.

_____: *Mary, Mother of the Redemption.* Sheed and Ward, New York, 1964.

Schnackenburg, Rudolf: *New Testament Theology Today.* Herder and Herder, New York, 1963.

_____: *Church in the New Testament.* Herder and Herder, New York, 1967.

_____: *The Truth Will Make You Free.* Herder and Herder, New York, 1967.

Sheets, John, S.J.: *The Theology of the Atonement: Readings in Soteriology.* Prentice-Hall, Englewood Cliffs, N.J., 1967.

Sillem, Edward: *Ways of Thinking About God.* Darton, Longmans and Todd, London, 1961.

Simon, Yves: *A General Theory of Authority.* University of Notre Dame Press, Notre Dame, Ind., 1962.

Smalley, B.: *The Study of the Bible in the Middle Ages.* 2d ed. Oxford University Press, New York, 1940.

Smith, Gerard, S.J.: *Natural Theology.* Macmillan, New York, 1951.

Sturzo, Luigi: *Church and State.* University of Notre Dame Press, Notre Dame, Ind., 1962.

Suhard, Emmanuel Cardinal: *Church Today: Growth or Decline?* Fides Publishers, Notre Dame, Ind., 1960.

Todd, John M.: *Problems of Authority.* Helicon, Baltimore, 1962.

Vawter, Bruce, C.M.: *A Path Through Genesis.* Sheed and Ward, New York, 1965.

_____: *The Four Gospels.* Doubleday, Garden City, N.Y., 1967.

Vollert, Cyril, S.J.: *A Theology of Mary.* Herder and Herder, New York, 1965.

Waddell, Helen: *The Desert Fathers.* University of Michigan Press, Ann Arbor, Mich., 1957.

Wikenhauser, A.: *New Testament Introduction.* Herder and Herder, New York, 1958.

Willis, John R.: *The Teaching of the Church Fathers.* Herder and Herder, New York, 1967.

Zamoyta, Vincent: *A Theology of Christ: Sources.* Bruce, Milwaukee, 1967.

Reference Works

Abbott, Walter, S.J.: *Documents of Vatican II.* Herder and Herder and Association Press, New York, 1966.

Cayré, F., A.A.: *Manual of Patrology* (two volumes). Desclée, New York, 1936.

Cronin, John F., Murphy, Francis X., C.SS.R., and Smith, Ferrer, O.P.: *The Encyclicals and Other Messages of Pope John* XXIII: *Commentaries.* The Pope Speaks Press, Washington, D.C., 1965.

Feiner, Johannes, Trütsch, Josef, and Böckle, Franz (editors): *Theology Today: Volume 1, Renewal in Dogma.* Bruce, Milwaukee, 1965.

Fremantle, Anne: *The Papal Encyclicals in Their Historical Context.* Mentor-Omega, New York, 1965.

Gilson, Étienne: *The Church Speaks to the Modern World: Encyclicals of Leo XIII.* Image Books, Garden City, N.Y., 1954.

McKenzie, John, S.J.: *Dictionary of the Bible.* Bruce, Milwaukee, 1965.

McLaughlin, Terence P., C.S.P.: *The Church and the Reconstruction of the Modern World: Encyclicals of Pius XI.* Image Books, Garden City, N.Y., 1957.

O'Brien, Elmer, S.J.: *Theology in Transition: A Bibliographical Evaluation.* Herder and Herder, New York, 1965.

Ott, Ludwig: *Fundamentals of Catholic Dogma.* 5th ed. B. Herder and Co., St. Louis, 1962.

Rahner, Karl, S.J., and Vorgrimler, Herbert, S.J., and Ernst, Cornelius, O.P. (editor): *Theological Dictionary.* Herder and Herder, New York, 1965.

Rahner, Karl, S.J.: *Theological Investigations.* 5 vols. Helicon, Baltimore, 1961–67.

Thomas Aquinas, St.: *Summa Theologica.* (Translated by the English Dominicans) Benizer Bros., New York, 1947–48.

_____: *On the Truth of the Catholic Faith.* 5 vols. *Contra Gentes.* Image Books, Garden City, N.Y., 1955.

Wolf, Donald J., S.J., and Schall, James V., S.J. (editors) : *Current Trends in Theology.* Image Books, Garden City, N.Y., 1966.

_____: *The New Catholic Encyclopedia.* McGraw-Hill, New York, 1967. (Prepared by an editorial staff of the Catholic University of America)

_____: *The Church and Mankind.* Paulist Press, Glen Rock, N.J., 1964. (Volume I of Concilium)

_____: *The Liturgical Movement* Hawthorn, New York, 1964.

(Prepared by the Societies of St. Severin and St. Joseph)

Index

CPSIA information can be obtained
at www.ICGtesting.com
Printed in the USA
FSHW010721021120
75382FS